grokking

Artificial Intelligence Algorithms

Rishal Hurbans

MANNING

SHELTER ISLAND

For online information and ordering of this and other Manning books, please visit
www.manning.com. The publisher offers discounts on this book when ordered in quantity. For more
information, please contact

    Special Sales Department
    Manning Publications Co.
    20 Baldwin Road, PO Box 761
    Shelter Island, NY 11964
    Email: orders@manning.com

Manning Publications Co.	Development editor: Elesha Hyde
20 Baldwin Road	Technical development editor: Frances Buontempo
Shelter Island, NY 11964	Review editor: Ivan Martinović
	Production editor: Deirdre Hiam
	Copy editor: Keir Simpson
	Proofreader: Jason Everett
	Technical proofreader: Krzysztof Kamyczek
	Typesetter: Jennifer Houle
	Cover designer: Marija Tudor

ISBN: 9781617296185
Printed in the United States of America

Get the eBooks FREE!

(PDF, ePub, Kindle, and liveBook all included)

We believe that once you buy a book from us, you should be able to read it in any format we have available. To get electronic versions of this book at no additional cost to you, purchase and then register this book at the Manning website.

Go to https://www.manning.com/freebook and follow the instructions to complete your pBook registration.

That's it!
Thanks from Manning!

To my parents, Pranil and Rekha. To making a positive difference.

contents

This preface aims to describe the evolution of technology, our need to automate, and our responsibility to make ethical decisions while using artificial intelligence in building the future.

Our obsession with technology and automation

Throughout history, we have had a hunger to solve problems while reducing manual labor and human effort. We have always strived for survival and conservation of our energy through the development of tools and automation of tasks. Some may argue that we are beautiful minds that seek innovation through creative problem-solving or creative works of literature, music, and art, but this book wasn't written to discuss philosophical questions about our being. This is an overview of artificial intelligence (AI) approaches that can be harnessed to address real-world problems practically. We solve hard problems to make living easier, safer, healthier, more fulfilling, and more enjoyable. All the advancements that you see in history and around the world today, including AI, address the needs of individuals, communities, and nations.

To shape our future, we must understand some key milestones in our past. In many revolutions, human innovation changed the way we live, and shaped the way we interact with the world and the way we think about it. We continue to do this as we iterate and improve the tools we use, which open future possibilities (figure 0.1).

This short high-level material on history and philosophy is provided purely to establish a baseline understanding of technology and AI, and to spur thought on responsible decision-making when embarking on your projects.

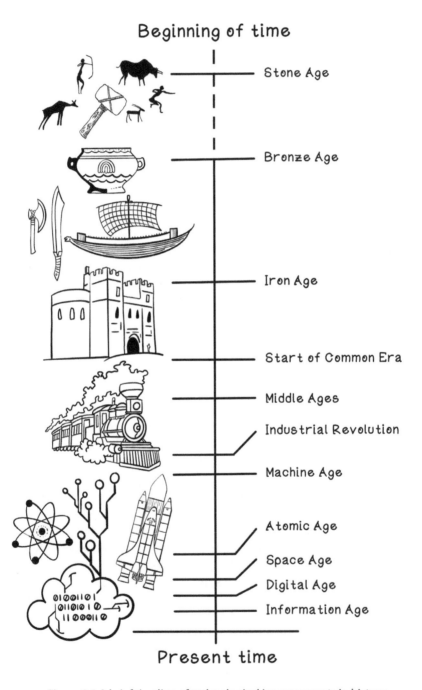

Figure 0.1 A brief timeline of technological improvements in history

In the timeline figure, notice the compression of the milestones in more recent times. In the past 30 years, the most notable advancements have been in the improvement of microchips, the wide adoption of personal computers, the boom of networked devices, and the digitization of industries to break physical borders and connect the world. These are also the reasons that artificial intelligence has become a feasible and sensible area to pursue.

- The internet has connected the world and made it possible to collect mass amounts of data about almost anything.

- Advancements in computing hardware has given us the means to compute previously known algorithms using the massive amounts of data that we have collected, while discovering new algorithms along the way.

- Industries have seen a need to leverage data and algorithms to make better decisions, solve harder problems, offer better solutions, and optimize our lives as people have done since the beginning of humanity.

Although we tend to think of technological progress as linear, by examining our history, we find that it is more likely that our progress is and will be exponential (figure 0.2). Advancements in technology will move faster each year that goes by. New tools and techniques need to be learned, but *problem solving fundamentals* underpin everything.

This book includes foundation-level concepts that help solve hard problems, but it also aims to make learning the more complex concepts easier.

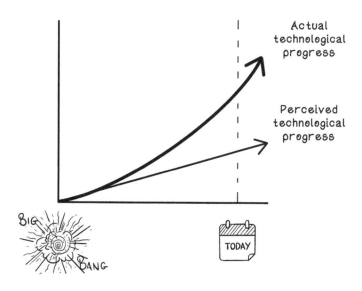

Figure 0.2 Perceived technological progress versus actual technological progress

Automation can be perceived differently by different people. For a technologist, automation may mean writing scripts that make software development, deployment, and distribution seamless and less error-prone. For an engineer, it may mean streamlining a factory line for more throughput or fewer defects. For a farmer, it may mean using tools to optimize the yield of crops through automatic tractors and irrigation systems. Automation is any solution that reduces the need for human energy to favor productivity or add superior value compared with what a manual intervention would have added (figure 0.3).

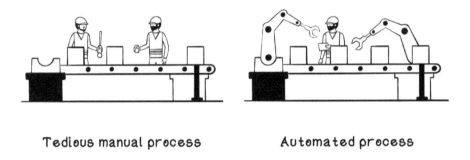

Figure 0.3 Manual processes versus automated processes

If we think about reasons not to automate, one prominent reason is simply that a person can do the task better, with less chance of failure and better accuracy, if the task requires intuition about several perspectives in a situation, when abstract creative thinking is required, or when understanding social interactions and the nature of people is important.

Nurses don't simply complete tasks, but connect with and take care of their patients. Studies show that the human interaction by caring people is a factor in the healing process. Teachers don't simply offload knowledge, but find creative ways to present knowledge, mentor, and guide students based on their ability, personality, and interests. That said, there is a place for automation through technology and a place for people. With the innovations of today, automation via technology will be a close companion to any occupation.

Ethics, legal matters, and our responsibility

You may be wondering why a section on ethics and responsibility is in a technical book. Well, as we progress towards a world in which technology is intertwined with the way of life, the ones who create the technology have more power than they know. Small contributions can have massive knock-on effects. It important that our intentions be benevolent and that the output of our work not be harmful (figure 0.4).

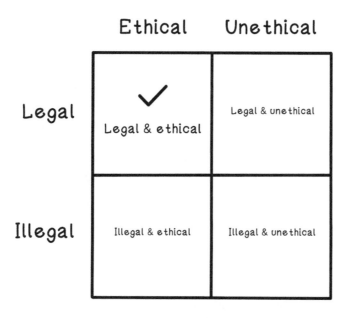

Figure 0.4 Aim for ethical and legal applications of technology

Intention and impact: Understanding your vision and goals

When you develop anything—such as a new physical product, service, or software—there's always a question about the intention behind it. Are you developing software that affects the world positively, or is your intention malevolent? Have you thought about the broader impact of what you're developing? Businesses always find ways to become more profitable and powerful, which is the whole point of growing a business. They use strategies to determine the best ways to beat the competition, gain more customers, and become even more influential. That said, businesses must ask themselves whether their intentions are pure, not only for the survival of the business, but also for the good of their customers and society in general. Many famous scientists, engineers, and technologists have expressed a need to govern the use of AI to prevent misuse. As individuals, we also have an ethical obligation to do what is right and establish a strong core set of values. When you're asked to do something that violates your principles, it is important to voice those principles.

Unintended use: Protecting against malicious use

It is important to identify and protect against unintended use. Although this may seem obvious and easy to accomplish, it is difficult to understand how people will use whatever you are creating, and even more difficult to predict whether it aligns with your values and the values of the organization.

An example is the loudspeaker, which was invented by Peter Jensen in 1915. The loudspeaker was originally called Magnavox, which was initially used to play opera music to large crowds in San Francisco, which is quite a benevolent use of the technology. The Nazi regime in Germany had other ideas, however: they placed loudspeakers in public places in such a way that everyone was subjected to hearing Hitler's speeches and announcements. Because the monologues were unavoidable, people became more susceptible to Hitler's ideas, and after this point in time, the Nazi regime gained the majority of its support in Germany. This is not what Jensen envisioned his invention being used for, but there's not much he could have done about it.

Times have changed, and we have more control of the things we build, especially software. It is still difficult to imagine how the technology you build may be used, but it is almost guaranteed that someone will find a way to use it in a way that you did not intend, with positive or negative consequences. Given this fact, we, as professionals in the technology industry and the organizations we work with must think of ways to mitigate malevolent use as far as possible.

Unintended bias: Building solutions for everyone

When building AI systems, we use our understanding of contexts and domains. We also use algorithms that find patterns in data and act on it. It can't be denied that there is bias all around us. A bias is a prejudice against a person or group of people, including, but not limited to their gender, race, and beliefs. Many of these biases arise from emergent behavior in social interactions, events in history, and cultural and political views around the world. These biases affect the data that we collect. Because AI algorithms work with this data, it is an inherent problem that the machine will "learn" these biases. From a technical perspective, we can engineer the system perfectly, but at the end of the day, humans interact with these systems, and it's our responsibility to minimize bias and prejudice as much as possible. The algorithms we use are only as good as the data provided to them. Understanding the data and the context in which it is being used is the first step in battling bias, and this understanding will help you build better solutions—because you will be well versed in the problem space. Providing balanced data with as little bias as possible should result in better solutions.

The law, privacy, and consent: Knowing the importance of core values

The legal aspect of what we do is hugely important. The law governs what we can and cannot do in the interest of society as a whole. Due to the fact that many laws were written in a time when computers and the internet were not as important in our lives as they are today, we find many gray areas in how we develop technology and what we are allowed to do with that technology. That said, laws are slowly changing to adapt to the rapid innovation in technology.

We are compromising our privacy almost every hour of every day via our interactions on computers, mobile phones, and other devices, for example. We are transmitting a vast amount of information about ourselves, some more personal than others. How is that data being processed and stored? We should consider these facts when building solutions. People should have a choice about what data is captured, processed, and stored about them; how that data is used; and who can potentially access that data. In my experience, people generally accept solutions that use their data to improve the products they use and add more value to their lives. Most important, people are more accepting when they are given a choice and that choice is respected.

Singularity: Exploring the unknown

The *singularity* is the idea that we create an AI that is so generally intelligent that it is capable of improving itself and expanding its intelligence to a stage where it becomes super intelligence. The concern is that something of this magnitude cannot be understood by humans which could change civilization as we know it for reasons we can't even comprehend. Some people are concerned that this intelligence may see humans as a threat; others propose that we may be to a super intelligence what ants are to us. We don't pay explicit attention to ants or concern ourselves with how they live, but if we are irritated by them, we deal with them in isolation.

Whether these assumptions are accurate representations of the future or not, we must be responsible and think about the decisions we make, as they ultimately affect a person, a group of people, or the world at large.

acknowledgments

Writing this book has been one of the most challenging yet rewarding things I've done to date. I needed to find time where I had none, find the right headspace while juggling many contexts, and find motivation while being caught up in the reality of life. I couldn't have done it without a number of amazing people. I have learned and grown through this experience. Thank you, Bert Bates, for being a fantastic editor and mentor to me. I've learned so much about effective teaching and written communication from you. Our discussions and debates, and your empathy throughout the process has helped mold this book into what it is. Every project needs someone organized with a finger on the pulse making sure things are happening. For this, I'd like to thank Elesha Hyde, my development editor. Working with you has been an absolute pleasure. You always provide direction and interesting insights about my work. We always need people to bounce ideas off, and who better to annoy than your friends. I'd like to especially thank Hennie Brink for being a great sounding board and pillar of support always. Next, I'd like to thank Frances Buontempo and Krzysztof Kamyczek for providing constructive criticism and objective feedback from a writing and technical perspective. Your input has helped fill gaps and make the teaching more accessible. I would also like to thank Deirdre Hiam, my project manager; my review editor, Ivan Martinovic; my copyeditor Kier Simpson; and my proofreader, Jason Everett.

Finally, I'd like to thank all the reviewers who took the time to read my manuscript throughout development and provided invaluable feedback that has made the book better in some or other way: Andre Weiner, Arav Agarwal, Charles Soetan, Dan Sheikh, David Jacobs, Dhivya Sivasubramanian, Domingo Salazar, GandhiRajan, Helen Mary Barrameda, James Zhijun Liu, Joseph Friedman, Jousef Murad, Karan Nih, Kelvin D. Meeks, Ken Byrne, Krzysztof Kamyczek, Kyle Peterson, Linda Ristevski, Martin Lopez, Peter Brown, Philip Patterson, Rodolfo Allendes, Tejas Jain, and Weiran Deng.

about this book

Grokking Artificial Intelligence Algorithms was written and illustrated to make understanding and implementing artificial intelligence algorithms and their uses in solving problems more accessible to the average person in the technology industry through the use of relatable analogies, practical examples, and visual explanations.

Who should read this book

Grokking Artificial Intelligence Algorithms is for software developers and anyone in the software industry who want to uncover the concepts and algorithms behind artificial intelligence through practical examples and visual explanations over theoretical deep dives and mathematical proofs.

This book is aimed at anyone with an understanding of basic computer programming concepts including variables, data types, arrays, conditional statements, iterators, classes, and functions—experience in any language is sufficient; and, anyone with an understanding of basic mathematical concepts such as data variables, the representation of functions, and plotting data and functions on a graph.

How this book is organized: A roadmap

This book contains 10 chapters, each focusing on a different artificial intelligence algorithm or algorithmic approach. The material covers fundamental algorithms and concepts at the start of the book that form a foundation for learning more sophisticated algorithms throughout the book.

- *Chapter 1—Intuition of artificial intelligence*, introduces the intuition and fundamental concepts that surround data, types of problems, categories of algorithms and paradigms, and use cases for artificial intelligence algorithms.

- *Chapter 2—Search fundamentals*, covers the core concepts of data structures and approaches for primitive search algorithms, and their uses.

- *Chapter 3—Intelligent search*, goes beyond primitive search algorithms and introduces search algorithms for finding solutions more optimally, and finding solutions in a competitive environment.

- *Chapter 4—Evolutionary algorithms*, dives into the workings of genetic algorithms where solutions to problems are iteratively generated and improved upon by mimicking evolution in nature.

- *Chapter 5—Advanced evolutionary approaches*, is a continuation of genetic algorithms but tackles advanced concepts involving how steps in the algorithm can be adjusted to solve different types of problems more optimally.

- *Chapter 6—Swarm intelligence: Ants*, digs into the intuition for swam intelligence and works through how the ant colony optimization algorithm uses a theory of how ants live and work to solve hard problems.

- *Chapter 7—Swarm intelligence: Particles*, continues with swarm algorithms while diving into what optimization problems are, and how they're solved using particle swarm optimization—as it seeks good solutions in large search spaces.

- *Chapter 8—Machine learning*, works through a machine learning workflow for data preparation, processing, modeling, and testing—to solve regression problems with linear regression, and classification problems with decision trees.

- *Chapter 9—Artificial neural networks*, uncovers the intuition, logical steps, and mathematical calculations in training and using an artificial neural network to find patterns in data and make predictions; while highlighting its place in a machine learning workflow.

- *Chapter 10—Reinforcement learning with Q-Learning*, covers the intuition of reinforcement learning from behavioral psychology, and works through the Q-Learning algorithm for agents to learn good and bad decisions to make in an environment.

The chapters should be read from start to end sequentially. Concepts and understandings are built up along the way as the chapters progress. It is useful to reference the Python code in the repository after reading each chapter to experiment and gain practical insight into how the respective algorithm can be implemented.

About the Code

This book contains Pseudocode to focus on the intuition and logical thinking behind the algorithms, as well as to ensure that the code is accessible to anyone, regardless of programming language preferences. Pseudocode is an informal way to describe instructions in code. It is intended to be more readable and understandable; basically more human-friendly.

With that said, all algorithms described in the book have examples of working Python code available on Github (http://mng.bz/Vgr0). Setup instructions and comments are provided in the source code to guide you as you learn. One potential learning approach would be to read each chapter then reference the code after to cement your understanding of the respective algorithms.

The Python source code is intended to be a reference for how the algorithms could be implemented. These examples are optimized FOR LEARNING and NOT PRODUCTION use. The code was written to serve as a tool for teaching. Using established libraries and frameworks is recommended for projects that will make their way into production, as they are usually optimized for performance, well tested, and well supported.

liveBook discussion forum

Purchase of *Grokking Artificial Intelligence Algorithms* includes free access to a private web forum run by Manning Publications where you can make comments about the book, ask technical questions, and receive help from the author and from other users. To access the forum, go to http://mng.bz/xWoe. You can also learn more about Manning's forums and the rules of conduct at https://livebook.manning.com/#!/discussion.

Manning's commitment to our readers is to provide a venue where a meaningful dialogue between individual readers and between readers and the author can take place. It is not a commitment to any specific amount of participation on the part of the author, whose contribution to the forum remains voluntary (and unpaid). We suggest you try asking the author some challenging questions lest his interest stray! The forum and the archives of previous discussions will be accessible from the publisher's website as long as the book is in print.

Other online resources

Source code for Grokking Artificial Intelligence Algorithms:
   http://mng.bz/Vgr0
Author website:
   https://rhurbans.com

about the author

Rishal has been obsessed with computers, technology, and crazy ideas since childhood. Throughout his career he has been involved in the leadership of teams and projects, hands-on software engineering, strategic planning, and the end-to-end design of solutions for various international businesses. He has also been responsible for actively growing a culture of pragmatism, learning and skills development within his company, community, and industry.

Rishal has a passion for business mechanics and strategy, growing people and teams, design thinking, artificial intelligence, and philosophy. Rishal has founded various digital products to help people and businesses be more productive and focus on what's important. He has also spoken at dozens of conferences around the globe to make complex concepts more accessible and help people elevate themselves.

This chapter covers

- Definition of AI as we know it

- Intuition of concepts that are applicable to AI

- Problem types in computer science and AI, and their properties

- Overview of the AI algorithms discussed in this book

- Real-world uses for AI

What is artificial intelligence?

Intelligence is a mystery—a concept that has no agreed-upon definition. Philosophers, psychologists, scientists, and engineers all have different opinions about what it is and how it emerges. We see intelligence in nature around us, such as groups of living creatures working together, and we see intelligence in the way that humans think and behave. In general, things that are autonomous yet adaptive are considered to be intelligent. *Autonomous* means that something does not need to be provided constant instructions; and *adaptive* means that it can change its behavior as the environment or problem space changes. When we look at living organisms and machines, we see that the core element for operation is data. Visuals that we see are data; sounds that we hear are data; measurements of the things around us are data. We consume data, process it all, and make decisions based on it; so a fundamental understanding of the concepts surrounding data is important for understanding artificial intelligence (AI) algorithms.

Defining AI

Some people argue that we don't understand what AI is because we struggle to define intelligence itself. Salvador Dalí believed that ambition is an attribute of intelligence; he said, "Intelligence without ambition is a bird without wings." Albert Einstein believed that imagination is a big factor in intelligence; he said, "The true sign of intelligence is not knowledge, but imagination." And Stephen Hawking said, "Intelligence is the ability to adapt," which focuses on being able to adapt to changes in the world. These three great minds had different outlooks on intelligence. With no true definitive answer to intelligence yet, we at least know that we base our understanding of intelligence on humans as being the dominant (and most intelligent) species.

For the sake of our sanity, and to stick to the practical applications in this book, we will loosely define AI as a synthetic system that exhibits "intelligent" behavior. Instead of trying to define something as AI or not AI, let's refer to the AI-likeness of it. Something might exhibit some aspects of intelligence because it helps us solve hard problems and provides value and utility. Usually, AI implementations that simulate vision, hearing, and other natural senses are seen to be AI-like. Solutions that are able to learn autonomously while adapting to new data and environments are also seen to be AI-likeness.

Here are some examples of things that exhibit AI-likeness:

- A system that succeeds at playing many types of complex games
- A cancer tumor detection system
- A system that generates artwork based on little input
- A self-driving car

Douglas Hofstadter said, "AI is whatever hasn't been done yet." In the examples just mentioned, a self-driving car may seem to be intelligent because it hasn't been perfected yet. Similarly, a computer that adds numbers was seen to be intelligent a while ago but is taken for granted now.

The bottom line is that *AI* is an ambiguous term that means different things to different people, industries, and disciplines. The algorithms in this book have been classified as AI algorithms in the past or present; whether they enable a specific definition of AI or not doesn't really matter. What matters is that they are useful for solving hard problems.

Understanding that data is core to AI algorithms

Data is the input to the wonderful algorithms that perform feats that almost appear to be magic. With the incorrect choice of data, poorly represented data, or missing data, algorithms perform poorly, so the outcome is only as good as the data provided. The world is filled with data, and that data exists in forms we can't even sense. Data can represent values that are measured numerically, such as the current temperature in the Arctic, the number of fish in a pond, or your current age in days. All these examples involve capturing accurate numeric values based on facts. It's difficult to misinterpret this data. The temperature at a specific location at a specific point in time is absolutely true and is not subject to any bias. This type of data is known as *quantitative data*.

Data can also represent values of observations, such as the smell of a flower or one's level of agreement with a politician's policies. This type of data is known as *qualitative data* and is sometimes difficult to interpret because it's not an absolute truth, but a perception of someone's truth. Figure 1.1 illustrates some examples of the quantitative and qualitative data around us.

Figure 1.1 Examples of data around us

Data is raw facts about things, so recordings of it usually have no bias. In the real world, however, data is collected, recorded, and related by people based on a specific context with a specific understanding of how the data may be used. The act of constructing meaningful insights to answer questions based on data is creating *information*. Furthermore, the act of utilizing information with experiences and consciously applying it creates *knowledge*. This is partly what we try to simulate with AI algorithms.

Figure 1.2 shows how quantitative and qualitative data can be interpreted. Standardized instruments such as clocks, calculators, and scales are usually used to measure quantitative data, whereas our senses of smell, sound, taste, touch, and sight, as well as our opinionated thoughts, are usually used to create qualitative data.

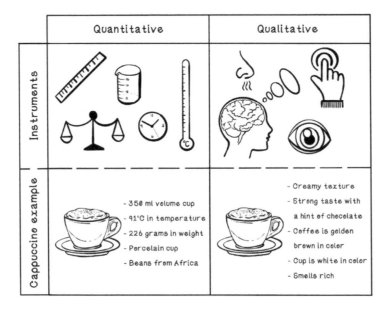

Figure 1.2 Qualitative data versus quantitative data

Data, information, and knowledge can be interpreted differently by different people, based on their level of understanding of that domain and their outlook on the world, and this fact has consequences for the quality of solutions—making the scientific aspect of creating technology hugely important. By following repeatable scientific processes to capture data, conduct experiments, and accurately report findings, we can ensure more accurate results and better solutions to problems when processing data with algorithms.

Viewing algorithms as instructions in recipes

We now have a loose definition of AI and an understanding of the importance of data. Because we will be exploring several AI algorithms throughout this book, it is useful to understand exactly what an algorithm is. An *algorithm* is a set of instructions and rules provided as a specification to accomplish a specific goal. Algorithms typically accept inputs, and after several finite steps in which the algorithm progresses through varying states, an output is produced.

Even something as simple as reading a book can be represented as an algorithm. Here's an example of the steps involved in reading this book:

1. Find the book *Grokking Artificial Intelligence Algorithms.*

2. Open the book.

3. While unread pages remain,

   a. Read page.

   b. Turn to next page.

   c. Think about what you have learned.

4. Think about how you can apply your learnings in the real world.

An algorithm can be viewed as a recipe, as seen in figure 1.3. Given some ingredients and tools as inputs, and instructions for creating a specific dish, a meal is the output.

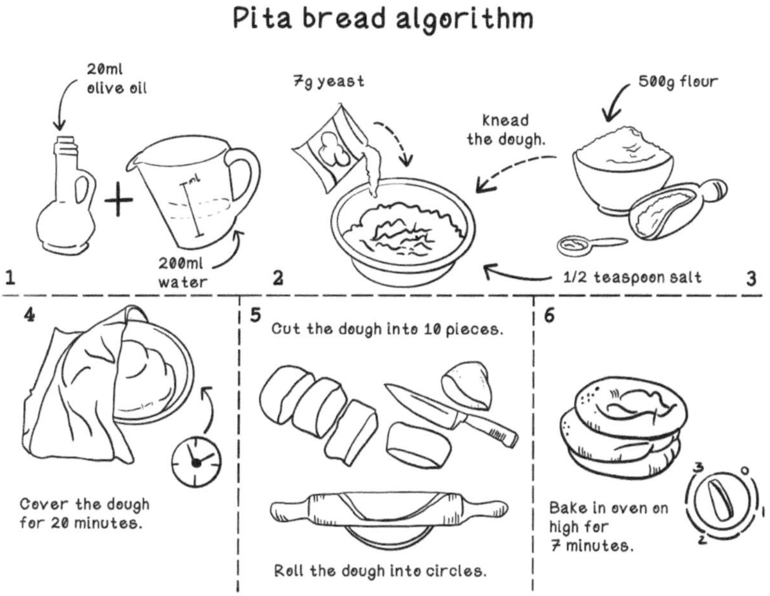

Pita bread algorithm

Figure 1.3 An example showing that an algorithm is like a recipe

Algorithms are used for many different solutions. For example, we can enable live video chat across the world through compression algorithms, and we can navigate cities through map applications that use real-time routing algorithms. Even a simple "Hello World" program has many algorithms at play to translate the human-readable programming language into machine code and execute the instructions on the hardware. You can find algorithms everywhere if you look closely enough.

To illustrate something more closely related to the algorithms in this book, figure 1.4 shows a number-guessing-game algorithm represented as a flow chart. The computer generates a random number in a given range, and the player attempts to guess that number. Notice that the algorithm has discrete steps that perform an action or determine a decision before moving to the next operation.

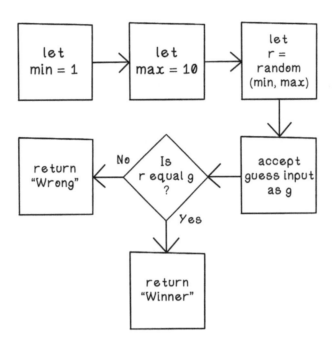

Figure 1.4 A number-guessing-game algorithm flow chart

Given our understanding of technology, data, intelligence, and algorithms: AI algorithms are sets of instructions that use data to create systems that exhibit intelligent behavior and solve hard problems.

A brief history of artificial intelligence

A brief look back at the strides made in AI is useful for understanding that old techniques and new ideas can be harnessed to solve problems in innovative ways. AI is not a new idea. History is filled with myths of mechanical men and autonomous "thinking" machines. Looking back, we find that we're standing on the shoulders of giants. Perhaps we ourselves can contribute to the pool of knowledge in a small way.

Looking at past developments highlights the importance of understanding the fundamentals of AI; algorithms from decades ago are critical in many modern AI implementations. This book starts with fundamental algorithms that help build the intuition of problem-solving and gradually moves to more interesting and modern approaches.

Figure 1.5 isn't an exhaustive list of achievements in AI—it is simply a small set of examples. History is filled with many more breakthroughs!

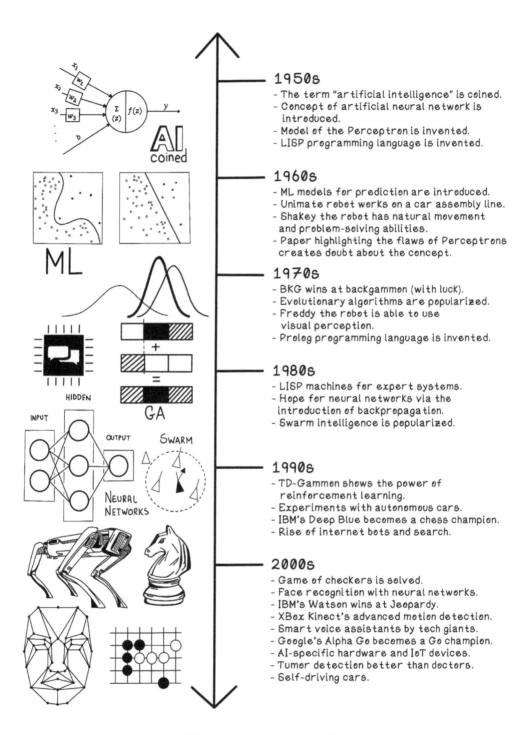

1950s
- The term "artificial intelligence" is coined.
- Concept of artificial neural network is introduced.
- Model of the Perceptron is invented.
- LISP programming language is invented.

1960s
- ML models for prediction are introduced.
- Unimate robot works on a car assembly line.
- Shakey the robot has natural movement and problem-solving abilities.
- Paper highlighting the flaws of Perceptrons creates doubt about the concept.

1970s
- BKG wins at backgammon (with luck).
- Evolutionary algorithms are popularized.
- Freddy the robot is able to use visual perception.
- Prolog programming language is invented.

1980s
- LISP machines for expert systems.
- Hope for neural networks via the introduction of backpropagation.
- Swarm intelligence is popularized.

1990s
- TD-Gammon shows the power of reinforcement learning.
- Experiments with autonomous cars.
- IBM's Deep Blue becomes a chess champion.
- Rise of internet bots and search.

2000s
- Game of checkers is solved.
- Face recognition with neural networks.
- IBM's Watson wins at Jeopardy.
- XBox Kinect's advanced motion detection.
- Smart voice assistants by tech giants.
- Google's Alpha Go becomes a Go champion.
- AI-specific hardware and IoT devices.
- Tumor detection better than doctors.
- Self-driving cars.

Figure 1.5 The evolution of AI

Problem types and problem-solving paradigms

AI algorithms are powerful, but they are not silver bullets that can solve any problem. But what are problems? This section looks at different types of problems that we usually experience in computer science, showing how we can start gaining intuition about them. This intuition can help us identify these problems in the real world and guide the choice of algorithms used in the solution.

Several terms in computer science and AI are used to describe problems. Problems are classified based on the *context* and the *goal*.

Search problems: Find a path to a solution

A *search problem* involves a situation that has multiple possible solutions, each of which represents a sequence of steps (path) toward a goal. Some solutions contain overlapping subsets of paths; some are better than others; and some are cheaper to achieve than others. A "better" solution is determined by the specific problem at hand; a "cheaper" solution means computationally cheaper to execute. An example is determining the shortest path between cities on a map. Many routes may be available, with different distances and traffic conditions, but some routes are better than others. Many AI algorithms are based on the concept of searching a solution space.

Optimization problems: Find a good solution

An *optimization problem* involves a situation in which there are a vast number of valid solutions and the absolute-best solution is difficult to find. Optimization problems usually have an enormous number of possibilities, each of which differs in how well it solves the problem. An example is packing luggage in the trunk of a car in such a way as to maximize the use of space. Many combinations are available, and if the trunk is packed effectively, more luggage can fit in it.

> *Local best versus global best*
>
> Because optimization problems have many solutions, and because these solutions exist at different points in the search space, the concept of local bests and global bests comes into play. A *local best* solution is the best solution within a specific area in the search space, and a *global best* is the best solution in the entire search space. Usually, there are many local best solutions and one global best solution. Consider searching for the best restaurant, for example. You may find the best restaurant in your local area, but it may not necessarily be the best restaurant in the country or the best restaurant in the world.

Prediction and classification problems: Learn from patterns in data

Prediction problems are problems in which we have data about something and want to try to find patterns. For example, we might have data about different vehicles and their engine sizes, as well as each vehicle's fuel consumption. Can we predict the fuel consumption of a new model of vehicle, given its engine size? If there's a correlation in the data between engine sizes and fuel consumption, this prediction is possible.

Classification problems are similar to prediction problems, but instead of trying to find an exact prediction such as fuel consumption, we try to find a category of something based on its features. Given the dimensions of a vehicle, its engine size, and the number of seats, can we predict whether that vehicle is a motorcycle, sedan, or sport-utility vehicle? Classification problems require finding patterns in the data that group examples into categories. Interpolation is an important concept when finding patterns in data because we estimate new data points based on the known data.

Clustering problems: Identify patterns in data

Clustering problems include scenarios in which trends and relationships are uncovered from data. Different aspects of the data are used to group examples in different ways. Given cost and location data about restaurants, for example, we may find that younger people tend to frequent locations where the food is cheaper.

Clustering aims to find relationships in data even when a precise question is not being asked. This approach is also useful for gaining a better understanding of data to inform what you might be able to do with it.

Deterministic models: Same result each time it's calculated

Deterministic models are models that, given a specific input, return a consistent output. Given the time as noon in a specific city, for example, we can always expect there to be daylight; and given the time as midnight, we can always expect darkness. Obviously this simple example doesn't take into account the unusual daylight durations near the poles of the planet.

Stochastic/probabilistic models: Potentially different result each time it's calculated

Probabilistic models are models that, given a specific input, return an outcome from a set of possible outcomes. Probabilistic models usually have an element of controlled randomness that contributes to the possible set of outcomes. Given the time as noon, for example, we can expect the weather to be sunny, cloudy, or rainy; there is no fixed weather at this time.

Intuition of artificial intelligence concepts

AI is a hot topic, as are machine learning and deep learning. Trying to make sense of these different but similar concepts can be a daunting experience. Additionally, within the domain of AI, distinctions exist among different levels of intelligence.

In this section, we demystify some of these concepts. The section is also a road map of the topics covered throughout this book.

Let's dive into the different levels of AI, introduced with figure 1.6.

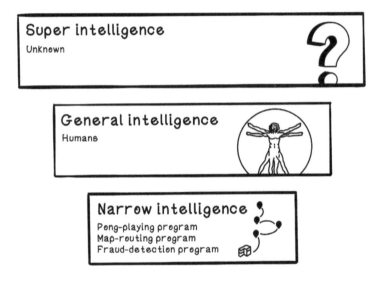

Figure 1.6 Levels of AI

Narrow intelligence: Specific-purpose solutions

Narrow intelligence systems solve problems in a specific context or domain. These systems usually cannot solve a problem in one context and apply that same understanding in another. A system developed to understand customer interactions and spending behavior, for example, would not be capable of identifying cats in an image. Usually, for something to be effective in solving a problem, it needs to be quite specialized in the domain of the problem, which makes it difficult to adapt to other problems.

Different narrow intelligence systems can be combined in sensible ways to create something greater that seems to be more general in its intelligence. An example is a voice assistant. This system can understand natural language, which alone is a narrow problem, but through integration with other narrow intelligence systems, such as web searches and music recommenders, it can exhibit qualities of general intelligence.

General intelligence: Humanlike solutions

General intelligence is humanlike intelligence. As humans, we are able to learn from various experiences and interactions in the world and apply that understanding from one problem to another. If you felt pain when touching something hot as a child, for example, you can extrapolate and know that other things that are hot may have a chance of hurting you. General intelligence in humans, however, is more than just reasoning something like "Hot things may be harmful." General intelligence encompasses memory, spatial reasoning through visual inputs, use of knowledge, and more. Achieving general intelligence in a machine seems to be an unlikely feat in the short term, but advancements in quantum computing, data processing, and AI algorithms could make it a reality in the future.

Super intelligence: The great unknown

Some ideas of *super intelligence* appear in science-fiction movies set in postapocalyptic worlds, in which all machines are connected, are able to reason about things beyond our understanding, and dominate humans. There are many philosophical differences about whether humans could create something more intelligent than ourselves and, if we could, whether we'd even know. Super intelligence is the great unknown, and for a long time, any definitions will be speculation.

Old AI and new AI

Sometimes, the notions of old AI and new AI are used. *Old AI* is often understood as being systems in which people encoded the rules that cause an algorithm to exhibit intelligent behavior—via in-depth knowledge of the problem or by trial and error. An example of old AI is a person manually creating a decision tree and the rules and options in the entire decision tree. *New AI* aims to create algorithms and models that learn from data and create their own rules that perform as accurately as, or better than, human-created rules. The difference is that the latter may find important patterns in the data that a person may never find or that would take a person much longer to find. Search algorithms are often seen as old AI, but a robust understanding of them is useful in learning more complex approaches. This book aims to introduce the most popular AI algorithms and gradually build on each concept. Figure 1.7 illustrates the relationship between some of the different concepts within artificial intelligence.

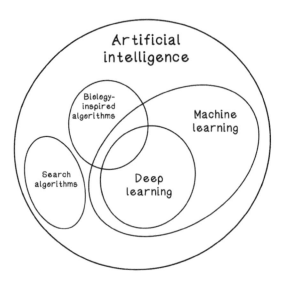

Figure 1.7 Categorization of concepts within AI

Search algorithms

Search algorithms are useful for solving problems in which several actions are required to achieve a goal, such as finding a path through a maze or determining the best move to make in a game. Search algorithms evaluate future states and attempt to find the optimal path to the most valuable goal. Typically, we have too many possible solutions to brute-force each one. Even small search spaces could result in thousands of hours of computing to find the best solution. Search algorithms provide smart ways to evaluate the search space. Search algorithms are used in online search engines, map routing applications, and even game-playing agents.

Biology-inspired algorithms

When we look at the world around us, we notice incredible things in various creatures, plants, and other living organisms. Examples include the cooperation of ants in gathering food, the flocking of birds when migrating, estimating how brains work, and the evolution of different organisms to produce stronger offspring. By observing and learning from various phenomena, we've gained knowledge of how these organic systems operate and of how simple rules can result in emergent intelligent behavior. Some of these phenomena have inspired algorithms that are useful in AI, such as evolutionary algorithms and swarm intelligence algorithms.

Evolutionary algorithms are inspired by the theory of evolution defined by Charles Darwin. The concept is that a population reproduces to create new individuals and that through this process, the mixture of genes and mutation produces individuals that perform better than their ancestors. *Swarm intelligence* is a group of seemingly "dumb" individuals exhibiting intelligent behavior. Ant-colony optimization and particle-swarm optimization are two popular algorithms that we will be exploring in this book.

Machine learning algorithms

Machine learning takes a statistical approach to training models to learn from data. The umbrella of machine learning has a variety of algorithms that can be harnessed to improve understanding of relationships in data, to make decisions, and to make predictions based on that data.

There are three main approaches in machine learning:

- *Supervised learning* means training models with algorithms when the training data has known outcomes for a question being asked, such as determining the type of fruit if we have a set of data that includes the weight, color, texture, and fruit label for each example.

- *Unsupervised learning* uncovers hidden relationships and structures within the data that guide us in asking the dataset relevant questions. It may find patterns in properties of similar fruits and group them accordingly, which can inform the exact questions we want to ask the data. These core concepts and algorithms helps us create a foundation for exploring advanced algorithms in the future.

- *Reinforcement learning* is inspired by behavioral psychology. In short, it describes rewarding an individual if a useful action was performed and penalizing that individual if an unfavorable action was performed. To explore a human example, when a child achieves good results on their report card, they are usually rewarded, but poor performance sometimes results in punishment, reinforcing the behavior of achieving good results. Reinforcement learning is useful for exploring how computer programs or robots interact with dynamic environments. An example is a robot that is tasked to open doors; it is penalized when it doesn't open a door and rewarded when it does. Over time, after many attempts, the robot "learns" the sequence of actions required to open a door.

Deep learning algorithms

Deep learning, which stems from machine learning, is a broader family of approaches and algorithms that are used to achieve narrow intelligence and strive toward general intelligence. Deep learning usually implies that the approach is attempting to solve a problem in a more general way like spatial reasoning, or it is being applied to problems that require more generalization such as computer vision and speech recognition. General problems are things humans are good at solving. For example, we can match visual patterns in almost any context. Deep learning also concerns itself with supervised learning, unsupervised learning, and reinforcement learning. Deep learning approaches usually employ many layers of artificial neural networks. By leveraging different layers of intelligent components, each layer solves specialized problems; together, the layers solve complex problems toward a greater goal. Identifying any object in an image, for example, is a general problem, but it can be broken into understanding color, recognizing shapes of objects, and identifying relationships among objects to achieve a goal.

Uses for artificial intelligence algorithms

The uses for AI techniques are potentially endless. Where there are data and problems to solve, there are potential applications of AI. Given the ever-changing environment, the evolution of interactions among humans, and the changes in what people and industries demand, AI can be applied in innovative ways to solve real-world problems. This section describes the application of AI in various industries.

Agriculture: Optimal plant growth

One of the most important industries that sustain human life is agriculture. We need to be able to grow quality crops for mass consumption economically. Many farmers grow crops on a commercial scale to enable us to purchase fruit and vegetables at stores conveniently. Crops grow differently based on the type of crop, the nutrients in the soil, the water content of the soil, the bacteria in the water, and the weather conditions in the area, among other things. The goal is to grow as much high-quality produce as possible within a season, because specific crops generally grow well only during specific seasons.

Farmers and other agriculture organizations have captured data about their farms and crops over the years. Using that data, we can leverage machines to find patterns and relationships among the variables in the crop-growing process and identify the factors that contribute most to successful growth. Furthermore, with modern digital sensors, we can record weather conditions, soil attributes, water conditions, and crop growth in real time. This data, combined with intelligent algorithms, can enable real-time recommendations and adjustments for optimal growth (figure 1.8).

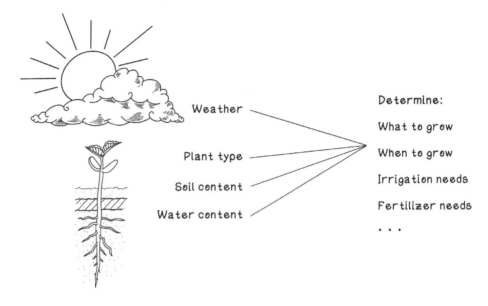

Figure 1.8 Using data to optimize crop farming

Banking: Fraud detection

The need for banking became obvious when we had to find a common consistent currency for trading goods and services. Banks have changed over the years to offer different options for storing money, investing money, and making payments. One thing that hasn't changed over time is people finding creative ways to cheat the system. One of the biggest problems—not only in banking but also in most financial institutions, such as insurance companies—is fraud. *Fraud* occurs when someone is dishonest or does something illegal to acquire something for themselves. Fraud usually happens when loopholes in a process are exploited or a scam fools someone into divulging information. Because the financial-services industry is highly connected through the internet and personal devices, more transactions happen electronically over a computer network than in person, with physical money. With the vast amounts of transaction data available, we can, in real-time, find patterns of transactions specific to an individual's spending behavior that may be out of the ordinary. This data helps save financial institutions enormous amounts of money and protects unsuspecting consumers from being robbed.

Cybersecurity: Attack detection and handling

One of the interesting side effects of the internet boom is cybersecurity. We send and receive sensitive information over the internet all the time—instant messages, credit-card details, emails, and other important confidential information that could be misused if it fell into the wrong hands. Thousands of servers across the globe receive data, process it, and store it. Attackers attempt to compromise these systems to gain access to the data, devices, or even facilities.

By using AI, we can identify and block potential attacks on servers. Some large internet companies store data about how specific individuals interact with their service, including their device IDs, geolocations, and usage behavior; when unusual behavior is detected, security measures limit access. Some internet companies can also block and redirect malicious traffic during a distributed denial of service (DDoS) attack, which involves overloading a service with bogus requests in an attempt to bring it down or prevent access by authentic users. These unauthentic requests can be identified and rerouted to minimize the impact of the attack by understanding the users' usage data, the systems, and the network.

Health care: Diagnosis of patients

Health care has been a constant concern throughout human history. We need access to diagnosis and treatment of different ailments in different locations in varying windows of time before a problem becomes more severe or even fatal. When we look at the diagnosis of a patient, we may look at the vast amounts of knowledge recorded about the human body, known problems, experience in dealing with these problems, and a myriad of scans of the body. Traditionally, doctors were required to analyze images of scans to detect the presence of tumors, but this approach resulted in the detection of only the largest, most advanced tumors. Advances in deep learning have improved the detection of tumors in images generated by scans. Now doctors can detect cancer earlier, which means that a patient can get the required treatment in time and have a higher chance of recovery.

Furthermore, AI can be used to find patterns in symptoms, ailments, hereditary genes, geographic locations, and the like. We could potentially know that someone has a high probability of developing a specific ailment and be prepared to manage that ailment before it develops. Figure 1.9 illustrates feature recognition of a brain scan using deep learning.

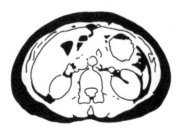 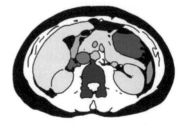

Brain scan   Brain scan with feature recognition

Figure 1.9 Using machine learning for feature recognition in brain scans

Logistics: Routing and optimization

The logistics industry is a huge market of different types of vehicles delivering different types of goods to different locations, with different demands and deadlines. Imagine the complexity in a large e-commerce site's delivery planning. Whether the deliverables are consumer goods, construction equipment, parts for machinery, or fuel, the system aims to be as optimal as possible to ensure that demand is met and costs are minimized.

You may have heard of the traveling-salesperson problem: a salesperson needs to visit several locations to complete their job, and the aim is to find the shortest distance to accomplish this task. Logistics problems are similar but usually immensely more complex due to the changing environment of the real world. Through AI, we can find optimal routes between locations in terms of time and distance. Furthermore, we can find the best routes based on traffic patterns, construction blockages, and even road types based on the vehicle being used. Additionally, we can compute the best way to pack each vehicle and what to pack in each vehicle in such a way that each delivery is optimized.

Telecoms: Optimizing networks

The telecommunications industry has played a huge role in connecting the world. These companies lay expensive infrastructure of cables, towers, and satellites to create a network that many consumers and organizations can use to communicate via the internet or private networks. Operating this equipment is expensive, so optimization of a network allows for more connections, which allows more people to access high-speed connections. AI can be used to monitor behavior on a network and optimize routing. Additionally, these networks record requests and responses; this data can be used to optimize the networks based on known load from certain individuals, areas, and specific local networks. The network data can also be instrumental for understanding where people are and who they are, which is useful for city planning.

Games: Creating AI agents

Since home and personal computers first became widely available, games have been a selling point for computer systems. Games were popular very early in the history of personal computers. If we think back, we may remember arcade machines, television consoles, and personal computers with gaming capabilities. The games of chess, backgammon, and others have been dominated by AI machines. If the complexity of a game is low enough, a computer can potentially find all possibilities and make a decision based on that knowledge faster than a human can. Recently, a computer was able to defeat human champions in the strategic game, Go. Go has simple rules for territory control but has huge complexity in terms of the decisions that need to be made for a winning scenario. A computer can't generate all possibilities for beating the best human players because the search space is so large; instead, it calls for a more-general algorithm that can "think" abstractly, strategize, and plan moves toward a goal. That algorithm has already been invented and has succeeded in defeating world champions. It has also been adapted to other applications, such as playing Atari games and modern multiplayer games. This system is called Alpha Go.

Several research organizations have developed AI systems that are capable of playing highly complex games better than human players and teams. The goal of this work is to create general approaches that can adapt to different contexts. At face value, these game-playing AI algorithms may seem unimportant, but the consequence of developing these systems is that the approach can be applied effectively in other important problem spaces. Figure 1.10 illustrates how a reinforcement learning algorithm can learn to play a classic video game like Mario.

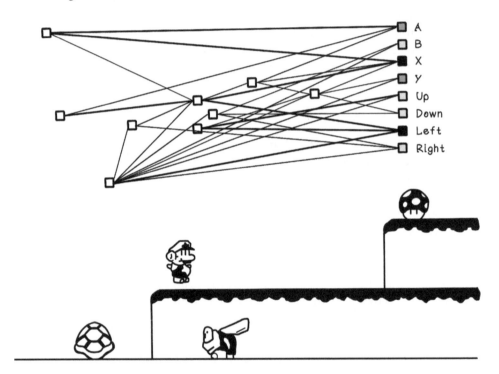

Figure 1.10 Using neural networks to learn how to play games

Art: Creating masterpieces

Unique, interesting artists have created beautiful paintings. Each artist has their own way of expressing the world around them. We also have amazing music compositions that are appreciated by the masses. In both cases, the quality of the art cannot be measured quantitatively; rather, it is measured qualitatively (by how much people enjoy the piece). The factors involved are difficult to understand and capture; the concept is driven by emotion.

Many research projects aim to build AI that generates art. The concept involves generalization. An algorithm would need to have a broad and general understanding of the subject to create something that fits those parameters. A Van Gogh AI, for example, would need to understand all of Van Gogh's work and extract the style and "feel" so that it can apply that data to other images. The same thinking can be applied to extracting hidden patterns in areas such as health care, cybersecurity, and finance.

Now that we have abstract intuition about what AI is, the categorization of themes within it, the problems it aims to solve, and some use cases, we will be diving into one of the oldest and simplest forms of mimicking intelligence: search algorithms. Search algorithms provide a good grounding in some concepts that are employed by other, more sophisticated AI algorithms explored throughout this book.

SUMMARY OF INTUITION OF ARTIFICIAL INTELLIGENCE

AI is difficult to define. There is no clear consensus.

Look at implementations as being AI-like things that exhibit intelligence.

Many disciplines are encompassed in AI.

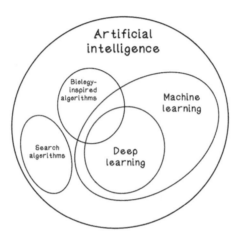

AI implementations almost always have room for error. Be cautious about the consequences of this.

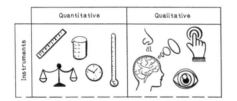 Quality and preparation of data is important.

AI has many uses and applications. Apply your mind!

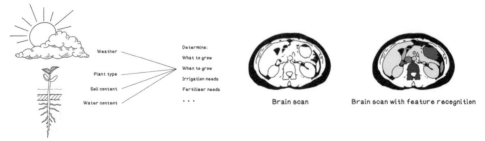

Be responsible when developing technology.

This chapter covers

- The intuition of planning and searching

- Identifying problems suited to be solved using search algorithms

- Representing problem spaces in a way suitable to be processed by search algorithms

- Understanding and designing fundamental search algorithms to solve problems

What are planning and searching?

When we think about what makes us intelligent, the ability to plan before carrying out actions is a prominent attribute. Before embarking on a trip to a different country, before starting a new project, before writing functions in code, planning happens. *Planning* happens at different levels of detail in different contexts to strive for the best possible outcome when carrying out the tasks involved in accomplishing goals (figure 2.1).

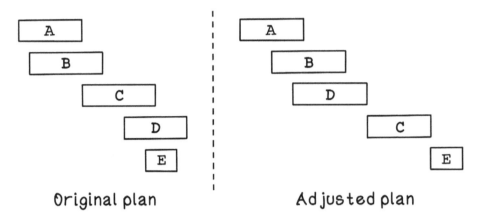

Figure 2.1 Example of how plans change in projects

Plans rarely work out perfectly in the way we envision at the start of an endeavor. We live in a world in which environments are constantly changing, so it is impossible to account for all the variables and unknowns along the way. Regardless of the plan we started with, we almost always deviate due to changes in the problem space. We need to (again) make a new plan from our current point going forward, if after we take more steps, unexpected events occur that require another iteration of planning to meet the goals. As a result, the final plan that is carried out is usually different from the original one.

Searching is a way to guide planning by creating steps in a plan. When we plan a trip, for example, we search for routes to take, evaluate the stops along the way and what they offer, and search for accommodations and activities that align with our liking and budget. Depending on the results of these searches, the plan changes.

Suppose that we have settled on a trip to the beach, which is 500 kilometers away, with two stops: one at a petting zoo and one at a pizza restaurant. We will sleep at a lodge close to the beach on arrival and partake in three activities. The trip to the destination will take approximately 8 hours. We're also taking a shortcut private road after the restaurant, but it's open only until 2:00.

We start the trip, and everything is going according to plan. We stop at the petting zoo and see some wonderful animals. We drive on and start getting hungry; it's time for the stop at the restaurant. But to our surprise, the restaurant recently went out of business. We need to adjust our plan and find another place to eat, which involves searching for a close-by establishment of our liking and adjusting our plan.

After driving around for a while, we find a restaurant, enjoy a pizza, and get back on the road. Upon approaching the shortcut private road, we realize that it's 2:20. The road is closed; yet again, we need to adjust our plan. We search for a detour and find that it will add 120 kilometers to our drive, and we will need to find accommodations for the night at a different lodge before we even get to the beach. We search for a place to sleep and plot out our new route. Due to lost time, we can partake in only two activities at the destination. The plan has been adjusted heavily through searching for different options that satisfy each new situation, but we end up having a great adventure en route to the beach.

This example shows how search is used for planning and influences planning toward desirable outcomes. As the environment changes, our goals may change slightly, and our path to them inevitably needs to be adjusted (figure 2.2). Adjustments in plans can almost never be anticipated and need to be made as required.

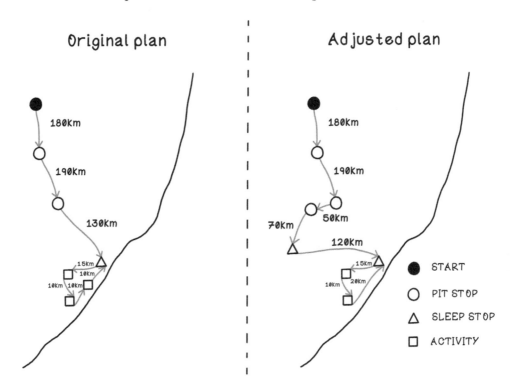

Figure 2.2 Original plan versus adjusted plan for a road trip

Searching involves evaluating future states toward a goal with the aim of finding an optimal path of states until the goal is reached. This chapter centers on different approaches to searching depending on different types of problems. Searching is an old but powerful tool for developing intelligent algorithms to solve problems.

Cost of computation:
The reason for smart algorithms

In programming, functions consist of operations, and due to the way that traditional computers work, different functions use different amounts of processing time. The more computation required, the more expensive the function is. *Big O notation* is used to describe the complexity of a function or algorithm. Big O notation models the number of operations required as the input size increases. Here are some examples and associated complexities:

- *A single operation that prints* `Hello World`—This operation is a single operation, so the cost of computation is O(1).

- *A function that iterates over a list and prints each item in the list*—The number of operations is dependent on the number of items in the list. The cost is O(n).

- *A function that compares every item in a list with every item in another list*—This operation costs O(n²).

Figure 2.3 depicts different costs of algorithms. Algorithms that require operations to explore as the size of the input increases are the worst-performing; algorithms that require a more constant number of operations as the number of inputs increases are better.

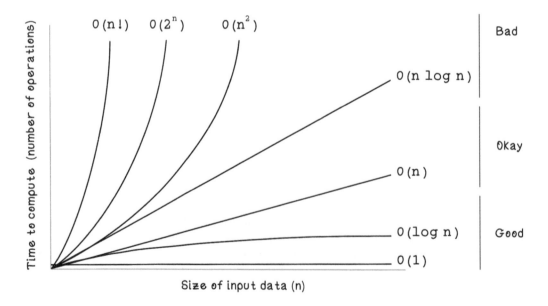

Figure 2.3 Big O complexity

Understanding that different algorithms have different computation costs is important because addressing this is the entire purpose of intelligent algorithms that solve problems well and quickly. Theoretically, we can solve almost any problem by brute-forcing every possible option until we find the best one, but in reality, the computation could take hours or even years, which makes it infeasible for real-world scenarios.

Problems applicable to searching algorithms

Almost any problem that requires a series of decisions to be made can be solved with search algorithms. Depending on the problem and the size of the search space, different algorithms may be employed to help solve it. Depending on the search algorithm selected and the configuration used, the optimal solution or a best available solution may be found. In other words, a good solution will be found, but it might not necessarily be the best solution. When we speak about a "good solution" or "optimal solution," we are referring to the performance of the solution in addressing the problem at hand.

One scenario in which search algorithms are useful is being stuck in a maze and attempting to find the shortest path to a goal. Suppose that we're in a square maze consisting of an area of 10 blocks by 10 blocks (figure 2.4). There exists a goal that we want to reach and barriers that we cannot step into. The objective is to find a path to the goal while avoiding barriers with as few steps as possible by moving north, south, east, or west. In this example, the player cannot move diagonally.

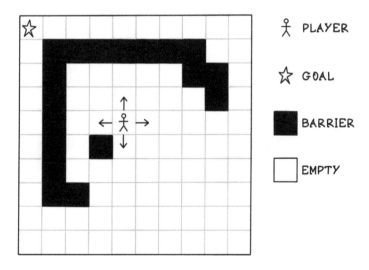

Figure 2.4 An example of the maze problem

How can we find the shortest path to the goal while avoiding barriers? By evaluating the problem as a human, we can try each possibility and count the moves. Using trial and error, we can find the paths that are the shortest, given that this maze is relatively small.

Using the example maze, figure 2.5 depicts some possible paths to reach the goal, although note that we don't reach the goal in option 1.

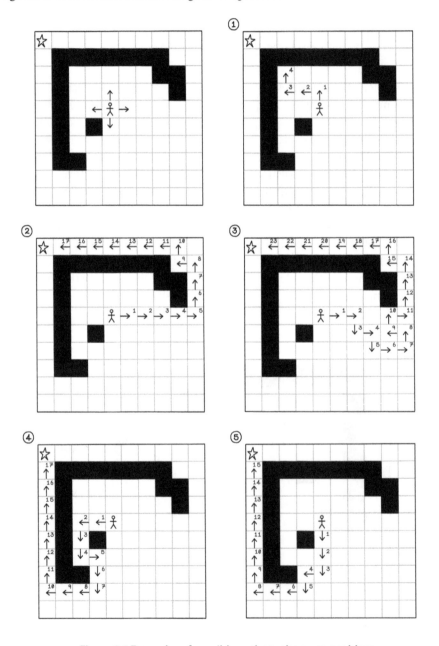

Figure 2.5 Examples of possible paths to the maze problem

By looking at the maze and counting blocks in different directions, we can find several solutions to the problem. Five attempts have been made to find four successful solutions out of an unknown number of solutions. It will take exhaustive effort to attempt to compute all possible solutions by hand:

- Attempt 1 is not a valid solution. It took 4 actions, and the goal was not found.

- Attempt 2 is a valid solution, taking 17 actions to find the goal.

- Attempt 3 is a valid solution, taking 23 actions to find the goal.

- Attempt 4 is a valid solution, taking 17 actions to find the goal.

- Attempt 5 is the best valid solution, taking 15 actions to find the goal. Although this attempt is the best one, it was found by chance.

If the maze were a lot larger, like the one in figure 2.6, it would take an immense amount of time to compute the best possible path manually. Search algorithms can help.

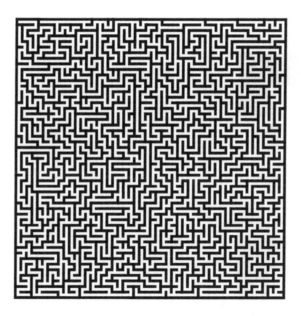

Figure 2.6 A large example of the maze problem

Our power as humans is to perceive a problem visually, understand it, and find solutions given the parameters. As humans, we understand and interpret data and information in an abstract way. A computer cannot yet understand generalized information in the natural form that we do. The problem space needs to be represented in a form that is applicable to computation and can be processed with search algorithms.

Representing state: Creating a framework to represent problem spaces and solutions

When representing data and information in a way that a computer can understand, we need to encode it logically so that it can be understood objectively. Although the data will be encoded subjectively by the person who performs the task, there should be a concise, consistent way to represent it.

Let's clarify the difference between data and information. *Data* is raw facts about something, and *information* is an interpretation of those facts that provides insight about the data in the specific domain. Information requires context and processing of data to provide meaning. As an example, each individual distance traveled in the maze example is data, and the sum of the total distance traveled is information. Depending on the perspective, level of detail, and desired outcome, classifying something as data or information can be subjective to the context and person or team (figure 2.7).

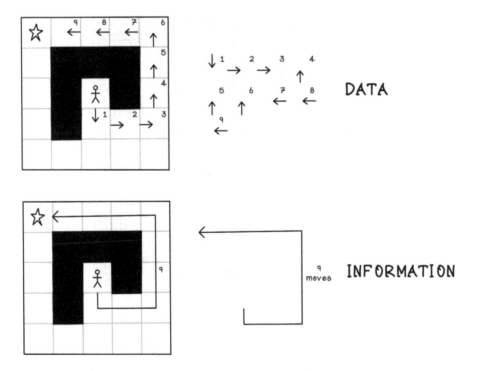

Figure 2.7 Data versus information

Data structures are concepts in computer science used to represent data in a way that is suitable for efficient processing by algorithms. A data structure is an abstract data type consisting of data and operations organized in a specific way. The data structure we use is influenced by the context of the problem and the desired goal.

An example of a data structure is an *array*, which is simply a collection of data. Different types of arrays have different properties that make them efficient for different purposes. Depending on the programming language used, an array could allow each value to be of a different type or require each value to be the same type, or the array may disallow duplicate values. These different types of arrays usually have different names. The features and constraints of different data structures also enable more efficient computation (figure 2.8).

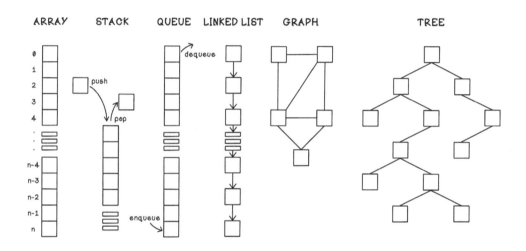

Figure 2.8 Data structures used with algorithms

Other data structures are useful in planning and searching. Trees and graphs are ideal for representing data in a way that search algorithms can use.

Graphs: Representing search problems and solutions

A *graph* is a data structure containing several states with connections among them. Each state in a graph is called a *node* (or sometimes a *vertex*), and a connection between two states is called an *edge*. Graphs are derived from graph theory in mathematics and used to model relationships among objects. Graphs are useful data structures that are easy for humans to understand, due to the ease of representing them visually as well as to their strong logical nature, which is ideal for processing via various algorithms (figure 2.9).

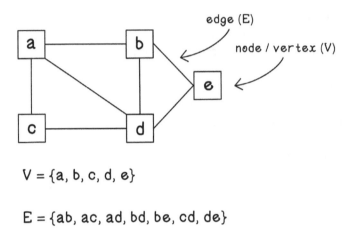

$$V = \{a, b, c, d, e\}$$

$$E = \{ab, ac, ad, bd, be, cd, de\}$$

Figure 2.9 The notation used to represent graphs

Figure 2.10 is a graph of the trip to the beach discussed in the first section of this chapter. Each stop is a node on the graph; each edge between nodes represent points traveled between; and the weights on each edge indicate the distance traveled.

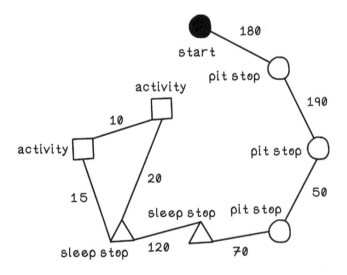

Figure 2.10 The example road trip represented as a graph

Representing a graph as a concrete data structure

A graph can be represented in several ways for efficient processing by algorithms. At its core, a graph can be represented by an array of arrays that indicates relationships among nodes, as shown in figure 2.11. It is sometimes useful to have another array that simply lists all nodes in the graph so that the distinct nodes do not need to be inferred from the relationships.

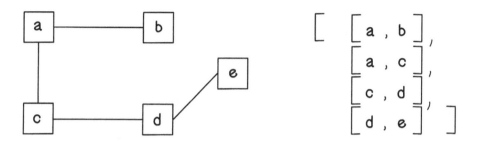

Figure 2.11 Representing a graph as an array of arrays

Other representations of graphs include an incidence matrix, an adjacency matrix, and an adjacency list. By looking at the names of these representations, you see that the adjacency of nodes in a graph is important. An *adjacent node* is a node that is connected directly to another node.

EXERCISE: REPRESENT A GRAPH AS A MATRIX
How would you represent the following graph using edge arrays?

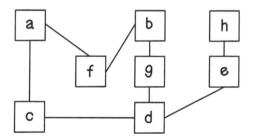

SOLUTION: REPRESENT A GRAPH AS A MATRIX

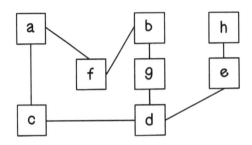

	a	b	c	d	e	f	g	h
a	0	0	1	0	0	1	0	0
b	0	0	0	0	0	1	1	0
c	1	0	0	1	0	0	0	0
d	0	0	1	0	1	0	1	0
e	0	0	0	1	0	0	0	1
f	1	1	0	0	0	0	0	0
g	0	1	0	1	0	0	0	0
h	0	0	0	0	1	0	0	0

```
[ [ a, c ],
  [ a, f ],
  [ b, g ],
  [ b, f ],
  [ c, d ],
  [ d, g ],
  [ d, e ],
  [ e, h ]  ]
```

Array of edges   Adjacency matrix

Trees: The concrete structures used to represent search solutions

A *tree* is a popular data structure that simulates a hierarchy of values or objects. A *hierarchy* is an arrangement of things in which a single object is related to several other objects below it. A tree is a *connected acyclic graph*—every node has an edge to another node, and no cycles exist.

In a tree, the value or object represented at a specific point is called a *node*. Trees typically have a single root node with zero or more child nodes that could contain subtrees. Let's take a deep breath and jump into some terminology. When a node has connected nodes, the root node is called the *parent*. You can apply this thinking recursively. A child node may have its own child nodes, which may also contain subtrees. Each child node has a single parent node. A node without any children is a leaf node.

Trees also have a total height. The level of specific nodes is called a *depth*.

The terminology used to relate family members is heavily used in working with trees. Keep this analogy in mind, as it will help you connect the concepts in the tree data structure. Note that in figure 2.12, the height and depth are indexed from 0 from the root node.

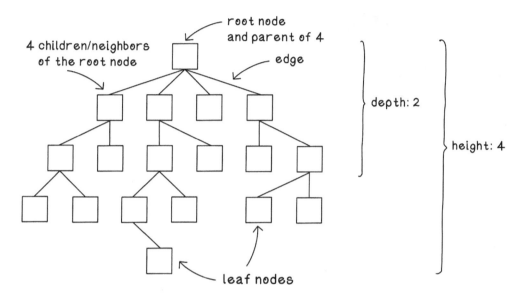

Figure 2.12 The main attributes of a tree

The topmost node in a tree is called the *root node*. A node directly connected to one or more other nodes is called a *parent node*. The nodes connected to a parent node are called *child nodes* **or** *neighbors*. Nodes connected to the same parent node are called *siblings*. A connection between two nodes is called an *edge*.

A *path* is a sequence of nodes and edges connecting nodes that are not directly connected. A node connected to another node by following a path away from the root node is called a *descendent*, and a node connected to another node by following a path toward the root node is called an *ancestor*. A node with no children is called a *leaf node*. The term *degree* is used to describe the number of children a node has; therefore, a leaf node has degree zero.

Figure 2.13 represents a path from the start point to the goal for the maze problem. This path contains nine nodes that represent different moves being made in the maze.

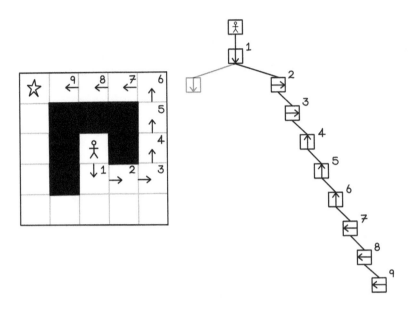

Figure 2.13 A solution to the maze problem represented as a tree

Trees are the fundamental data structure for search algorithms, which we will be diving into next. Sorting algorithms are also useful in solving certain problems and computing solutions more efficiently. If you're interested in learning more about sorting algorithms, take a look at *Grokking Algorithms* (Manning Publications).

Uninformed search: Looking blindly for solutions

Uninformed search is also known as *unguided search*, *blind search*, or *brute-force search*. Uninformed search algorithms have no additional information about the domain of the problem apart from the representation of the problem, which is usually a tree.

Think about exploring things you want to learn. Some people might look at a wide breadth of different topics and learn the basics of each, whereas other people might choose one narrow topic and explore its subtopics in depth. This is what breadth-first search (BFS) and depth-first search (DFS) involve, respectively. *Depth-first search* explores a specific path from the start until it finds a goal at the utmost depth. *Breadth-first search* explores all options at a specific depth before moving to options deeper in the tree.

Consider the maze scenario (figure 2.14). In attempting to find an optimal path to the goal, assume the following simple constraint to prevent getting stuck in an endless loop and prevent cycles in our tree: *the player cannot move into a block that they have previously occupied.* Because uninformed algorithms attempt every possible option at every node, creating a cycle will cause the algorithm to fail catastrophically.

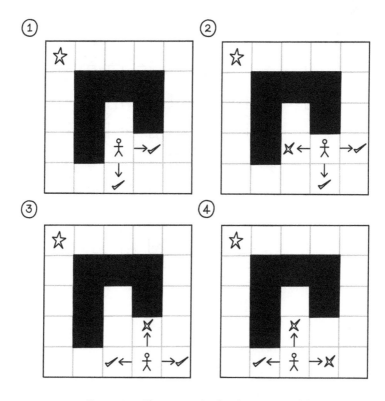

Figure 2.14 The constraint for the maze problem

This constraint prevents cycles in the path to the goal in our scenario. But this constraint will introduce problems if, in a different maze with different constraints or rules, moving into a previously occupied block more than once is required for the optimal solution.

In figure 2.15, all possible paths in the tree are represented to highlight the different options available. This tree contains seven paths that lead to the goal and one path that results in an invalid solution, given the constraint of not moving to previously occupied blocks. It's important to understand that in this small maze, representing all the possibilities is feasible. The entire point of search algorithms, however, is to search or generate these trees iteratively, because generating the entire tree of possibilities up front is inefficient due to being computationally expensive.

It is also important to note that the term *visiting* is used to indicate different things. The player visits blocks in the maze. The algorithm also visits nodes in the tree. The order of choices will influence the order of nodes being visited in the tree. In the maze example, the priority order of movement is north, south, east, and then west.

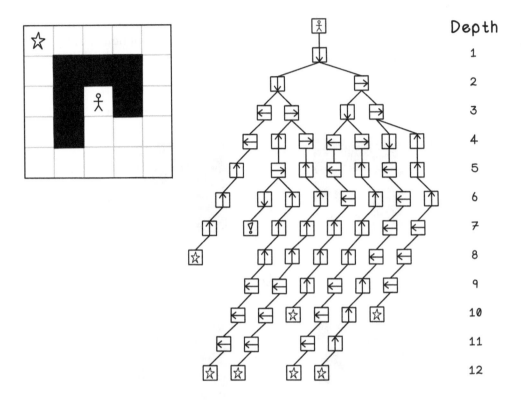

Figure 2.15 All possible movement options represented as a tree

Now that we understand the ideas behind trees and the maze example, let's explore how search algorithms can generate trees that seek out paths to the goal.

Breadth-first search:
Looking wide before looking deep

Breadth-first search is an algorithm used to traverse or generate a tree. This algorithm starts at a specific node, called the *root*, and explores every node at that depth before exploring the next depth of nodes. It essentially visits all children of nodes at a specific depth before visiting the next depth of child until it finds a *goal* leaf node.

The breadth-first search algorithm is best implemented by using a first-in, first-out queue in which the current depths of nodes are processed, and their children are queued to be processed later. This order of processing is exactly what we require when implementing this algorithm.

Figure 2.16 is a flow chart describing the sequence of steps involved in the breadth-first search algorithm.

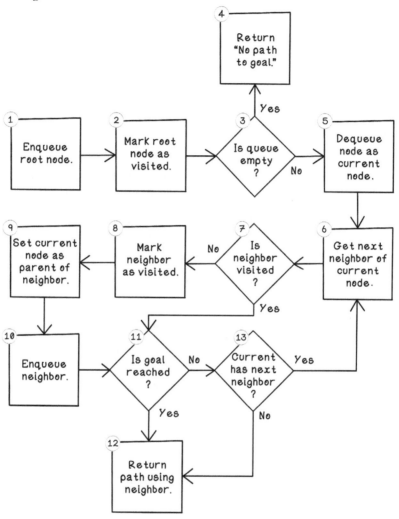

Figure 2.16 Flow of the breadth-first search algorithm

Here are some notes and additional remarks about each step in the process:

1. *Enqueue root node.* The breadth-first search algorithm is best implemented with a queue. Objects are processed in the sequence in which they are added to the queue. This process is also known as *first in, first out* (FIFO). The first step is adding the root node to the queue. This node will represent the starting position of the player on the map.

2. *Mark root node as visited.* Now that the root node has been added to the queue for processing, it is marked as visited to prevent it from being revisited for no reason.

3. *Is queue empty?* If the queue is empty (all nodes have been processed after many iterations), and if no path has been returned in step 12 of the algorithm, there is no path to the goal. If there are still nodes in the queue, the algorithm can continue its search to find the goal.

4. *Return* `No path to goal`. This message is the one possible exit from the algorithm if no path to the goal exists.

5. *Dequeue node as current node.* By pulling the next object from the queue and setting it as the current node of interest, we can explore its possibilities. When the algorithm starts, the current node will be the root node.

6. *Get next neighbor of current node.* This step involves getting the next possible move in the maze from the current position by referencing the maze and determining whether a north, south, east, or west movement is possible.

7. *Is neighbor visited?* If the current neighbor has not been visited, it hasn't been explored yet and can be processed now.

8. *Mark neighbor as visited.* This step indicates that this neighbor node has been visited.

9. *Set current node as parent of neighbor.* Set the origin node as the parent of the current neighbor. This step is important for tracing the path from the current neighbor to the root node. From a map perspective, the origin is the position that the player moved from, and the current neighbor is the position that the player moved to.

10. *Enqueue neighbor.* The neighbor node is queued for its children to be explored later. This queuing mechanism allows nodes from each depth to be processed in that order.

11. *Is goal reached?* This step determines whether the current neighbor contains the goal that the algorithm is searching for.

12. *Return path using neighbor.* By referencing the parent of the neighbor node, then the parent of that node, and so on, the path from the goal to the root will be described. The root node will be a node without a parent.

13. *Current has next neighbor?* If the current node has more possible moves to make in the maze, jump to step 6 for that move.

Let's walk through what that would look like in a simple tree. Notice that as the tree is explored and nodes are added to the FIFO queue, the nodes are processed in the order desired by leveraging the queue (figures 2.17 and 2.18).

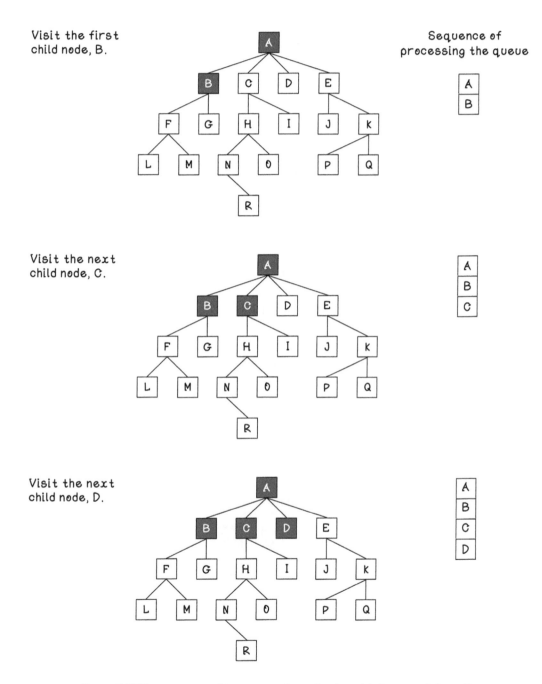

Figure 2.17 The sequence of tree processing using breadth-first search (part 1)

Visit the final
node on this
depth, E.

Sequence of
processing the queue

Visit the first
child of the
first neighbor
of A. This is F,
first child of B.

Visit the next
child of B. This
is G.

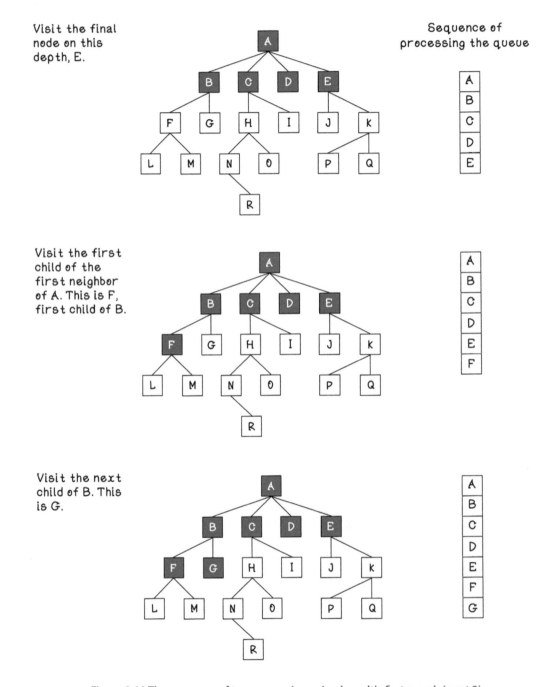

Figure 2.18 The sequence of tree processing using breadth-first search (part 2)

EXERCISE: DETERMINE THE PATH TO THE SOLUTION

What would be the order of visits using breadth-first search for the following tree?

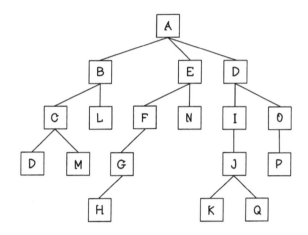

SOLUTION: DETERMINE THE PATH TO THE SOLUTION

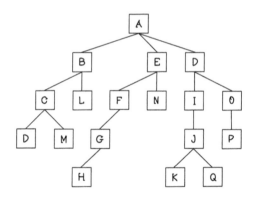

Breadth-first search order:
A, B, E, D, C, L, F, N, I, O, D, M, G, J, P, H, K, Q

In the maze example, the algorithm needs to understand the current position of the player in the maze, evaluate all possible choices for movement, and repeat that logic for each choice of movement made until the goal is reached. By doing this, the algorithm generates a tree with a single path to the goal.

It is important to understand that the processes of visiting nodes in a tree is used to generate nodes in a tree. We are simply finding related nodes through a mechanism.

Each path to the goal consists of a series of moves to reach the goal. The number of moves in the path is the distance to reach the goal for that path, which we will call the *cost*. The number of moves also equals the number of nodes visited in the path, from the root node to the leaf node that contains the goal. The algorithm moves down the tree depth by depth until it finds a goal; then it returns the first path that got it to the goal as the solution. There may be a more optimal path to the goal, but because breadth-first search is uninformed, it is not guaranteed to find that path.

> **NOTE** In the maze example, all search algorithms used terminate when they've found a solution to the goal. It is possible to allow these algorithms to find multiple solutions with a small tweak to each algorithm, but the best use cases for search algorithms find a single goal, as it is often too expensive to explore the entire tree of possibilities.

Figure 2.19 shows the generation of a tree using movements in the maze. Because the tree is generated using breadth-first search, each depth is generated to completion before looking at the next depth (figure 2.20).

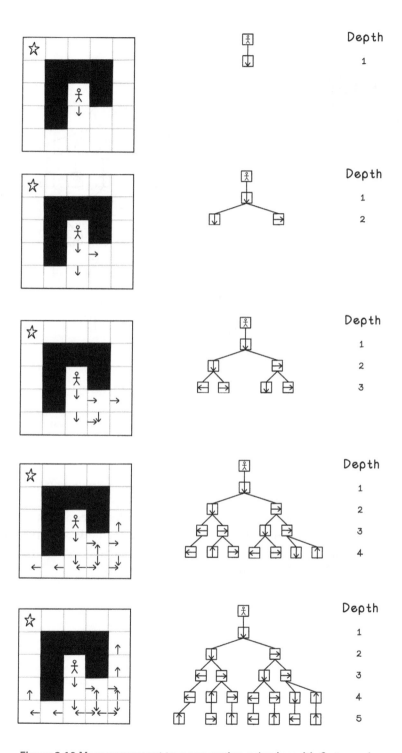

Figure 2.19 Maze movement tree generation using breadth-first search

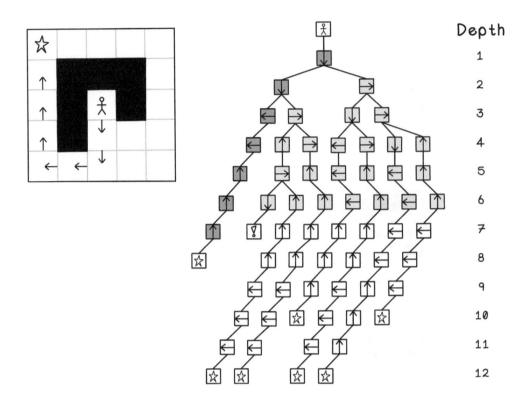

Figure 2.20 Nodes visited in the entire tree after breadth-first search

Pseudocode

As mentioned previously, the breadth-first search algorithm uses a queue to generate a tree one depth at a time. Having a structure to store visited nodes is critical to prevent getting stuck in cyclic loops; and setting the parent of each node is important for determining a path from the starting point in the maze to the goal:

```
run_bfs(maze, current_point, visited_points):
  let q equal a new queue
  push current_point to q
  mark current_point as visited
  while q is not empty:
    pop q and let current_point equal the returned point
    add available cells north, east, south, and west to a list neighbors
    for each neighbor in neighbors:
      if neighbor is not visited:
        set neighbor parent as current_point
        mark neighbor as visited
        push neighbor to q
        if value at neighbor is the goal:
          return path using neighbor
  return "No path to goal"
```

Depth-first search: Looking deep before looking wide

Depth-first search is another algorithm used to traverse a tree or generate nodes and paths in a tree. This algorithm starts at a specific node and explores paths of connected nodes of the first child, doing this recursively until it reaches the farthest leaf node before backtracking and exploring other paths to leaf nodes via other child nodes that have been visited. Figure 2.21 illustrates the general flow of the depth-first search algorithm.

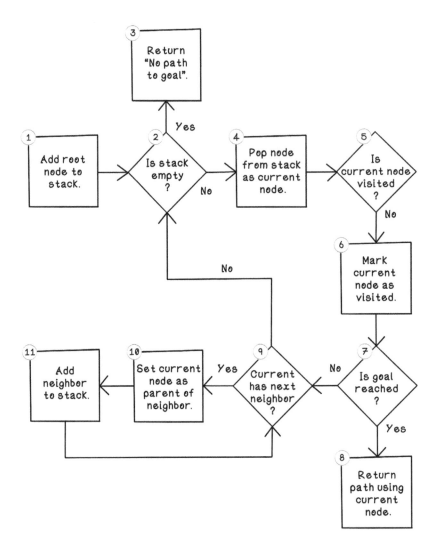

Figure 2.21 Flow of the depth-first search algorithm

Let's walk through the flow of the depth-first search algorithm:

1. *Add root node to stack.* The depth-first search algorithm can be implemented by using a stack in which the last object added is processed first. This process is known as *last in, first out* (LIFO). The first step is adding the root node to the stack.

2. *Is stack empty?* If the stack is empty and no path has been returned in step 8 of the algorithm, there is no path to the goal. If there are still nodes in the stack, the algorithm can continue its search to find the goal.

3. *Return* `No path to goal`. This return is the one possible exit from the algorithm if no path to the goal exists.

4. *Pop node from stack as current node.* By pulling the next object from the stack and setting it as the current node of interest, we can explore its possibilities.

5. *Is current node visited?* If the current node has not been visited, it hasn't been explored yet and can be processed now.

6. *Mark current node as visited.* This step indicates that this node has been visited to prevent unnecessary repeat processing of it.

7. *Is goal reached?* This step determines whether the current neighbor contains the goal that the algorithm is searching for.

8. *Return path using current node.* By referencing the parent of the current node, then the parent of that node, and so on, the path from the goal to the root is described. The root node will be a node without a parent.

9. *Current has next neighbor?* If the current node has more possible moves to make in the maze, that move can be added to the stack to be processed. Otherwise, the algorithm can jump to step 2, where the next object in the stack can be processed if the stack is not empty. The nature of the LIFO stack allows the algorithm to process all nodes to a leaf node depth before backtracking to visit other children of the root node.

10. *Set current node as parent of neighbor.* Set the origin node as the parent of the current neighbor. This step is important for tracing the path from the current neighbor to the root node. From a map perspective, the origin is the position that the player moved from, and the current neighbor is the position that the player moved to.

11. *Add neighbor to stack.* The neighbor node is added to the stack for its children to be explored later. Again, this stacking mechanism allows nodes to be processed to the utmost depth before processing neighbors at shallow depths.

Figures 2.22 and 2.23 explore how the LIFO stack is used to visit nodes in the order desired by depth-first search. Notice that nodes get pushed onto and popped from the stack as the depths of the nodes visited progress. The term *push* describes adding objects to a stack, and the term *pop* describes removing the topmost object from the stack.

Similarly to breadth-first search, visit the first child of node A. This is B.

Instead of visiting other child nodes of A, the first child of B is visited — in this case, F.

Again, the first child of F is visited. This is L.

Sequence of processing the stack

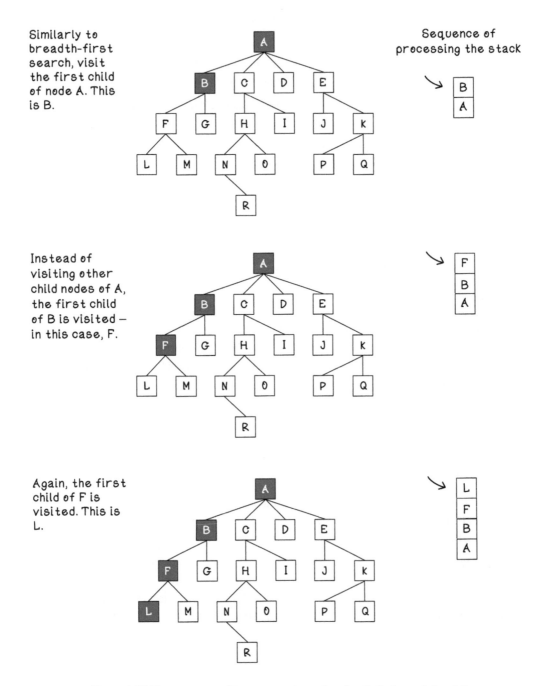

Figure 2.22 The sequence of tree processing using depth-first search (part 1)

Because L is a
leaf node (it
has no children),
the algorithm
backtracks to
visit the next
child of F, which
is M.

Sequence of
processing the stack

Because M is a
leaf node, the
algorithm
backtracks to
visit the next
child of B.
Because F has
no unvisited
children, this
child is G.

Finally, because all
children of B
have been visited,
the algorithm
backtracks to the
next child of A,
which is C.

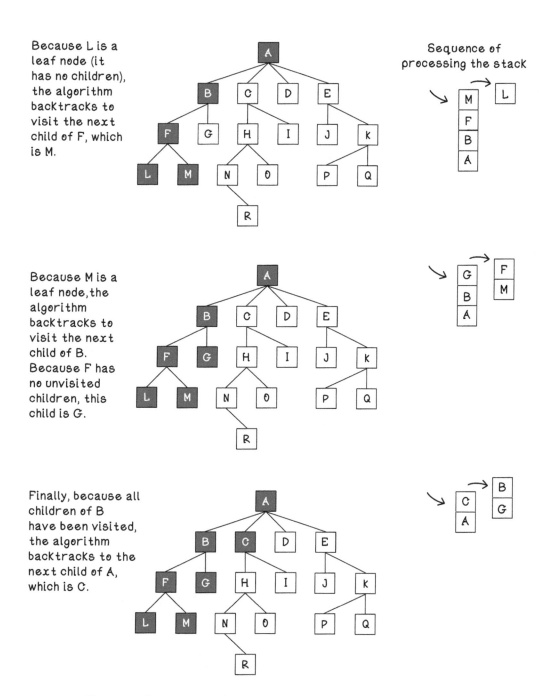

Figure 2.23 The sequence of tree processing using depth-first search (part 2)

EXERCISE: DETERMINE THE PATH TO THE SOLUTION

What would the order of visits be in depth-first search for the following tree?

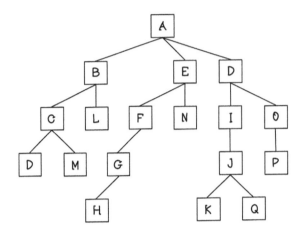

SOLUTION: DETERMINE THE PATH TO THE SOLUTION

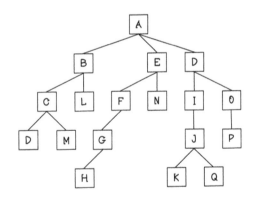

Depth-first search order:
A, B, C, D, M, L, E, F, G, H, N, D, I, J, K, Q, O, P

It is important to understand that the order of children matters substantially when using depth-first search, as the algorithm explores the first child until it finds leaf nodes before backtracking.

In the maze example, the order of movement (north, south, east, and west) influences the path to the goal that the algorithm finds. A change in order will result in a different solution. The forks represented in figures 2.24 and 2.25 don't matter; what matters is the order of the movement choices in our maze example.

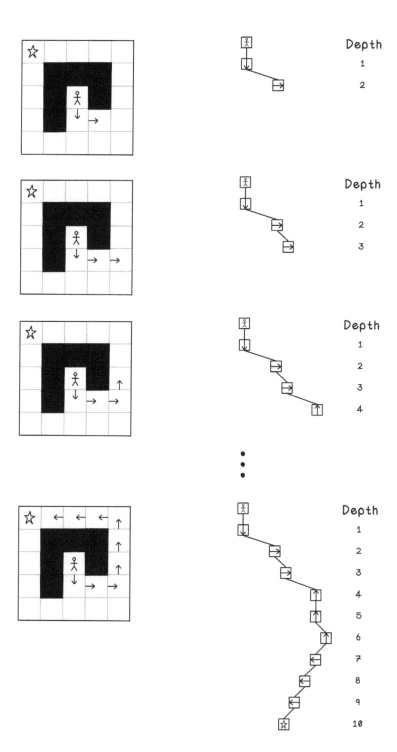

Figure 2.24 Maze movement tree generation using depth-first search

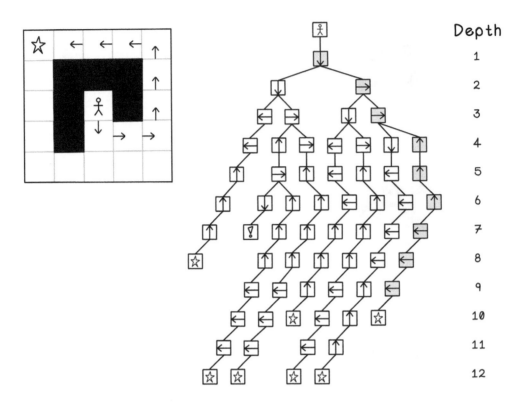

Figure 2.25 Nodes visited in the entire tree after depth-first search

Pseudocode

Although the depth-first search algorithm can be implemented with a recursive function, we're looking at an implementation that is achieved with a stack to better represent the order in which nodes are visited and processed. It is important to keep track of the visited points so that the same nodes do not get visited unnecessarily, creating cyclic loops:

```
run_dfs(maze, root_point, visited_points):
  let s equal a new stack
  add root_point to s
  while s is not empty
    pop s and let current_point equal the returned point
    if current_point is not visited:
      mark current_point as visited
      if value at current_node is the goal:
        return path using current_point
      else:
        add available cells north, east, south, and west to a list neighbors
        for each neighbor in neighbors:
          set neighbor parent as current_point
          push neighbor to s
  return "No path to goal"
```

Use cases for uninformed search algorithms

Uninformed search algorithms are versatile and useful in several real-world use cases, such as

- *Finding paths between nodes in a network*—When two computers need to communicate over a network, the connection passes through many connected computers and devices. Search algorithms can be used to establish a path in that network between two devices.

- *Crawling web pages*—Web searches allow us to find information on the internet across a vast number of web pages. To index these web pages, crawlers typically read the information on each page, as well as follow each link on that page recursively. Search algorithms are useful for creating crawlers, metadata structures, and relationships between content.

- *Finding social network connections*—Social media applications contain many people and their relationships. Bob may be friends with Alice, for example, but not direct friends with John, so Bob and John are indirectly related via Alice. A social media application can suggest that Bob and John should become friends because they may know each other through their mutual friendship with Alice.

Optional: More about graph categories

Graphs are useful for many computer science and mathematical problems, and due to the nature of different types of graphs, different principles and algorithms may apply to specific categories of graphs. A graph is categorized based on its overall structure, number of nodes, number of edges, and interconnectivity between nodes.

These categories of graphs are good to know about, as they are common and sometimes referenced in search and other AI algorithms:

- *Undirected graph*—No edges are directed. Relationships between two nodes are mutual. As with roads between cities, there are roads traveling in both directions.

- *Directed graph*—Edges indicate direction. Relationships between two nodes are explicit. As in a graph representing a child of a parent, the child cannot be the parent of its parent.

- *Disconnected graph*—One or more nodes are not connected by any edges. As in a graph representing physical contact between continents, some nodes are not connected. Like continents, some are connected by land, and others are separated by oceans.

- *Acyclic graph*—A graph that contains no cycles. As with time as we know it, the graph does not loop back to any point in the past (yet).

- *Complete graph*—Every node is connected to every other node by an edge. As in the lines of communication in a small team, everyone talks to everyone else to collaborate.

- *Complete bipartite graph*—A *vertex partition* is a grouping of vertices. Given a vertex partition, every node from one partition is connected to every node of the other partition with edges. As at a cheese-tasting event, typically, every person tastes every type of cheese.

- *Weighted graph*—A graph in which the edges between nodes have a weight. As in the distance between cities, some cities are farther than others. The connections "weigh" more.

It is useful to understand the different types of graphs to best describe the problem and use the most efficient algorithm for processing (figure 2.26). Some of these categories of graphs are discussed in upcoming chapters, such as chapter 6 on ant colony optimization and chapter 8 on neural networks.

UNDIRECTED

No edges are directed.
Relationships between two
nodes are mutual.

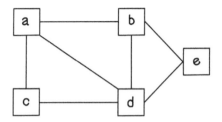

DIRECTED

Edges indicate direction.
Relationships between two
nodes are explicit.

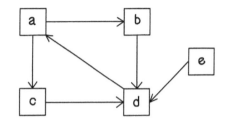

DISCONNECTED

One or more nodes are not
connected by any edges.

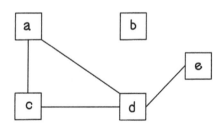

ACYCLIC

A graph that contains
no cycles.

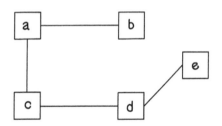

COMPLETE

Every node is connected
to every other node by an
edge.

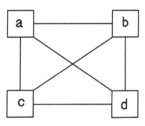

COMPLETE BIPARTITE

Every node from one partition is
connected to every node of the
other partition.

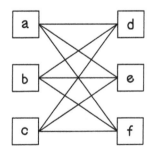

WEIGHTED

A graph where the
edges between nodes
have a weight.

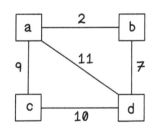

Figure 2.26 Types of graphs

Optional: More ways to represent graphs

Depending on the context, other encodings of graphs may be more efficient for processing or easier to work with, depending on the programming language and tools you're using.

Incidence matrix

An *incidence matrix* uses a matrix in which the height is the number of nodes in the graph and the width is the number of edges. Each row represents a node's relationship with a specific edge. If a node is not connected by a specific edge, the value 0 is stored. If a node is connected by a specific edge as the receiving node in the case of a directed graph, the value -1 is stored. If a node is connected by a specific edge as an outgoing node or connected in an undirected graph, the value 1 is stored. An incidence matrix can be used to represent both directed and undirected graphs (figure 2.27).

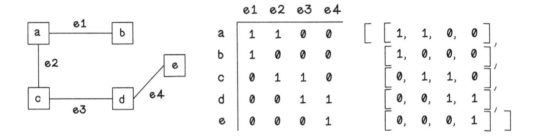

Figure 2.27 Representing a graph as an incidence matrix

Adjacency list

An *adjacency list* uses linked lists in which the size of the initial list is the number of nodes in the graph and each value represents the connected nodes for a specific node. An adjacency list can be used to represent both directed and undirected graphs (figure 2.28).

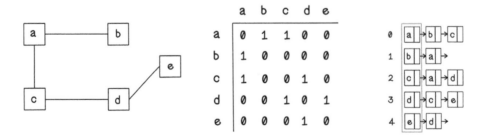

Figure 2.28 Representing a graph as an adjacency list

Graphs are also interesting and useful data structures because they can easily be represented as mathematical equations, which are the backing for all algorithms we use. You can find more information about this topic throughout the book.

SUMMARY OF SEARCH FUNDAMENTALS

Data structures are important to solve problems.

Search algorithms are useful in planning and finding solutions in some changing environments.

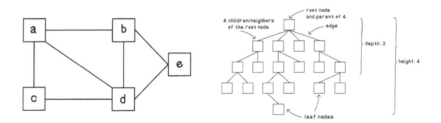

Graph and tree data structures are useful in AI.

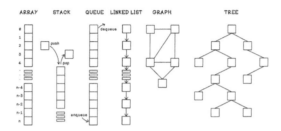

Uninformed search is blind and can be computationally expensive. Using the correct data structures helps.

Depth-first search looks deep before looking wide. Breadth-first search looks wide before looking deep.

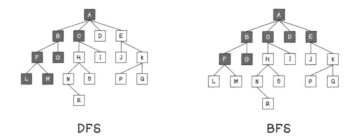

DFS   BFS

This chapter covers

- Understanding and designing heuristics for guided search

- Identifying problems suited to being solved with guided search approaches

- Understanding and designing a guided search algorithm

- Designing a search algorithm to play a two-player game

Defining heuristics: Designing educated guesses

Now that we have an idea of how uninformed search algorithms work from chapter 2, we can explore how they can be improved by seeing more information about the problem. For this purpose, we use informed search. *Informed search* means that the algorithm has some context of the specific problem being solved. Heuristics are a way to represent this context. Often described as a *rule of thumb*, a *heuristic* is a rule or set of rules used to evaluate a state. It can be used to define criteria that a state must satisfy or measure the performance of a specific state. A heuristic is used when a clear method of finding an optimal solution is not possible. A heuristic can be interpreted as an educated guess in social terms and should be seen more as a guideline than as a scientific truth with respect to the problem that is being solved.

When you're ordering a pizza at a restaurant, for example, your heuristic of how good it is may be defined by the ingredients and type of base used. If you enjoy extra tomato sauce, extra cheese, mushrooms, and pineapple on a thick base with crunchy crust, a pizza that includes more of these attributes will be more appealing to you and achieve a better score for your heuristic. A pizza that contains fewer of those attributes will be less appealing to you and achieve a poorer score.

Another example is writing algorithms to solve a GPS routing problem. The heuristic may be "Good paths minimize time in traffic and minimize distance traveled" or "Good paths minimize toll fees and maximize good road conditions." A poor heuristic for a GPS routing program would be to minimize straight-line distance between two points. This heuristic might work for birds or planes, but in reality, we walk or drive; these methods of transport bind us to roads and paths between buildings and obstacles. Heuristics need to make sense for the context of use.

Take the example of checking whether an uploaded audio clip is an audio clip in a library of copyrighted content. Because audio clips are frequencies of sound, one way to achieve this goal is to search every time slice of the uploaded clip with every clip in the library. This task will require an extreme amount of computation. A primitive start to building a better search could be defining a heuristic that minimizes the difference of distribution of frequencies between the two clips, as shown in figure 3.1. Notice that the frequencies are identical apart from the time difference; they don't have differences in their frequency distributions. This solution may not be perfect, but it is a good start toward a less-expensive algorithm.

Figure 3.1 Comparison of two audio clips using frequency distribution

Heuristics are context-specific, and a good heuristic can help optimize solutions substantially. The maze scenario from chapter 2 will be adjusted to demonstrate the concept of creating heuristics by introducing an interesting dynamic. Instead of treating all movements the same way and measuring better solutions purely by paths with fewer actions (shallow depth in the tree), movements in different directions now cost different amounts to execute. There's been some strange shift in the gravity of our maze, and moving north or south now costs five times as much as moving east or west (figure 3.2).

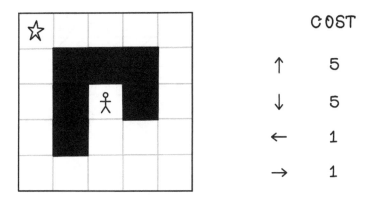

Figure 3.2 Adjustments to the maze example: gravity

In the adjusted maze scenario, the factors influencing the best possible path to the goal are the number of actions taken and the sum of the cost for each action in a respective path.

In figure 3.3, all possible paths in the tree are represented to highlight the options available, indicating the costs of the respective actions. Again, this example demonstrates the search space in the trivial maze scenario and does not often apply to real-life scenarios. The algorithm will be generating the tree as part of the search.

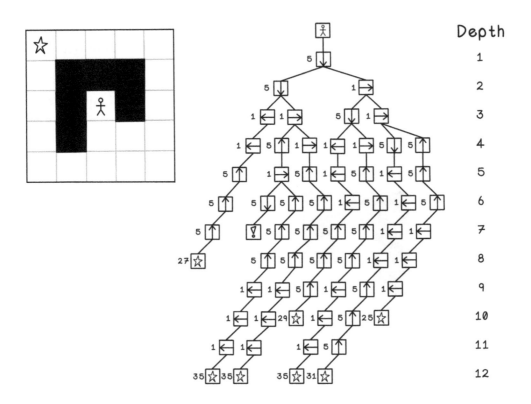

Figure 3.3 All possible movement options represented as a tree

A heuristic for the maze problem can be defined as follows: "Good paths minimize cost of movement and minimize total moves to reach the goal." This simple heuristic helps guide which nodes are visited because we are applying some domain knowledge to solve the problem.

THOUGHT EXPERIMENT: GIVEN THE FOLLOWING SCENARIO,
WHAT HEURISTIC CAN YOU IMAGINE?

> Several miners specialize in different types of mining, including diamond, gold, and platinum. All the miners are productive in any mine, but they mine faster in mines that align with their specialties. Several mines that can contain diamonds, gold, and platinum are spread across an area, and depots appear at different distances between mines. If the problem is to distribute miners to maximize their efficiency and reduce travel time, what could a heuristic be?

THOUGHT EXPERIMENT: POSSIBLE SOLUTION

A sensible heuristic would include assigning each miner to a mine of their specialty and tasking them with traveling to the depot closest to that mine. This can also be interpreted as minimizing assigning miners to mines that are not their specialty and minimizing the distance traveled to depots.

Informed search: Looking for solutions with guidance

Informed search, also known as *heuristic search*, is an algorithm that uses both breadth-first search and depth-first search approaches combined with some intelligence. The search is guided by heuristics, given some predefined knowledge of the problem at hand.

We can employ several informed search algorithms, depending on the nature of the problem, including Greedy Search (also known as Best-first Search). The most popular and useful informed search algorithm, however, is A*.

A* search

A* search is pronounced "A star search." The A* algorithm usually improves performance by estimating heuristics to minimize the cost of the next node visited.

Total cost is calculated with two metrics: the total distance from the start node to the current node and the estimated cost of moving to a specific node by using a heuristic. When we are attempting to minimize cost, a lower value indicates a better-performing solution (figure 3.4).

$$\mathbf{f}(n) = \mathbf{g}(n) + \mathbf{h}(n)$$

$g(n)$: cost of the path from the start node to node n

$h(n)$: the cost from the heuristic function for node n

$f(n)$: the cost of the path from the start node to node n plus the cost from the heuristic function for node n

Figure 3.4 The function for the A* search algorithm

The following example of processing is an abstract example of how a tree is visited using heuristics to guide the search. The focus is on the heuristic calculations for the different nodes in the tree.

Breadth-first search visits all nodes on each depth before moving to the next depth. Depth-first search visits all nodes down to the final depth before traversing back to the root and visiting the next path. A* search is different, in that it does not have a pre-defined pattern to follow; nodes are visited in the order based on their heuristic costs. Note that the algorithm does not know the costs of all nodes up front. Costs are calculated as the tree is explored or generated, and each node visited is added to a stack, which means nodes that cost more than nodes already visited are ignored, saving computation time (figures 3.5, 3.6, and 3.7).

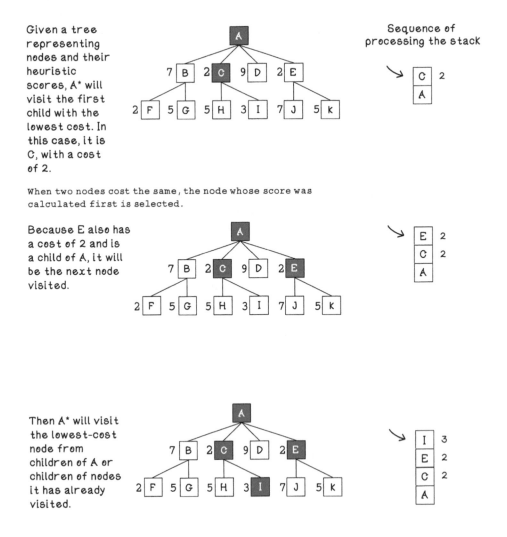

Figure 3.5 The sequence of tree processing using A* search (part 1)

The next lowest-cost node is K, a child of E.

Sequence of processing the stack

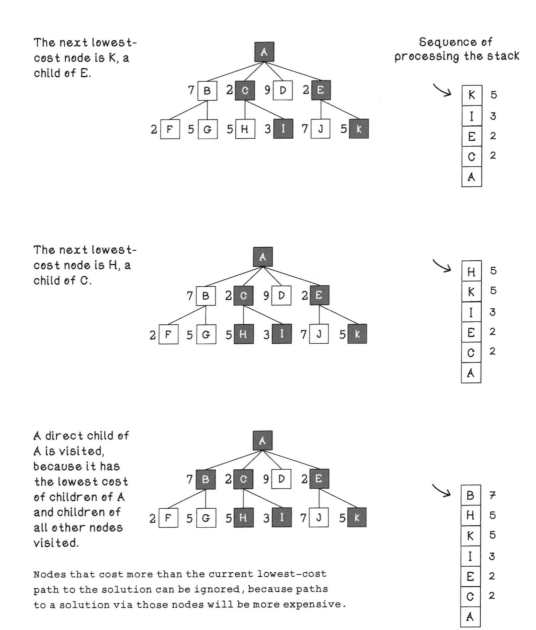

The next lowest-cost node is H, a child of C.

A direct child of A is visited, because it has the lowest cost of children of A and children of all other nodes visited.

Nodes that cost more than the current lowest-cost path to the solution can be ignored, because paths to a solution via those nodes will be more expensive.

Figure 3.6 The sequence of tree processing using A* search (part 2)

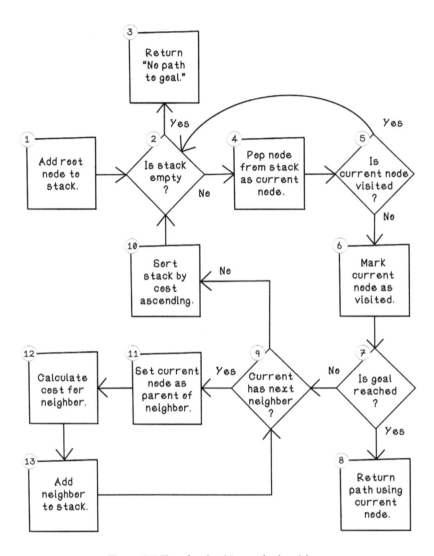

Figure 3.7 Flow for the A* search algorithm

Let's walk through the flow of the A* search algorithm:

1. *Add root node to stack.* The A* search algorithm can be implemented with a stack in which the last object added is processed first (last-in, first-out, or LIFO). The first step is adding the root node to the stack.

2. *Is stack empty?* If the stack is empty, and no path has been returned in step 8 of the algorithm, there is no path to the goal. If there are still nodes in the queue, the algorithm can continue its search.

3. *Return* No path to goal. This step is the one possible exit from the algorithm if no path to the goal exists.

4. *Pop node from stack as current node.* By pulling the next object from the stack and setting it as the current node of interest, we can explore its possibilities.

5. *Is current node visited?* If the current node has not been visited, it hasn't been explored yet and can be processed now.

6. *Mark current node as visited.* This step indicates that this node has been visited to prevent unnecessary repeat processing.

7. *Is goal reached?* This step determines whether the current neighbor contains the goal that the algorithm is searching for.

8. *Return path using current node.* By referencing the parent of the current node, then the parent of that node, and so on, the path from the goal to the root is described. The root node will be a node without a parent.

9. *Current has next neighbor?* If the current node has more possible moves to make in the maze example, that move can be added to be processed. Otherwise, the algorithm can jump to step 2, in which the next object in the stack can be processed if it is not empty. The nature of the LIFO stack allows the algorithm to process all nodes to a leaf-node depth before backtracking to visit other children of the root node.

10. *Sort stack by cost ascending.* When the stack is sorted by the cost of each node in the stack ascending, the lowest-cost node is processed next, allowing the cheapest node always to be visited.

11. *Set current node as parent of neighbor.* Set the origin node as the parent of the current neighbor. This step is important for tracing the path from the current neighbor to the root node. From a map perspective, the origin is the position that the player moved from, and the current neighbor is the position that the player moved to.

12. *Calculate cost for neighbor.* The cost function is critical for guiding the A* algorithm. The cost is calculated by summing the distance from the root node with the heuristic score for the next move. More-intelligent heuristics will directly influence the A* algorithm for better performance.

13. *Add neighbor to stack.* The neighbor node is added to the stack for its children to be explored later. Again, this stacking mechanism allows nodes to be processed to the utmost depth before processing neighbors at shallow depths.

Similar to depth-first search, the order of child nodes influences the path selected, but less drastically. If two nodes have the same cost, the first node is visited before the second (figures 3.8, 3.9, and 3.10).

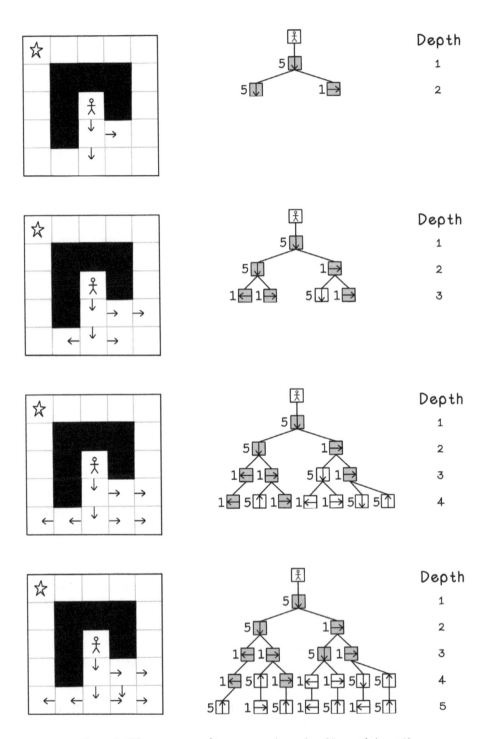

Figure 3.8 The sequence of tree processing using A* search (part 1)

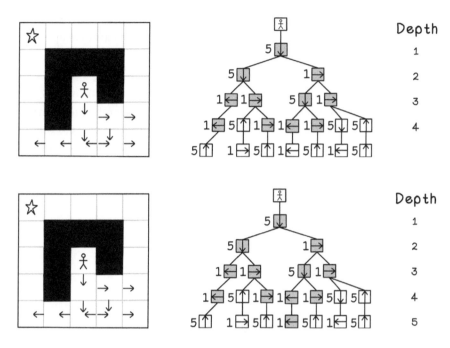

Figure 3.9 The sequence of tree processing using A* search (part 2)

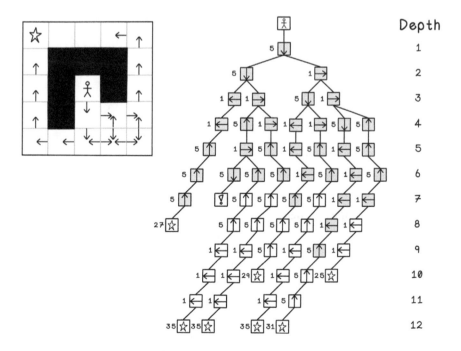

Figure 3.10 Nodes visited in the entire tree after A* search

Notice that there are several paths to the goal, but the A* algorithm finds a path to the goal while minimizing the cost to achieve it, with fewer moves and cheaper move costs based on north and south moves being more expensive.

Pseudocode

The A* algorithm uses a similar approach to the depth-first search algorithm but intentionally targets nodes that are cheaper to visit. A stack is used to process the nodes, but the stack is ordered by cost ascending every time a new calculation happens. This order ensures that the object popped from the stack is always the cheapest, because the cheapest is first in the stack after ordering:

```
run_astar(maze, root_point, visited_points):
  let s equal a new stack
  add root_point to s
  while s is not empty
    pop s and let current_point equal the returned point
    if current_point is not visited:
      mark current_point as visited
      if value at current_node is the goal:
        return path using current_point
      else:
        add available cells north, east, south, and west to a list neighbors
        for each neighbor in neighbors:
          set neighbor parent as current_point
          set neighbor cost as calculate_cost(current_point, neighbor)
          push neighbor to s
        sort s by cost ascending
  return "No path to goal"
```

The functions for calculating the cost are critical to the operation of A* search. The cost function provides the information for the algorithm to seek the cheapest path. In our adjusted maze example, a higher cost is associated with moving up or down. If there is a problem with the cost function, the algorithm may not work.

The following two functions describe how cost is calculated. The distance from the root node is added to the cost of the next movement. Based on our hypothetical example, the cost of moving north or south influences the total cost of visiting that node:

```
calculate_cost(origin, target):
  let distance_to_root equal length of path from origin to target
  let cost_to_move equal get_move_cost(origin, target)
  return distance_to_root + cost_to_move

move_cost(origin, target):
  if target is north or south of origin:
    return 5
  else:
    return 1
```

Uninformed search algorithms such as breadth-first search and depth-first search explore every possibility exhaustively and result in the optimal solution. A* search is a good approach when a sensible heuristic can be created to guide the search. It computes more efficiently than uninformed search algorithms, because it ignores nodes that cost more than nodes already visited. If the heuristic is flawed, however, and doesn't make sense for the problem and context, poor solutions will be found instead of optimal ones.

Use cases for informed search algorithms

Informed search algorithms are versatile and useful for several real-world use cases in which heuristics can be defined, such as the following:

- *Path finding for autonomous game characters in video games*—Game developers often use this algorithm to control the movement of enemy units in a game in which the goal is to find the human player within an environment.

- *Parsing paragraphs in natural language processing (NLP)*—The meaning of a paragraph can be broken into a composition of phrases, which can be broken into a composition of words of different types (like nouns and verbs), creating a tree structure that can be evaluated. Informed search can be useful in extracting meaning.

- *Telecommunications network routing*—Guided search algorithms can be used to find the shortest paths for network traffic in telecommunications networks to improve performance. Servers/network nodes and connections can be represented as searchable graphs of nodes and edges.

- *Single-player games and puzzles*—Informed search algorithms can be used to solve single-player games and puzzles such as the Rubik's Cube, because each move is a decision in a tree of possibilities until the goal state is found.

Adversarial search: Looking for solutions in a changing environment

The search example of the maze game involves a single actor: the player. The environment is affected only by the single player; thus, that player generates all possibilities. The goal until now was to maximize the benefit for the player: choosing paths to the goal with the shortest distance and cost.

Adversarial search is characterized by opposition or conflict. Adversarial problems require us to anticipate, understand, and counteract the actions of the opponent in pursuit of a goal. Examples of adversarial problems include two-player turn-based games such as Tic-Tac-Toe and Connect Four. The players take turns for the opportunity to change the state of the environment of the game to their favor. A set of rules dictates how the environment may be changed and what the winning and end states are.

A simple adversarial problem

This section uses the game of Connect Four to explore adversarial problems. Connect Four (figure 3.11) is a game consisting of a grid in which players take turns dropping tokens into a specific column. The tokens in a specific column pile up, and any player who manages to create four adjacent sequences of their tokens—vertically, horizontally, or diagonally—wins. If the grid is full, with no winner, the game results in a draw.

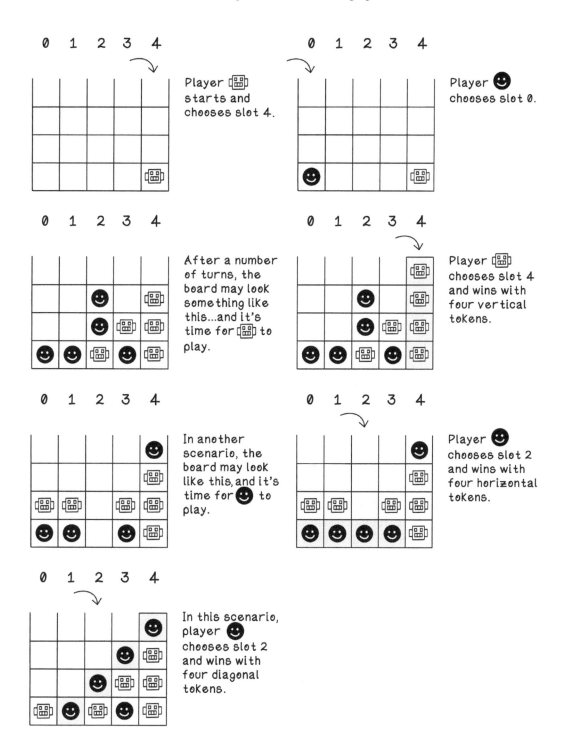

Player 🤖 starts and chooses slot 4.

Player 😊 chooses slot 0.

After a number of turns, the board may look something like this...and it's time for 🤖 to play.

Player 🤖 chooses slot 4 and wins with four vertical tokens.

In another scenario, the board may look like this, and it's time for 😊 to play.

Player 😊 chooses slot 2 and wins with four horizontal tokens.

In this scenario, player 😊 chooses slot 2 and wins with four diagonal tokens.

Figure 3.11 The game of Connect Four

Min-max search: Simulate actions and choose the best future

Min-max search aims to build a tree of possible outcomes based on moves that each player could make and favor paths that are advantageous to the agent while avoiding paths that are favorable to the opponent. To do so, this type of search simulates possible moves and scores the state based on a heuristic after making the respective move. Min-max search attempts to discover as many states in the future as possible; but due to memory and computation limitations, discovering the entire game tree may not be realistic, so it searches to a specified depth. Min-max search simulates the turns taken by each player, so the depth specified is directly linked to the number of turns between both players. A depth of 4, for example, means that each player has had 2 turns. Player A makes a move, player B makes a move, player A makes another move, and Player B makes another move.

Heuristics

The min-max algorithm uses a heuristic score to make decisions. This score is defined by a crafted heuristic and is not learned by the algorithm. If we have a specific game state, every possible valid outcome of a move from that state will be a child node in the game tree.

Assume that we have a heuristic that provides a score in which positive numbers are better than negative numbers. By simulating every possible valid move, the min-max search algorithm tries to minimize making moves where the opponent will have an advantage or a winning state and maximize making moves that give the agent an advantage or a winning state.

Figure 3.12 illustrates a min-max search tree. In this figure, the leaf nodes are the only nodes where the heuristic score is calculated, since these states indicate a winner or a draw. The other nodes in the tree indicate states that are in progress. Starting at the depth where the heuristic is calculated and moving upward, either the child with the minimum score or the child with the maximum score is chosen, depending on whose turn is next in the future simulated states. Starting at the top, the agent attempts to maximize its score; and after each alternating turn, the intention changes, because the aim is to maximize the score for the agent and minimize the score for the opponent.

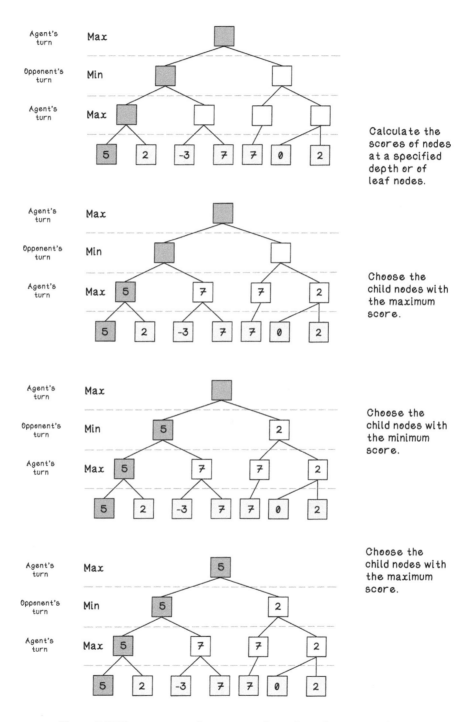

Calculate the scores of nodes at a specified depth or of leaf nodes.

Choose the child nodes with the maximum score.

Choose the child nodes with the minimum score.

Choose the child nodes with the maximum score.

Figure 3.12 The sequence of tree processing using min-max search

EXERCISE: WHAT VALUES WOULD PROPAGATE IN THE FOLLOWING MIN-MAX TREE?

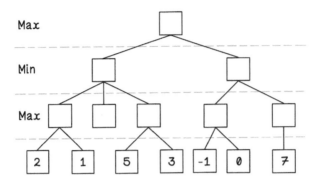

SOLUTION: WHAT VALUES WOULD PROPAGATE IN THE FOLLOWING MIN-MAX TREE?

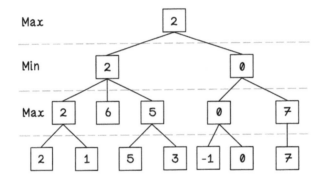

Because the min-max search algorithm simulates possible outcomes, in games that offer a multitude of choices, the game tree explodes, and it quickly becomes too computationally expensive to explore the entire tree. In the simple example of Connect Four played on a 5 × 4 block board, the number of possibilities already makes exploring the entire game tree on every turn inefficient (figure 3.13).

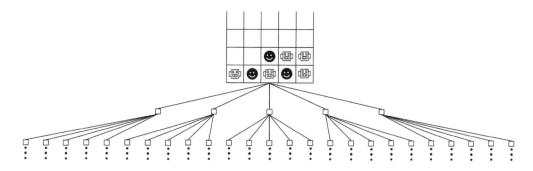

Figure 3.13 The explosion of possibilities while searching the game tree

To use min-max search in the Connect Four example, the algorithm essentially makes all possible moves from a current game state; then it determines all possible moves from each of those states until it finds the path that is most favorable. Game states that result in a win for the agent return a score of 10, and states that result in a win for the opponent return a score of -10. Min-max search tries to maximize the positive score for the agent (figures 3.14 and 3.15).

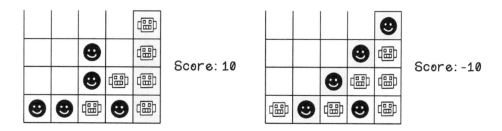

Figure 3.14 Scoring for the agent versus scoring for the opponent

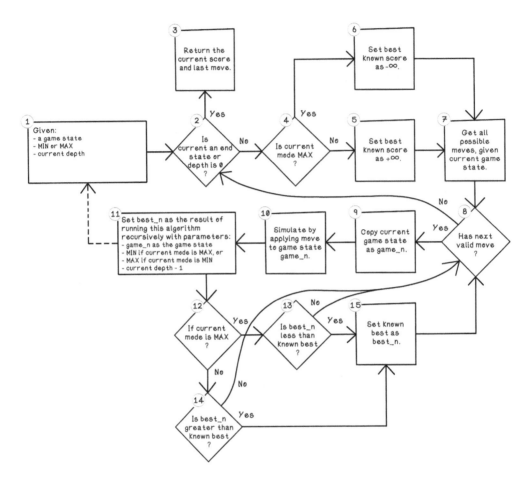

Figure 3.15 Flow for the min-max search algorithm

Although the flow chart for the min-max search algorithm looks complex due to its size, it really isn't. The number of conditions that check whether the current state is to maximize or minimize causes the chart to bloat.

Let's walk through the flow of the min-max search algorithm:

1. *Given a game state, whether the current mode is minimization or maximization, and a current depth, the algorithm can start.* It is important to understand the inputs for the algorithm, as the min-max search algorithm is recursive. A recursive algorithm calls itself in one or more of its steps. It is important for a recursive algorithm to have an exit condition to prevent it from calling itself forever.

2. *Is current an end state or depth is 0?* This condition determines whether the current state of the game is a terminal state or whether the desired depth has been reached. A terminal state is one in which one of the players has won or the game is a draw. A score of 10 represents a win for the agent, and a score of -10 represents a win for the opponent, and a score of 0 indicates a draw. A depth is specified, because traversing the entire tree of possibilities to all end states is computationally expensive and will likely take too long on the average computer. By specifying a depth, the algorithm can look a few turns into the future to determine whether a terminal state exists.

3. *Return the current score and last move.* The score for the current state is returned if the current state is a terminal game state or if the specified depth has been reached.

4. *Is current mode MAX?* If the current iteration of the algorithm is in the maximize state, it tries to maximize the score for the agent.

5. *Set best known score as +∞.* If the current mode is to minimize the score, the best score is set to positive infinity, because we know that the scores returned by the game states will always be less. In actual implementation, a really large number is used rather than infinity.

6. *Set best known score as -∞.* If the current mode is to maximize the score, the best score is set to negative infinity, because we know that the scores returned by the game states will always be more. In actual implementation, a really large negative number is used rather than infinity.

7. *Get all possible moves, given current game state.* This step specifies a list of possible moves that can be made, given the current game state. As the game progresses, not all moves available at the start may be available anymore. In the Connect Four example, a column may be filled; therefore, a move selecting that column is invalid.

8. *Has next valid move?* If any possible moves have not been simulated yet and there are no more valid moves to make, the algorithm short-circuits to returning the best move in that instance of the function call.

9. *Copy current game state as game_n.* A copy of the current game state is required to perform simulations of possible future moves on it.

10. *Simulate by applying move to game state game_n.* This step applies the current move of interest to the copied game state.

11. *Set best_n as the result of running this algorithm recursively.* Here's where recursion comes into play. *best_n* is a variable used to store the next best move, and we're making the algorithm explore future possibilities from this move.

12. *If current mode is MAX?* When the recursive call returns a best candidate, this condition determines whether the current mode is to maximize the score.

13. *Is best_n less than known best?* This step determines whether the algorithm has found a better score than one previously found if the mode is to maximize the score.

14. *Is best_n greater than known best?* This step determines whether the algorithm has found a better score than one previously found if the mode is to minimize the score.

15. *Set known best as best_n.* If the new best score is found, set the known best as that score.

Given the Connect Four example at a specific state, the min-max search algorithm generates the tree shown in figure 3.16. From the start state, every possible move is explored. Then each move from that state is explored until a terminal state is found—either the board is full or a player has won.

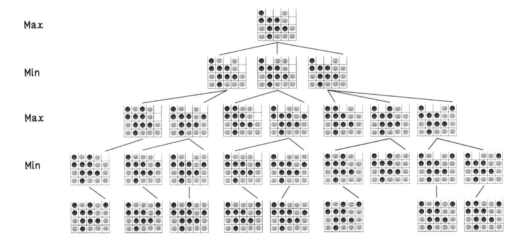

Figure 3.16 A representation of the possible states in a Connect Four game

The highlighted nodes in figure 3.17 are terminal state nodes in which draws are scored as 0, losses are scored as -10, and wins are scored as 10. Because the algorithm aims to maximize its score, a positive number is required, whereas opponent wins are scored with a negative number.

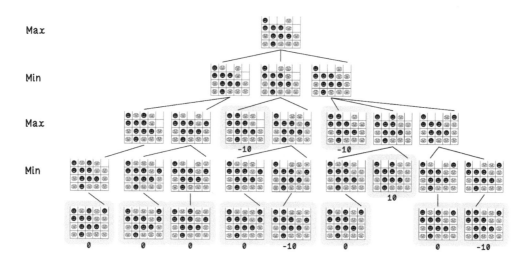

Figure 3.17 The possible end states in a Connect Four game

When these scores are known, the min-max algorithm starts at the lowest depth and chooses the node whose score is the minimum value (figure 3.18).

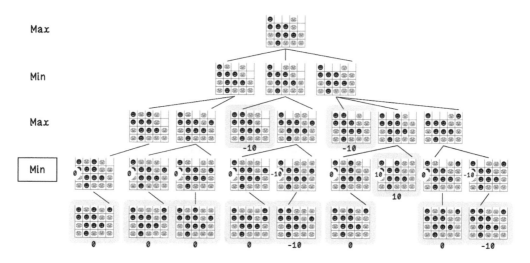

Figure 3.18 The possible scores for end states in a Connect Four game (part 1)

Then, at the next depth, the algorithm chooses the node whose score is the maximum value (figure 3.19).

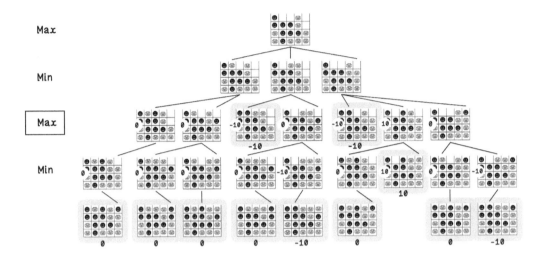

Figure 3.19 The possible scores for end states in a Connect Four game (part 2)

Finally, at the next depth, nodes whose score is the minimum are chosen, and the root node chooses the maximum of the options. By following the nodes and score selected and intuitively applying ourselves to the problem, we see that the algorithm selects a path to a draw to avoid a loss. If the algorithm selects the path to the win, there is a high likelihood of a loss in the next turn. The algorithm assumes that the opponent will always make the smartest move to maximize their chance of winning (figure 3.20).

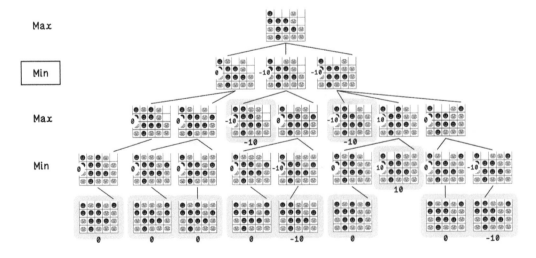

Figure 3.20 The possible scores for end states in a Connect Four game (part 3)

The simplified tree in figure 3.21 represents the outcome of the min-max search algorithm for the given game state example.

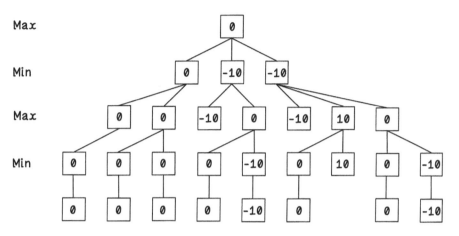

Figure 3.21 Simplified game tree with min-max scoring

Pseudocode

The min-max search algorithm is implemented to be a recursive function. The function is provided with the current state, desired depth to search, minimization or maximization mode, and last move. The algorithm terminates by returning the best move and score for every child at every depth in the tree. Comparing the code with the flow chart in figure 3.15, we notice that the tedious conditions of checking whether the current mode is maximizing or minimizing are not as apparent. In the pseudocode, 1 or -1 represents the intention to maximize or minimize, respectively. By using some clever logic, the best score, conditions, and switching states can be done via the principle of negative multiplication, in which a negative number multiplied by another negative number results in a positive. So if -1 indicates the opponent's turn, multiplying it by -1 results in 1, which indicates the agent's turn. Then, for the next turn, 1 multiplied by -1 results in -1 to indicate the opponent's turn again:

```
minmax(state, depth, min_or_max, last_move):
    let current score equal state.get_score
    if current_score is not equal to 0 or state.is_full or depth is equal to 0:
        return new Move(last_move, current_score)
    let best_score equal to min_or_max multiplied by -∞
    let best_move = -1
    for each possible choice (0 to 4 in a 5x4 board) as move:
        let neighbor equal to a copy of state
        execute current move on neighbor
        let best_neighbor equal minmax(neighbor, depth -1, min_or_max * -1, move)
        if (best_neighbor.score is greater than best_score and min_or_max is MAX)
        or (best_neighbor.score is less than best_score and min_or_max is MIN):
            let best_score = best_neighbor.score
            let best_move = best_neighbor.move
    return new Move(best_move, best_score)
```

Alpha-beta pruning: Optimize by exploring the sensible paths only

Alpha-beta pruning is a technique used with the min-max search algorithm to short-circuit exploring areas of the game tree that are known to produce poor solutions. This technique optimizes the min-max search algorithm to save computation, because insignificant paths are ignored. Because we know how the Connect Four example game tree explodes, we clearly see that ignoring more paths will improve performance significantly (figure 3.22).

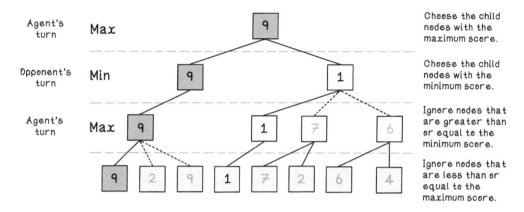

Figure 3.22 An example of alpha-beta pruning

The alpha-beta pruning algorithm works by storing the best score for the maximizing player and the best score for the minimizing player as alpha and beta, respectively. Initially, alpha is set as -∞, and beta is set as ∞—the worst score for each player. If the best score of the minimizing player is less than the best score of the maximizing player, it is logical that other child paths of the nodes already visited would not affect the best score.

Figure 3.23 illustrates the changes made in the min-max search flow to accommodate the optimization of alpha-beta pruning. The highlighted blocks are the additional steps in the min-max search algorithm flow.

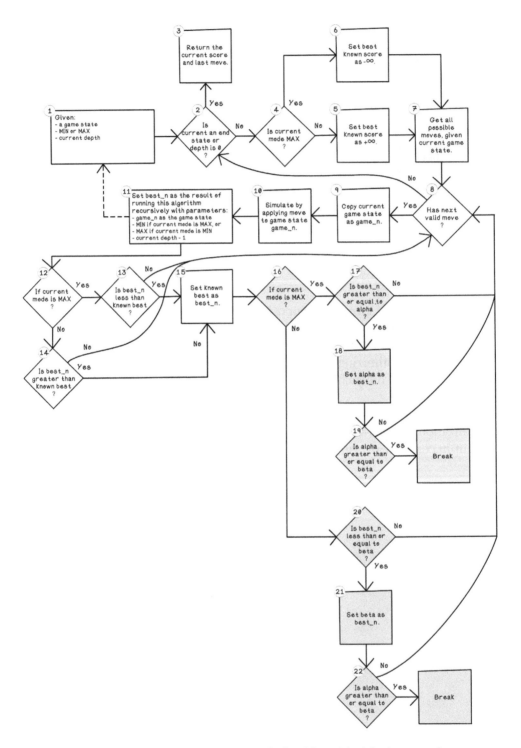

Figure 3.23 Flow for the min-max search algorithm with alpha-beta pruning

The following steps are additions to the min-max search algorithm. These conditions allow termination of exploration of paths when the best score found will not change the outcome:

16. *Is current mode MAX?* Again, determine whether the algorithm is currently attempting to maximize or minimize the score.

17. *Is best_n greater than or equal to alpha?* If the current mode is to maximize the score and the current best score is greater than or equal to alpha, no better scores are contained in that node's children, allowing the algorithm to ignore that node.

18. *Set alpha as best_n.* Set the variable *alpha* as *best_n*.

19. *Is alpha greater than or equal to beta?* The score is as good as other scores found, and the rest of the exploration of that node can be ignored by breaking.

20. *Is best_n less than or equal to beta?* If the current mode is to minimize the score and the current best score is less than or equal to beta, no better scores are contained in that node's children, allowing the algorithm to ignore that node.

21. *Set beta as best_n.* Set the variable *beta* as *best_n*.

22. *Is alpha greater than or equal to beta?* The score is as good as other scores found, and the rest of the exploration of that node can be ignored by breaking.

Pseudocode

The pseudocode for achieving alpha-beta pruning is largely the same as the code for min-max search, with the addition of keeping track of the alpha and beta values and maintaining those values as the tree is traversed. Note that when minimum(min) is selected the variable *min_or_max* is -1, and when maximum(max) is selected, the variable *min_or_max is* 1:

```
minmax_ab_pruning(state,depth,min_or_max,last_move, alpha,beta):
  let current score equal state.get_score
  if current_score is not equal to 0 or state.is_full or depth is equal to 0:
    return new Move(last_move, current_score)
  let best_score equal to min_or_max multiplied by -∞
  let best_move = -1
  for each possible choice (0 to 4 in a 5x4 board) as move:
    let neighbor equal to a copy of state
    execute current move on neighbor
    let best_neighbor equal
      minmax(neighbor, depth -1, min_or_max * -1, move, alpha,beta)
    if (best_neighbor.score is greater than best_score and min_or_max is MAX)
    or (best_neighbor.score is less than best_score and min_or_max is MIN):
      let best_score = best_neighbor.score
      let best_move = best_neighbor.move
      if best_score >= alpha:
        alpha = best_score
      if best_score <= beta:
        beta = best_score
    if alpha >= beta:
      break
  return new Move(best_move, best_score)
```

Use cases for adversarial search algorithms

Informed search algorithms are versatile and useful in real-world use cases such as the
following:

- *Creating game-playing agents for turn-based games with perfect information*—In
  some games, two or more players act on the same environment. There have been
  successful implementations of chess, checkers, and other classic games. Games
  with perfect information are games that do not have hidden information or
  random chance involved.

- *Creating game-playing agents for turn-based games with imperfect information*—
  Unknown future options exist in these games, including games like poker and
  Scrabble.

- *Adversarial search and ant colony optimization (ACO) for route optimization—* Adversarial search is used in combination with the ACO algorithm (discussed in chapter 6) to optimize package-delivery routes in cities.

SUMMARY OF INTELLIGENT SEARCH

Informed search gives algorithms some intelligence.

Heuristics can be tricky to think up, but a good heuristic is powerful in finding solutions efficiently.

A* search uses heuristics and the distance from the root to find solutions optimally.

$$f(n) = g(n) + h(n)$$

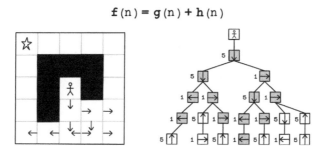

Adverserial search such as min-max is useful when something else affects the environment.

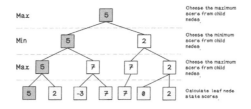

Alpha-beta pruning helps optimize the min-max algorithm by eliminating undesirable paths.

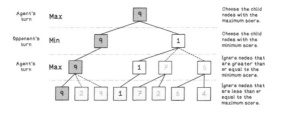

This chapter covers

- The inspiration for evolutionary algorithms

- Solving problems with evolutionary algorithms

- Understanding the life cycle of a genetic algorithm

- Designing and developing a genetic algorithm to solve
  optimization problems

What is evolution?

When we look at the world around us, we sometimes wonder how everything we see and interact with came to be. One way to explain this is the theory of evolution. The theory of evolution suggests that the living organisms that we see today did not suddenly exist that way, but evolved through millions of years of subtle changes, with each generation adapting to its environment. This implies that the physical and cognitive characteristics of each living organism are a result of best fitting to its environment for survival. Evolution suggests that organisms evolve through reproduction by producing children of mixed genes from their parents. Given the fitness of these individuals in their environment, stronger individuals have a higher likelihood of survival.

We often make the mistake of thinking that evolution is a linear process, with clear changes in successors. In reality, evolution is far more chaotic, with divergence in a species. A multitude of variants of a species are created through reproduction and mixing of genes. Noticeable differences in a species could take thousands of years to manifest and be realized only by comparing the average individual in each of those time points. Figure 4.1 depicts actual evolution versus the commonly mistaken version of the evolution of humans.

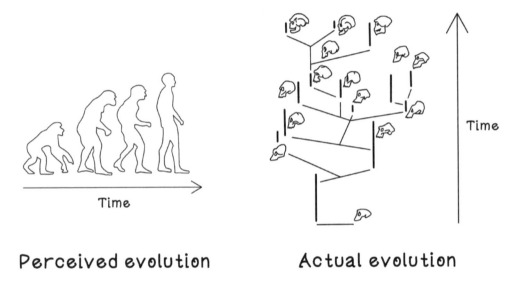

Figure 4.1 The idea of linear human evolution vs. actual human evolution

Charles Darwin proposed a theory of evolution that centers on natural selection. *Natural selection* is the concept that stronger members of a population are more likely to survive due to being more fit for their environment, which means they reproduce more and, thus, carry traits that are beneficial to survival to future generations—that could potentially perform better than their ancestors.

A classic example of evolution for adaption is the peppered moth. The peppered moth was originally light in color, which made for good camouflage against predators as the moth could blend in with light-colored surfaces in its environment. Only around 2% of the moth population was darker in color. After the Industrial Revolution, around 95% of the species were of the darker color variant. One explanation is that the lighter-colored moths could not blend in with as many surfaces anymore because pollution had darkened surfaces; thus lighter-colored moths were eaten more by predators because those moths were more visible. The darker moths had a greater advantage in blending in with the darker surfaces, so they survived longer and reproduced more, and their genetic information was more widely spread to successors.

Among the peppered moths, the attribute that changed on a high level was the color of the moth. This property didn't just magically switch, however. For the change to happen, genes in moths with the darker color had to be carried to successors.

In other examples of natural evolution, we may see dramatic changes in more than simply color between different individuals, but in actuality, these changes are influenced by lower-level genetic differences over many generations (figure 4.2).

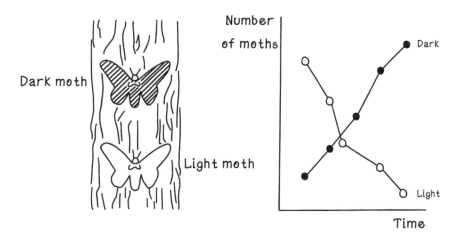

Figure 4.2 The evolution of the peppered moth

Evolution encompasses the idea that in a population of a species, pairs of organisms reproduce. The offspring are a combination of the parent's genes, but small changes are made in that offspring through a process called *mutation*. Then the offspring become part of the population. Not all members of a population live on, however. As we know, disease, injury, and other factors cause individuals to die. Individuals that are more adaptive to the environment around them are more likely to live on, a situation that gave rise to the term *survival of the fittest*. Based on Darwinian evolution theory, a population has the following attributes:

- *Variety*—Individuals in the population have different genetic traits.

- *Hereditary*—A child inherits genetic properties from its parents.

- *Selection*—A mechanism that measures the fitness of individuals. Stronger individuals have the highest likelihood of survival (survival of the fittest).

These properties imply that the following things happen during the process of evolution (figure 4.3):

- *Reproduction*—Usually, two individuals in the population reproduce to create offspring.

- *Crossover and mutation*—The offspring created through reproduction contain a mix of their parents' genes and have slight random changes in their genetic code.

Figure 4.3 A simple example of reproduction and mutation

In summary, evolution is a marvelous and chaotic system that produces variations of life forms, some of which are better than others for specific things in specific environments. This theory also applies to evolutionary algorithms; learnings from biological evolution are harnessed for finding optimal solutions to practical problems by generating diverse solutions and converging on better-performing ones over many generations.

This chapter and chapter 5 are dedicated to exploring evolutionary algorithms, which are powerful but underrated approaches to solving hard problems. Evolutionary algorithms can be used in isolation or in conjunction with constructs such as neural networks. Having a solid grasp of this concept opens many possibilities for solving different novel problems.

Problems applicable to evolutionary algorithms

Evolutionary algorithms aren't applicable to solving all problems, but they are powerful for solving optimization problems in which the solution consists of a large number of permutations or choices. These problems typically consist of many valid solutions, with some being more optimal than others.

Consider the Knapsack Problem, a classic problem used in computer science to explore how algorithms work and how efficient they are. In the Knapsack Problem, a knapsack has a specific maximum weight that it can hold. Several items are available to be stored in the knapsack, and each item has a different weight and value. The goal is to fit as many items into the knapsack as possible so that the total value is maximized and the total weight does not exceed the knapsack's limit. The physical size and dimensions of the items are ignored in the simplest variation of the problem (figure 4.4).

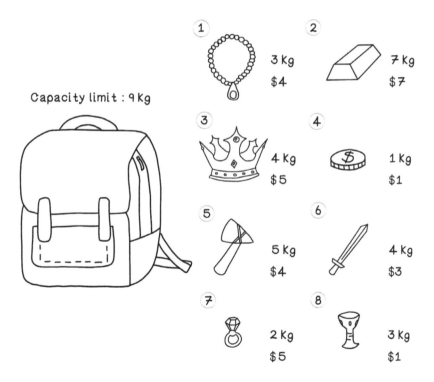

Figure 4.4 A simple Knapsack Problem example

As a trivial example, given the specification of the problem in table 4.1, a knapsack can hold a total weight capacity of 9 kg, and it could contain any of the eight items of varying weight and value.

Table 4.1 Knapsack weight capacity: 9 kg

Item ID	Item name	Weight (kg)	Value ($)
1	Pearls	3	4
2	Gold	7	7
3	Crown	4	5
4	Coin	1	1
5	Axe	5	4
6	Sword	4	3
7	Ring	2	5
8	Cup	3	1

This problem has 255 possible solutions, including the following (figure 4.5):

- *Solution 1*—Include Item 1, Item 4, and Item 6. The total weight is 8 kg, and the total value is $8.

- *Solution 2*—Include Item 1, Item 3, and Item 7. The total weight is 9 kg, and the total value is $14.

- *Solution 3*—Include Item 2, Item 3, and Item 6. The total weight is 15 kg, which exceeds the knapsack's capacity.

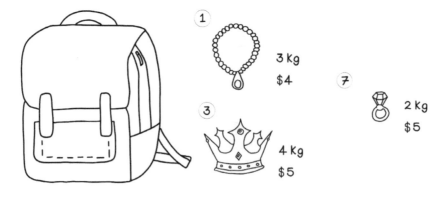

Figure 4.5 The optimal solution for the simple Knapsack Problem example

Clearly, the solution with the most value is *Solution 2*. Don't concern yourself too much about how the number of possibilities is calculated, but understand that the possibilities explode as the number of potential items increases.

Although this trivial example can be solved by hand, the Knapsack Problem could have varying weight constraints, a varying number of items, and varying weights and values for each item, making it impossible to solve by hand as the variables grow larger. It will also be computationally expensive to try to brute-force every combination of items when the variables grow; thus, we look for algorithms that are efficient at finding a desirable solution.

Note that we qualify the best solution we can find as a *desirable* solution rather than the *optimal* solution. Although some algorithms attempt to find the one true optimal solution to the Knapsack Problem, an evolutionary algorithm attempts to find the optimal solution but is not guaranteed to find it. The algorithm will find a solution that is acceptable for the use case, however—a subjective opinion of what an acceptable solution is, based on the problem. For a mission-critical health system, for example, a "good enough" solution may not cut it; but for a song-recommender system, it may be acceptable.

Now consider the larger dataset (yes, a giant knapsack) in table 4.2, in which the number of items and varying weights and values makes the problem difficult to solve by hand. By understanding the complexity of this dataset, you can easily see why many computer science algorithms are measured by their performance in solving such problems. Performance is defined as how well a specific solution solves a problem, not necessarily computational performance. In the Knapsack Problem, a solution that yields a higher total value would be better-performing. Evolutionary algorithms provide one method of finding solutions to the Knapsack Problem.

Table 4.2 Knapsack capacity: 6,404,180 kg

Item ID	Item name	Weight (kg)	Value ($)
1	Axe	32,252	68,674
2	Bronze coin	225,790	471,010
3	Crown	468,164	944,620
4	Diamond statue	489,494	962,094
5	Emerald belt	35,384	78,344
6	Fossil	265,590	579,152
7	Gold coin	497,911	902,698
8	Helmet	800,493	1,686,515
9	Ink	823,576	1,688,691
10	Jewel box	552,202	1,056,157
11	Knife	323,618	677,562
12	Long sword	382,846	833,132
13	Mask	44,676	99,192
14	Necklace	169,738	376,418
15	Opal badge	610,876	1,253,986
16	Pearls	854,190	1,853,562
17	Quiver	671,123	1,320,297
18	Ruby ring	698,180	1,301,637
19	Silver bracelet	446,517	859,835
20	Timepiece	909,620	1,677,534
21	Uniform	904,818	1,910,501
22	Venom potion	730,061	1,528,646
23	Wool scarf	931,932	1,827,477
24	Crossbow	952,360	2,068,204
25	Yesteryear book	926,023	1,746,556
26	Zinc cup	978,724	2,100,851

One way to solve this problem is to use a brute-force approach. This approach involves calculating every possible combination of items and determining the value of each combination that satisfies the knapsack's weight constraint until the best solution is encountered.

Figure 4.6 shows some benchmark analytics for the brute-force approach. Note that the computation is based on the hardware of an average personal computer.

Combinations	2^26 = 67,108,864
Iterations	2^26 = 67,108,864
Accuracy	100%
Compute time	~7 minutes

Figure 4.6 Performance analytics of brute-forcing the Knapsack Problem

Keep the Knapsack Problem in mind, as it will be used throughout this chapter as we attempt to understand, design, and develop a genetic algorithm to find acceptable solutions to this problem.

> **NOTE** A note about the term *performance*: From the perspective of an individual solution, performance is how well the solution solves the problem. From the perspective of the algorithm, performance may be how well a specific configuration does in finding a solution. Finally, performance may mean computational cycles. Bear in mind that this term is used differently based on the context.

The thinking behind using a genetic algorithm to solve the Knapsack Problem can be applied to a range of practical problems. If a logistics company wants to optimize the packing of trucks based on their destinations, for example, a genetic algorithm would be useful. If that same company wanted to find the shortest route between several destinations, a genetic algorithm would be useful as well. If a factory refined items into raw material via a conveyor-belt system, and the order of the items influenced productivity, a genetic algorithm would be useful in determining that order.

When we dive into the thinking, approach, and life cycle of the genetic algorithm, it should become clear where this powerful algorithm can be applied, and perhaps you will think of other uses in your work. It is important to keep in mind that a genetic algorithm is *stochastic*, which means that the output of the algorithm is likely to be different each time it is run.

Genetic algorithm: Life cycle

The genetic algorithm is a specific algorithm in the family of evolutionary algorithms. Each algorithm works on the same premise of evolution but has small tweaks in the different parts of the life cycle to cater to different problems. We explore some of these parameters in chapter 5.

Genetic algorithms are used to evaluate large search spaces for a good solution. It is important to note that a genetic algorithm is not guaranteed to find the absolute best solution; it attempts to find the global best while avoiding local best solutions.

A *global best* is the best possible solution, and a *local best* is a solution that is less optimal. Figure 4.7 represents the possible best solutions if the solution must be minimized—that is, the smaller the value, the better. If the goal was to maximize a solution, the larger the value, the better. Optimization algorithms like genetic algorithms aim to incrementally find local best solutions in search of the global best solution.

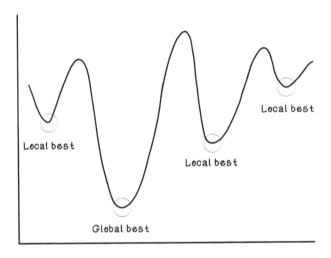

Figure 4.7 Local best vs. global best

Careful attention is needed when configuring the parameters of the algorithm so that it strives for diversity in solutions at the start and gradually gravitates toward better solutions through each generation. At the start, potential solutions should vary widely in individual genetic attributes. Without divergence at the start, the risk of getting stuck in a local best increases (figure 4.8).

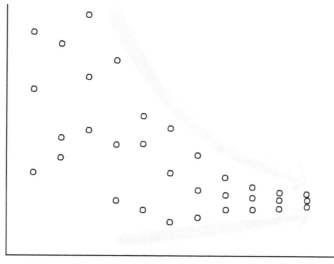

Generations

Figure 4.8 Diversity to convergence

The configuration for a genetic algorithm is based on the problem space. Each problem has a unique context and a different domain in which data is represented, and solutions are evaluated differently.

The general life cycle of a genetic algorithm is as follows:

- *Creating a population*—Creating a random population of potential solutions.

- *Measuring the fitness of individuals in the population*—Determining how good a specific solution is. This task is accomplished by using a fitness function that scores solutions to determine how good they are.

- *Selecting parents based on their fitness*—Selecting pairs of parents that will reproduce offspring.

- *Reproducing individuals from parents*—Creating offspring from their parents by mixing genetic information and applying slight mutations to the offspring.

- *Populating the next generation*—Selecting individuals and offspring from the population that will survive to the next generation.

Several steps are involved in implementing a genetic algorithm. These steps encompass the stages of the algorithm life cycle (figure 4.9).

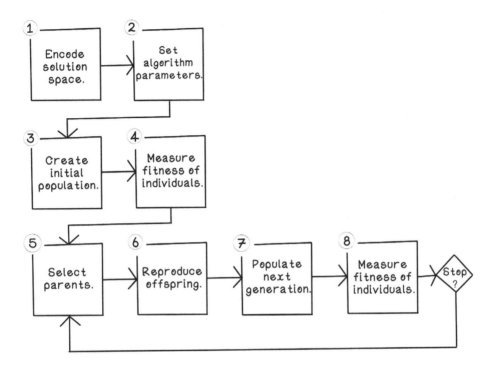

Figure 4.9 Genetic algorithm life cycle

With the Knapsack Problem in mind, how would we use a genetic algorithm to find solutions to the problem? The next section dives into the process.

Encoding the solution spaces

When we use a genetic algorithm, it is paramount to do the encoding step correctly, which requires careful design of the representation of possible states. The *state* is a data structure with specific rules that represents possible solutions to a problem. Furthermore, a collection of states forms a population (figure 4.10).

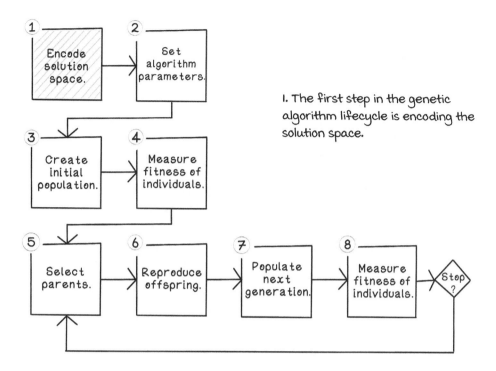

1. The first step in the genetic algorithm lifecycle is encoding the solution space.

Figure 4.10 Encode the solution.

Terminology

With respect to evolutionary algorithms, an individual candidate solution is called a *chromosome*. A chromosome is made up of genes. The *gene* is the logical type for the unit, and the *allele* is the actual value stored in that unit. A *genotype* is a representation of a solution, and a *phenotype* is a unique solution itself. Each chromosome always has the same number of genes. A collection of chromosomes forms a *population* (figure 4.11).

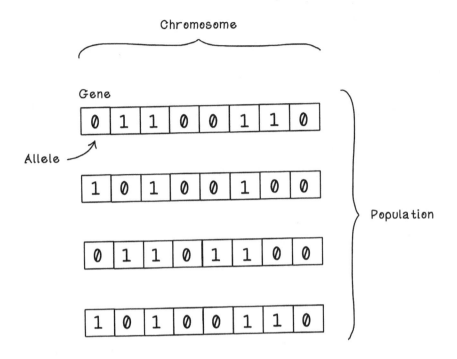

Figure 4.11 Terminology of the data structures representing a population of solutions

In the Knapsack Problem, several items can be placed in the knapsack. A simple way to describe a possible solution that contains some items but not others is binary encoding (figure 4.12). *Binary encoding* represents excluded items with 0s and included items with 1s. If the value at gene index 3 is 1, for example, that item is marked to be included. The complete binary string is always the same size: the number of items available for selection. Several alternative encoding schemes exist, however, and are described in chapter 5.

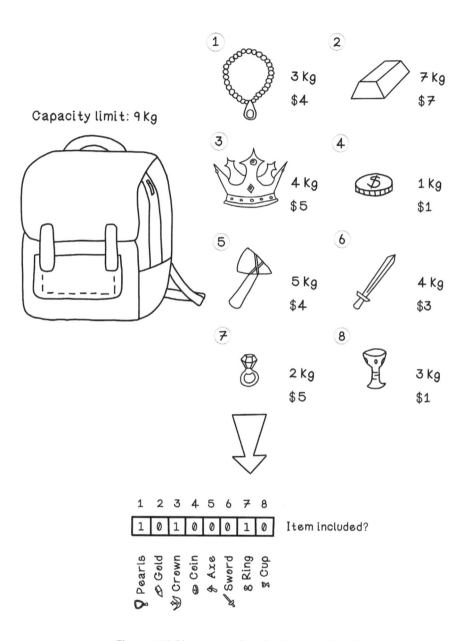

Figure 4.12 Binary-encoding the Knapsack Problem

Binary encoding: Representing possible solutions with zeros and ones

Binary encoding represents a gene in terms of 0 or 1, so a chromosome is represented by a string of binary bits. Binary encoding can be used in versatile ways to express the presence of a specific element or even encoding numeric values as binary numbers. The advantage of binary encoding is that it is usually more performant due to the use of primitive types. Using binary encoding places less demand on working memory, and depending on the language used, binary operations are computationally faster. But critical thought must be used to ensure that the encoding makes sense for the respective problem and represents potential solutions well; otherwise, the algorithm may perform poorly (figure 4.13).

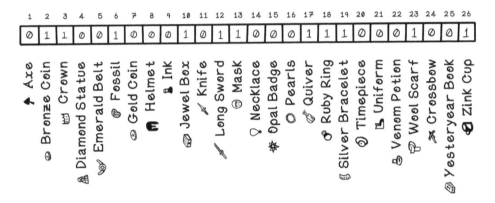

Figure 4.13 Binary-encoding the larger dataset for the Knapsack Problem

Given the Knapsack Problem with a dataset that consists of 26 items of varying weight and value, a binary string can be used to represent the inclusion of each item. The result is a 26-character string in which for each index, 0 means that the respective item is excluded and 1 means that the respective item is included.

Other encoding schemes—including real-value encoding, order encoding, and tree encoding—are discussed in chapter 5.

EXERCISE: WHAT IS A POSSIBLE ENCODING FOR THE FOLLOWING PROBLEM?

Suppose we have the following sentence and want to find which words can be
excluded or included to maintain a meaningful phrase using a genetic algorithm:

```
THE QUICK BROWN FOX JUMPS OVER THE LAZY DOG
```

Incorrect phrases
```
THE          BROWN       JUMPS OVER
     QUICK        FOX          OVER THE
THE               FOX               THE LAZY
```

Correct phrases
```
THE QUICK         FOX
     QUICK        FOX JUMPS
THE          BROWN FOX                         DOG
THE          BROWN                   LAZY DOG
THE QUICK                            DOG
     QUICK                 OVER THE  DOG
THE QUICK                            LAZY DOG
```
*Punctuation is excluded.

SOLUTION: WHAT IS A POSSIBLE ENCODING FOR THE FOLLOWING PROBLEM?

Because the number of possible words is always the same, and the words are
always in the same position, binary encoding can be used to describe which
words are included and which are excluded. The chromosome consists of 9
genes, each gene indicating a word in the phrase.

```
THE QUICK BROWN FOX JUMPS OVER THE LAZY DOG
┌──┬──┬──┬──┬──┬──┬──┬──┬──┐
│  │  │  │  │  │  │  │  │  │
└──┴──┴──┴──┴──┴──┴──┴──┴──┘

THE          BROWN       JUMPS OVER
┌──┬──┬──┬──┬──┬──┬──┬──┬──┐
│ 1│ 0│ 1│ 0│ 1│ 1│ 0│ 0│ 0│
└──┴──┴──┴──┴──┴──┴──┴──┴──┘

THE          BROWN                   LAZY DOG
┌──┬──┬──┬──┬──┬──┬──┬──┬──┐
│ 1│ 0│ 1│ 0│ 0│ 0│ 0│ 1│ 1│
└──┴──┴──┴──┴──┴──┴──┴──┴──┘
```

Creating a population of solutions

In the beginning, the population was created. The first step in a genetic algorithm is initializing random potential solutions to the problem at hand. In the process of initializing the population, although the chromosomes are generated randomly, the constraints of the problem must be taken into consideration, and the potential solutions should be valid or assigned a terrible fitness score if they violate the constraints. Each individual in the population may not solve the problem well, but the solution is valid. As mentioned in the earlier example of packing items into a knapsack, a solution that specifies packing the same item more than once should be an invalid solution and should not form part of the population of potential solutions (figure 4.14).

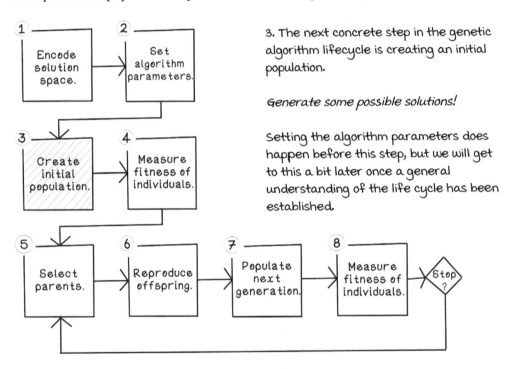

3. The next concrete step in the genetic algorithm lifecycle is creating an initial population.

Generate some possible solutions!

Setting the algorithm parameters does happen before this step, but we will get to this a bit later once a general understanding of the life cycle has been established.

Figure 4.14 Create an initial population.

Given how the Knapsack Problem's solution state is represented, this implementation randomly decides whether each item should be included in the bag. That said, only solutions that satisfy the weight-limit constraint should be considered. The problem with simply moving from left to right and randomly choosing whether the item is included is that it creates a bias toward the items on the left end of the chromosome. Similarly, if we start from the right, we will be biased toward items on the right. One possible way to get around this is to generate an entire individual with random genes and then determine whether the solution is valid and does not violate any constraints. Assigning a terrible score to invalid solutions can solve this problem (figure 4.15).

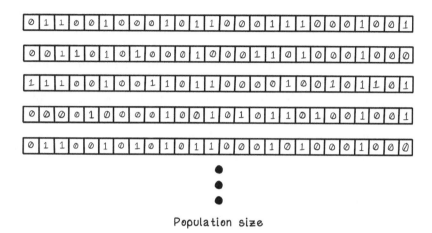

Figure 4.15 An example of a population of solutions

To generate an initial population of possible solutions, an empty array is created to hold the individuals. Then, for each individual in the population, an empty array is created to hold the genes of the individual. Each gene is randomly set to 1 or 0, indicating whether the item at that gene index is included:

```
generate_initial_population (population_size, individual_size)
    let population be an empty array
    for individual in range 0 to population_size
        let current_individual be an empty array
        for gene in range 0 to individual_size
            let random_gene be 0 or 1 randomly
            append random_gene to current_individual
        append current_individual to population
    return population
```

Measuring fitness of individuals in a population

When a population has been created, the fitness of each individual in the population needs to be determined. Fitness defines how well a solution performs. The fitness function is critical to the life cycle of a genetic algorithm. If the fitness of the individuals is measured incorrectly or in a way that does not attempt to strive for the optimal solution, the selection process for parents of new individuals and new generations will be influenced; the algorithm will be flawed and cannot strive to find the best possible solution.

Fitness functions are similar to the heuristics that we explored in chapter 3. They are guidelines for finding good solutions (figure 4.16).

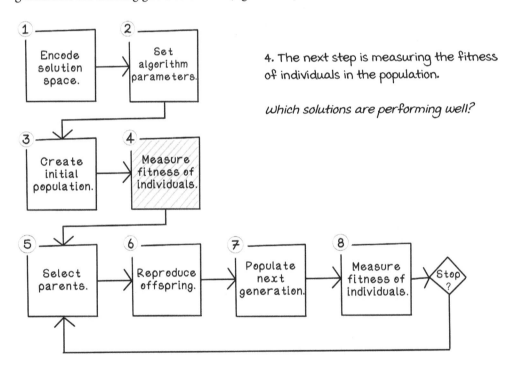

Figure 4.16 Measure the fitness of individuals.

In our example, the solution attempts to maximize the value of the items in the knapsack while respecting the weight-limit constraints. The fitness function measures the total value of the items in the knapsack for each individual. The result is that individuals with higher total values are more fit. Note that an invalid individual appears in figure 4.17, to highlight that its fitness score would result in 0—a terrible score, because it exceeds the weight capacity for this instance of the problem, which is 6,404,180.

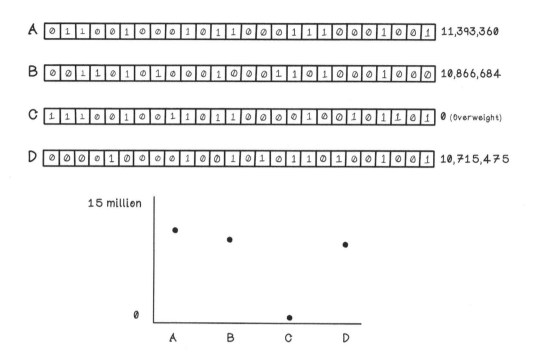

Figure 4.17 Measuring the fitness of individuals

Depending on the problem being solved, the result of the fitness function may be required to be minimized or maximized. In the Knapsack Problem, the contents of the knapsack can be maximized within constraints, or the empty space in the knapsack could be minimized. The approach depends on the interpretation of the problem.

Pseudocode

To calculate the fitness of an individual in the Knapsack Problem, the sums of the values of each item that the respective individual includes must be determined. This task is accomplished by setting the total value to 0 and then iterating over each gene to determine whether the item it represents is included. If the item is included, the value of the item represented by that gene is added to the total value. Similarly, the total weight is calculated to ensure that the solution is valid. The concepts of calculating fitness and checking constraints can be split for clearer separation of concerns:

```
calculate_individual_fitness (individual,
                              knapsack_items,
                              knapsack_max_weight)
   let total_weight equal 0
   let total_value equal 0
   for gene_index in range 0 to length of individual
      let current_bit equal individual[gene_index]
      if current_bit equals 1
         add weight of knapsack_items[gene_index] to total_weight
         add value of knapsack_items[gene_index] to total_value
   if total_weight is greater than knapsack_max_weight
      return value as 0 since it exceeds the weight constraint
   return total_value as individual fitness
```

Selecting parents based on their fitness

The next step in a genetic algorithm is selecting parents that will produce new individuals. In Darwinian theory, the individuals that are more fit have a higher likelihood of reproduction than others because they typically live longer. Furthermore, these individuals contain desirable attributes for inheritance due to their superior performance in their environment. That said, some individuals are likely to reproduce even if they are not the fittest in the entire group, and these individuals may contain strong traits even though they are not strong in their entirety.

Each individual has a calculated fitness that is used to determine the probability of it being selected to be a parent to a new individual. This attribute makes the genetic algorithm stochastic in nature (figure 4.18).

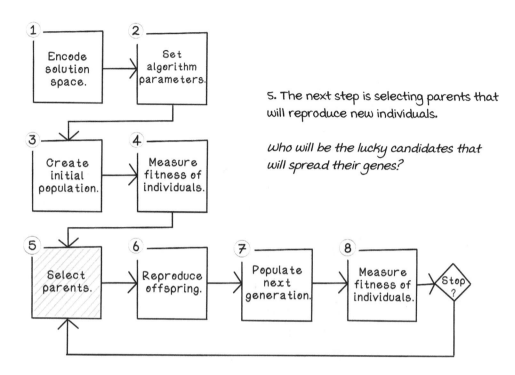

5. The next step is selecting parents that will reproduce new individuals.

Who will be the lucky candidates that will spread their genes?

Figure 4.18 Select parents.

A popular technique in choosing parents based on their fitness is *roulette-wheel selection*. This strategy gives different individuals portions of a wheel based on their fitness. The wheel is "spun," and an individual is selected. Higher fitness gives an individual a larger slice of the wheel. This process is repeated until the desired number of parents is reached.

By calculating the probabilities of 16 individuals of varying fitness, the wheel allocates a slice to each. Because many individuals perform similarly, there are many slices of similar size (figure 4.19).

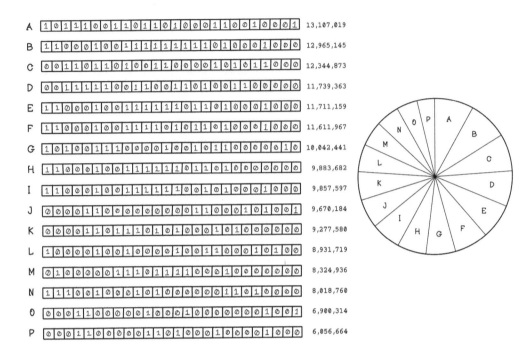

A `1 0 1 1 1 0 0 1 1 0 1 1 0 1 0 0 0 1 1 0 0 1 0 0 0 1` 13,107,019

B `1 1 0 0 0 1 0 0 1 1 1 1 1 1 1 1 1 0 1 0 0 0 1 0 0 0` 12,965,145

C `0 0 1 1 0 1 1 0 1 0 0 1 1 0 0 0 0 1 0 1 0 1 1 0 0 0` 12,344,873

D `0 0 1 1 1 1 1 1 0 0 1 1 0 0 1 1 0 1 0 0 1 1 0 0 0 0` 11,739,363

E `1 1 0 0 0 1 0 0 1 1 1 1 1 1 0 1 1 0 1 0 0 0 1 0 0 0` 11,711,159

F `1 1 0 0 0 1 0 0 1 1 1 1 0 1 0 1 1 0 1 0 0 0 1 0 0 0` 11,611,967

G `1 0 1 0 0 1 1 1 0 0 0 0 1 0 0 1 0 1 1 0 0 0 0 0 1 0` 10,042,441

H `1 1 0 0 0 1 0 0 1 1 1 1 1 1 0 1 1 0 1 0 0 0 0 0 0 0` 9,883,682

I `1 1 0 0 0 1 0 0 0 1 1 1 1 1 0 0 1 0 1 0 0 0 1 0 0 0` 9,857,597

J `0 0 0 0 1 1 0 0 0 0 0 0 0 0 1 1 0 0 0 1 0 1 0 0 0 1` 9,670,184

K `0 0 0 0 1 1 0 1 1 1 0 1 0 1 0 0 0 1 0 1 0 0 0 0 0 0` 9,277,580

L `1 0 0 0 0 1 0 0 1 0 0 0 0 1 0 0 1 1 0 0 0 1 0 1 0 0` 8,931,719

M `0 1 0 0 0 0 0 1 1 1 0 1 1 1 1 0 0 0 1 0 0 0 0 0 0 0` 8,324,936

N `1 1 1 0 0 1 0 0 0 1 0 1 0 0 0 0 0 0 1 1 0 1 0 0 0 0` 8,018,760

O `0 0 0 1 1 0 0 0 0 0 1 0 0 0 1 0 0 0 0 0 0 1 0 0 1` 6,900,314

P `0 0 0 1 1 0 0 0 0 0 1 1 0 1 0 0 0 1 0 0 0 0 1 0 0 0` 6,056,664

Figure 4.19 Determining the probability of selection for each individual

The number of parents selected to be used for reproducing new offspring is determined by the intended total number of offspring required, which is determined by the desired population size for each generation. Two parents are selected, and offspring are created. This process repeats with different parents selected (with a chance of the same individuals being a parent more than once) until the desired number of offspring have been generated. Two parents can reproduce a single mixed child or two mixed children. This concept will be made clearer later in this chapter. In our Knapsack Problem example, the individuals with greater fitness are those that fill the bag with the most combined value while respecting the weight-limit constraint.

Population models are ways to control the diversity of the population. Steady state and generational are two population models that have their own advantages and disadvantages.

Steady state: Replacing a portion of the population each generation

This high-level approach to population management is not an alternative to the other selection strategies, but a scheme that uses them. The idea is that the majority of the population is retained, and a small group of weaker individuals are removed and replaced with new offspring. This process mimics the cycle of life and death, in which weaker individuals die and new individuals are made through reproduction. If there were 100 individuals in the population, a portion of the population would be existing individuals, and a smaller portion would be new individuals created via reproduction. There may be 80 individuals from the current generation and 20 new individuals.

Generational: Replacing the entire population each generation

This high-level approach to population management is similar to the steady-state model but is not an alternative to selection strategies. The generational model creates a number of offspring individuals equal to the population size and replaces the entire population with the new offspring. If there were 100 individuals in the population, each generation would result in 100 new individuals via reproduction. Steady state and generational are overarching ideas for designing the configuration of the algorithm.

Roulette wheel: Selecting parents and surviving individuals

Chromosomes with higher fitness scores are more likely to be selected, but chromosomes with lower fitness scores still have a small chance of being selected. The term *roulette-wheel selection* comes from a roulette wheel at a casino, which is divided into slices. Typically, the wheel is spun, and a marble is released into the wheel. The selected slice is the one that the marble lands on when the wheel stops turning.

In this analogy, chromosomes are assigned to slices of the wheel. Chromosomes with higher fitness scores have larger slices of the wheel, and chromosomes with lower fitness scores have smaller slices. A chromosome is selected randomly, much as a ball randomly lands on a slice.

This analogy is an example of probabilistic selection. Each individual has a chance of being selected, whether that chance is small or high. The chance of selection of individuals influences the diversity of the population and convergence rates mentioned earlier in this chapter. Figure 4.19, also earlier in this chapter, illustrates this concept.

Pseudocode

First, the probability of selection for each individual needs to be determined. This probability is calculated for each individual by dividing its fitness by the total fitness of the population. Roulette-wheel selection can be used. The "wheel" is "spun" until the desired number of individuals have been selected. For each selection, a random decimal number between 0 and 1 is calculated. If an individual's fitness is within that probability, it is selected. Other probabilistic approaches may be used to determine the probability of each individual, including standard deviation, in which an individual's value is compared with the mean value of the group:

```
set_probabilities_of_population (population)
  let total_fitness equal the sum of fitness of the population
  for individual in population
    let the probability_of_selection of individual...
        ...equal it's fitness/total_fitness


roulette_wheel_selection(population, number_of_selections):
  let possible_probabilities equal
      set_probabilities_of_population (population)
  let slices equal empty array
  let total equal 0
  for i in range(0, number_of_selections):
    append [i, total, total + possible_probabilities[i]]
      to slices
    total += possible_probabilities[i]
  let spin equal random(0, 1)
  let result equal [slice for slice in slices if slice[1] < spin <= slice[2]]
  return result
```

Reproducing individuals from parents

When parents are selected, reproduction needs to happen to create new offspring from the parents. Generally, two steps are related to creating children from two parents. The first concept is *crossover*, which means mixing part of the chromosome of the first parent with part of the chromosome of the second parent, and vice versa. This process results in two offspring that contain inversed mixes of their parents. The second concept is *mutation*, which means randomly changing the offspring slightly to create variation in the population (figure 4.20).

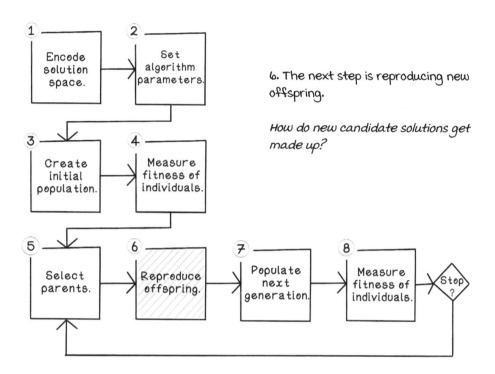

Figure 4.20 Reproduce offspring.

Crossover

Crossover involves mixing genes between two individuals to create one or more offspring individuals. Crossover is inspired by the concept of reproduction. The offspring individuals are parts of their parents, depending on the crossover strategy used. The crossover strategy is highly affected by the encoding used.

Single-point crossover: Inheriting one part from each parent

One point in the chromosome structure is selected. Then, by referencing the two parents in question, the first part of the first parent is used, and the second part of the second parent is used. These two parts combined create a new offspring. A second offspring can be made by using the first part of the second parent and the second part of the first parent.

Single-point crossover is applicable to binary encoding, order/permutation encoding, and real-value encoding (figure 4.21). These encoding schemes are discussed in chapter 5.

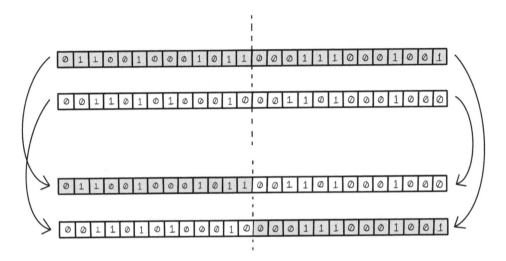

Figure 4.21 Single-point crossover

To create two new offspring individuals, an empty array is created to hold the new individuals. All genes from index 0 to the desired index of parent A are concatenated with all genes from the desired index to the end of the chromosome of parent B, creating one offspring individual. The inverse creates the second offspring individual:

```
one_point_crossover (parent_a, parent_b, xover_point)

    let children equal empty array


    let child_1 equal genes 0 to xover_point from parent_a plus...
    ...genes xover_point to parent_b length from parent_b
    append child_1 to children


    let child_2 equal genes 0 to xover_point from parent_b plus...
    ...genes xover_point to parent_a length from parent_a
    append child_2 to children


    return children
```

Two-point crossover: Inheriting more parts from each parent

Two points in the chromosome structure are selected; then, referencing the two parents in question, parts are chosen in an alternating manner to make a complete offspring individual. This process is similar to single-point crossover, discussed earlier. To describe the process completely, the offspring consist of the first part of the first parent, the second part of the second parent, and the third part of the first parent. Think about two-point crossover as splicing arrays to create new ones. Again, a second individual can be made by using the inverse parts of each parent. Two-point crossover is applicable to binary encoding and real-value encoding (figure 4.22).

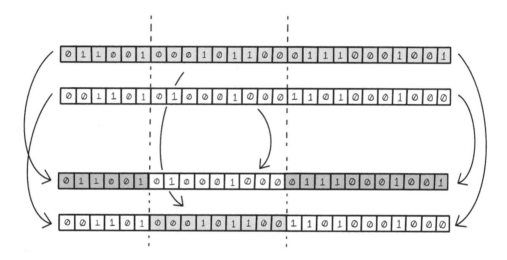

Figure 4.22 Two-point crossover

Uniform crossover: Inheriting many parts from each parent

Uniform crossover is a step beyond two-point crossover. In uniform crossover, a mask is created that represents which genes from each parent will be used to generate the child offspring. The inverse process can be used to make a second offspring. The mask can be generated randomly each time offspring are created to maximize diversity. Generally speaking, uniform crossover creates more-diverse individuals because the attributes of the offspring are quite different compared with any of their parents. Uniform crossover is applicable to binary encoding and real-value encoding (figure 4.23).

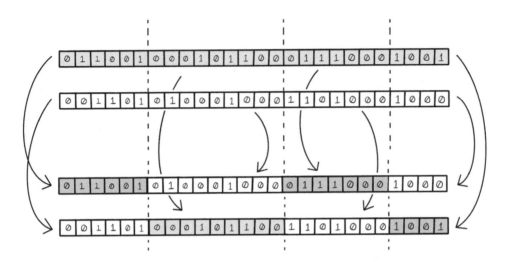

Figure 4.23 Uniform crossover

Mutation

Mutation involves changing offspring individuals slightly to encourage diversity in the population. Several approaches to mutation are used based on the nature of the problem and the encoding method.

One parameter in mutation is the mutation rate—the likelihood that an offspring chromosome will be mutated. Similarly to living organisms, some chromosomes are mutated more than others; an offspring is not an exact combination of its parents' chromosomes but contains minor genetic differences. Mutation can be critical to encouraging diversity in a population and preventing the algorithm from getting stuck in local best solutions.

A high mutation rate means that individuals have a high chance of being selected to be mutated or that genes in the chromosome of an individual have a high chance of being mutated, depending on the mutation strategy. High mutation means more diversity, but too much diversity may result in the deterioration of good solutions.

EXERCISE: WHAT OUTCOME WOULD UNIFORM CROSSOVER GENERATE
FOR THESE CHROMOSOMES?

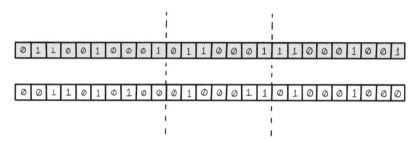

SOLUTION: WHAT OUTCOME WOULD UNIFORM CROSSOVER GENERATE
FOR THESE CHROMOSOMES?

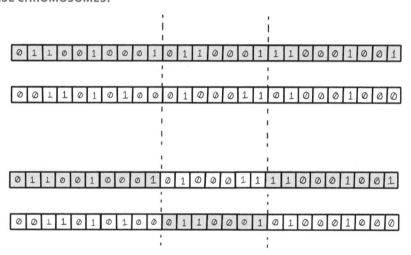

Bit-string mutation for binary encoding

In bit-string mutation, a gene in a binary-encoded chromosome is selected randomly and changed to another valid value (figure 4.24). Other mutation mechanisms are applicable when nonbinary encoding is used. The topic of mutation mechanisms will be explored in chapter 5.

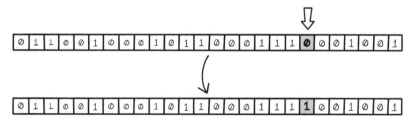

Figure 4.24 Bit-string mutation

To mutate a single gene of an individual's chromosome, a random gene index is selected. If that gene represents 1, change it to represent 0, and vice versa:

```
mutate_individual (individual, chromosome_length)
  let random_index equal a random number between 0 and chromosome_length
  if gene at index random_index of individual is equal to 1:
    let gene at index random_index of individual equal 0
  else:
    let gene at index random_index of individual equal 1
  return individual
```

Flip-bit mutation for binary encoding

In flip-bit mutation, all genes in a binary-encoded chromosome are inverted to the opposite value. Where there were 1s are 0s, and where there were 0s are 1s. This type of mutation could degrade good-performing solutions dramatically and usually is used when diversity needs to be introduced into the population constantly (figure 4.25).

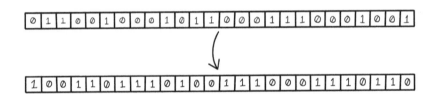

Figure 4.25 Flip-bit mutation

Populating the next generation

When the fitness of the individuals in the population has been measured and offspring have been reproduced, the next step is selecting which individuals live on to the next generation. The size of the population is usually fixed, and because more individuals have been introduced through reproduction, some individuals must die off and be removed from the population.

It may seem like a good idea to take the top individuals that fit into the population size and eliminate the rest. This strategy, however, could create stagnation in the diversity of individuals if the individuals that survive are similar in genetic makeup (figure 4.26).

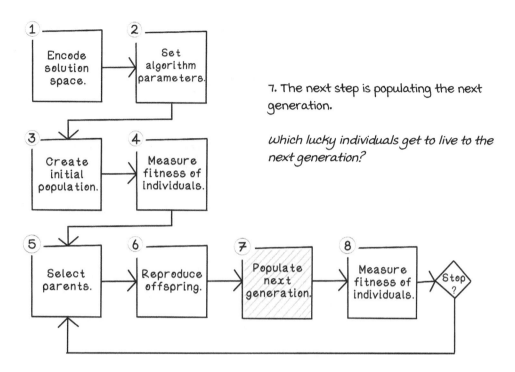

Figure 4.26 Populate the next generation.

The selection strategies mentioned in this section can be used to determine the individuals that are selected to form part of the population for the next generation.

Exploration vs. exploitation

Running a genetic algorithm always involves striking a balance between exploration and exploitation. The ideal situation is one in which there is diversity in individuals and the population as a whole seeks out wildly different potential solutions in the search space; then stronger local solution spaces are exploited to find the most desirable solution. The beauty of this situation is that the algorithm explores as much of the search space as possible while exploiting strong solutions as individuals evolve (figure 4.27).

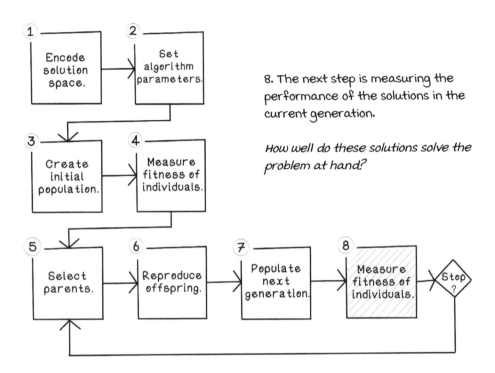

8. The next step is measuring the performance of the solutions in the current generation.

How well do these solutions solve the problem at hand?

Figure 4.27 Measure the fitness of individuals.

Stopping conditions

Because a genetic algorithm is iterative in finding better solutions through each generation, a stopping condition needs to be established; otherwise, the algorithm might run forever. A *stopping condition* is the condition that is met where the algorithm ends; the strongest individual of the population at that generation is selected as the best solution.

The simplest stopping condition is a *constant*—a constant value that indicates the number of generations for which the algorithm will run. Another approach is to stop when a certain fitness is achieved. This method is useful when a desired minimum fitness is known but the solution is unknown.

Stagnation is a problem in evolutionary algorithms in which the population yields solutions of similar strength for several generations. If a population stagnates, the likelihood of generating strong solutions in future generations is low. A stopping condition could look at the change in the fitness of the best individual in each generation and, if the fitness changes only marginally, choose to stop the algorithm.

The various steps of a genetic algorithm are used in a main function that outlines the life cycle in its entirety. The variable parameters include the population size, the number of generations for the algorithm to run, and the knapsack capacity for the fitness function, in addition to the variable crossover position and mutation rate for the crossover and mutation steps:

```
run_ga (population_size, number_of_generations, knapsack_capacity):
  let best_global_fitness equal 0
  let global_population equal...
  ...generate_initial_population(population_size)
  for generation in range(number_of_generations):
    let current_best_fitness equal...
    ...calculate_population_fitness(global_population, knapsack_capacity)
    if current_best_fitness is greater than best_global_fitness:
      let best_global_fitness equal current_best_fitness
    let the_chosen equal...
    ...roulette_wheel_selection(global_population, population_size)
    let the_children equal...
    ...reproduce_children(the_chosen)
    let the_children equal...
    ...mutate_children(the_children)
    let global_population equal...
    ...merge_population_and_children(global_population, the_children)
```

As mentioned at the beginning of this chapter, the Knapsack Problem could be solved using a brute-force approach, which requires more than 60 million combinations to be generated and analyzed. When comparing genetic algorithms that aim to solve the same problem, we can see far more efficiency in computation if the parameters for exploration and exploitation are configured correctly. Remember, in some cases, a genetic algorithm produces a "good enough" solution that is not necessarily the best possible solution but is desirable. Again, using a genetic algorithm for a problem depends on the context (figure 4.28).

	Brute force	Genetic algorithm
Iterations	2^26 = 67,108,864	10,000 - 100,000
Accuracy	100%	100%
Compute time	~7 minutes	~3 seconds
Best value	13,692,887	13,692,887

Figure 4.28 Brute-force performance vs. genetic algorithm performance

Configuring the parameters of a genetic algorithm

In designing and configuring a genetic algorithm, several decisions need to be made that influence the performance of the algorithm. The performance concerns fall into two areas: the algorithm should strive to perform well in finding good solutions to the problem, and the algorithm should perform efficiently from a computation perspective. It would be pointless to design a genetic algorithm to solve a problem if the solution will be more computationally expensive than other traditional techniques. The approach used in encoding, the fitness function used, and the other algorithmic parameters influence both types of performances in achieving a good solution and computation. Here are some parameters to consider:

- *Chromosome encoding*—The chromosome encoding method requires thought to ensure that it is applicable to the problem and that the potential solutions strive for global maxima. The encoding scheme is at the heart of the success of the algorithm.

- *Population size*—The population size is configurable. A larger population encourages more diversity in possible solutions. Larger populations, however, require more computation at each generation. Sometimes, a larger population balances out the need for mutation, which results in diversity at the start but no diversity during generations. A valid approach is to start with a smaller population and grow it based on performance.

- *Population initialization*—Although the individuals in a population are initialized randomly, ensuring that the solutions are valid is important for optimizing the computation of the genetic algorithm and initializing individuals with the right constraints.

- *Number of offspring*—The number of offspring created in each generation can be configured. Given that after reproduction, part of the population is killed off to ensure that the population size is fixed, more offspring means more diversity, but there is a risk that good solutions will be killed off to accommodate those offspring. If the population is dynamic, the population size may change after every generation, but this approach requires more parameters to configure and control.

- *Parent selection method*—The selection method used to choose parents can be configured. The selection method must be based on the problem and the desired explorability versus exploitability.

- *Crossover method*—The crossover method is associated with the encoding method used but can be configured to encourage or discourage diversity in the population. The offspring individuals must still yield a valid solution.

- *Mutation rate*—The mutation rate is another configurable parameter that induces more diversity in offspring and potential solutions. A higher mutation rate means more diversity, but too much diversity may deteriorate good-performing individuals. The mutation rate can change over time to create more diversity in earlier generations and less in later generations. This result can be described as exploration at the start followed by exploitation.

- *Mutation method*—The mutation method is similar to the crossover method in that it is dependent on the encoding method used. An important attribute of the mutation method is that it must still yield a valid solution after the modification or assigned a terrible fitness score.

- *Generation selection methods*—Much like the selection method used to choose parents, a generation selection method must choose the individuals that will survive the generation. Depending on the selection method used, the algorithm may converge too quickly and stagnate or explore too long.

- *Stopping condition*—The stopping condition for the algorithm must make sense based on the problem and desired outcome. Computational complexity and time are the main concerns for the stopping condition.

Use cases for evolutionary algorithms

Evolutionary algorithms have a wide variety of uses. Some algorithms address isolated problems; others combine evolutionary algorithms with other techniques to create novel approaches to solving difficult problems, such as the following:

- *Predicting investor behavior in the stock market*—Consumers who invest make decisions every day about whether to buy more of a specific stock, hold on to what they have, or sell stock. Sequences of these actions can be evolved and mapped to outcomes of an investor's portfolio. Financial institutions can use this insight to proactively provide valuable customer service and guidance.

- *Feature selection in machine learning*—Machine learning is discussed in chapter 8, but a key aspect of machine learning is: given a number of features about something, determining what it is classified as. If we're looking at houses, we may find many attributes related to houses, such as age, building material, size, color, and location. But to predict market value, perhaps only age, size, and location matter. A genetic algorithm can uncover the isolated features that matter the most.

- *Code breaking and ciphers*—A *cipher* is a message encoded in a certain way to look like something else and is often used to hide information. If the receiver does not know how to decipher the message, it cannot be understood. Evolutionary algorithms can generate many possibilities for changing the ciphered message to uncover the original message.

Chapter 5 dives into advanced concepts of genetic algorithms that adapt them to different problem spaces. We explore different techniques for encoding, crossover, mutation, and selection, as well as uncover effective alternatives.

SUMMARY OF EVOLUTIONARY ALGORITHMS

GAs use smart randomness to find good solutions fast.

Encoding is critial to the algorithm.

1	2	3	4	5	6	7	8	9	10	11	12	13	14	15	16	17	18	19	20	21	22	23	24	25	26
0	1	1	0	0	1	0	0	0	1	0	1	1	0	0	0	1	1	1	0	0	0	1	0	0	1

The fitness function is paramount to finding good solutions to the problem at hand.

Crossover aims to reproduce better solutions at each generation.

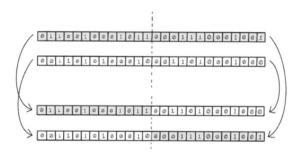

Selection favors stronger individuals but gives weaker ones an opportunity to possibly reproduce good solutions in the future.

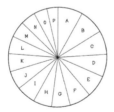 Roulette-wheel selection

Explore at the start and exploit toward the end.

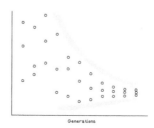

Generations

This chapter covers

- Considering options for the various steps in the genetic algorithm
  life cycle

- Adjusting a genetic algorithm to solve varying problems

- The advanced parameters for configuring a genetic algorithm life
  cycle based on different scenarios, problems, and datasets

  NOTE Chapter 4 is a prerequisite to this chapter.

Evolutionary algorithm life cycle

The general life cycle of a genetic algorithm is outlined in chapter 4. In this chapter, we consider other problems that may be suitable to be solved with a genetic algorithm, why some of the approaches demonstrated thus far won't work, and alternative approaches.

As a reminder, the general life cycle of a genetic algorithm is as follows:

- *Creating a population*—Creating a random population of potential solutions.

- *Measuring fitness of individuals in the population*—Determining how good a specific solution is. This task is accomplished by using a fitness function that scores solutions to determine how good they are.

- *Selecting parents based on their fitness*—Selecting pairs of parents that will reproduce offspring.

- *Reproducing individuals from parents*—Creating offspring from their parents by mixing genetic information and applying slight mutations to the offspring.

- *Populating the next generation*—Selecting individuals and offspring from the population that will survive to the next generation.

Keep the life cycle flow (depicted in figure 5.1) in mind as we work through this chapter.

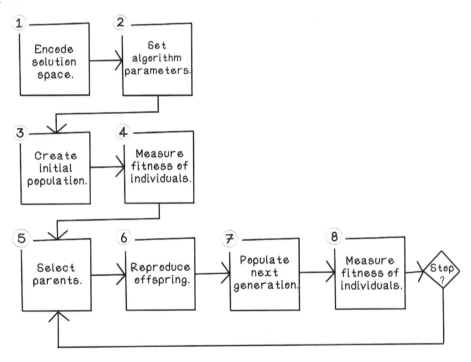

Figure 5.1 Genetic algorithm life cycle

This chapter starts by exploring alternative selection strategies; these individual approaches can be generically swapped in and out for any genetic algorithm. Then it follows three scenarios that are tweaks of the Knapsack Problem (chapter 4) to highlight the utility of the alternative encoding, crossover, and mutation approaches (figure 5.2).

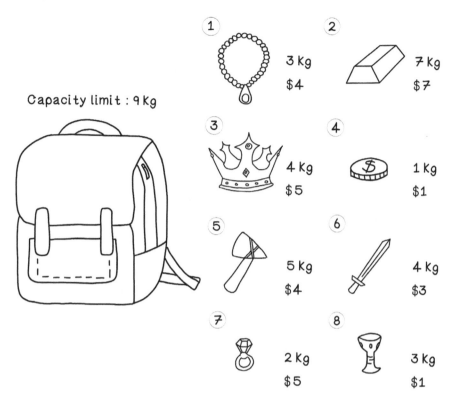

Figure 5.2 The example Knapsack Problem

Alternative selection strategies

In chapter 4, we explored one selection strategy: roulette-wheel selection, which is one of the simplest methods for selecting individuals. The following three selection strategies help mitigate the problems of roulette-wheel selection; each has advantages and disadvantages that affect the diversity of the population, which ultimately affects whether an optimal solution is found.

Rank selection: Even the playing field

One problem with roulette-wheel selection is the vast differences in the magnitude of fitness between chromosomes. This heavily biases the selection toward choosing individuals with high fitness scores or giving poor-performing individuals a larger chance of selection than desired. This problem affects the diversity of the population. More diversity means more exploration of the search space, but it can also make finding optimal solutions take too many generations.

Rank selection aims to solve this problem by ranking individuals based on their fitness and then using each individual's rank as the value for calculating the size of its slice on the wheel. In the Knapsack Problem, this value is a number between 1 and 16, because we're choosing among 16 individuals. Although strong individuals are more likely to be selected and weaker ones are less likely to be selected even though they are average, each individual has a fairer chance of being selected based on rank rather than exact fitness. When 16 individuals are ranked, the wheel looks slightly different from roulette-wheel selection (figure 5.3).

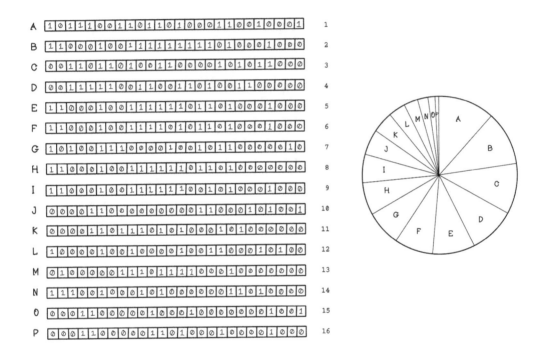

Figure 5.3 Example of rank selection

Figure 5.4 compares roulette-wheel selection and rank selection. It is clear that rank selection gives better-performing solutions a better chance of selection.

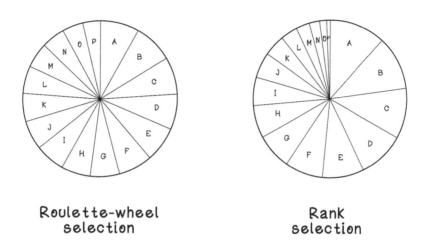

Figure 5.4 Roulette-wheel selection vs. rank selection

Tournament selection: Let them fight

Tournament selection plays chromosomes against one other. Tournament selection randomly chooses a set number of individuals from the population and places them in a group. This process is performed for a predetermined number of groups. The individual with the highest fitness score in each respective group is selected. The larger the group, the less diverse it is, because only one individual from each group is selected. As with rank selection, the actual fitness score of each individual is not the key factor in selecting individuals globally.

When 16 individuals are allocated to four groups, selecting only 1 individual from each group results in the choice of 4 of the strongest individuals from those groups. Then the 4 winning individuals can be paired to reproduce (figure 5.5).

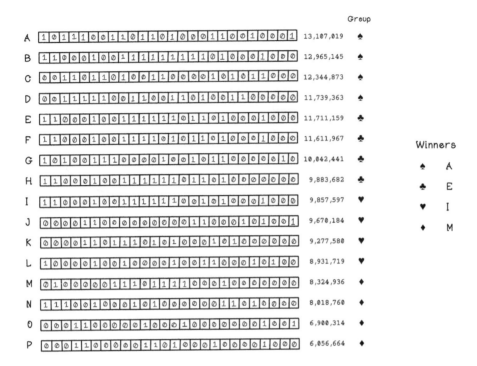

Figure 5.5 Example of tournament selection

Elitism selection: Choose only the best

The elitism approach selects the best individuals in the population. Elitism is useful for retaining strong-performing individuals and eliminating the risk that they will be lost through other selection methods. The disadvantage of elitism is that the population can fall into a local best solution space and never be diverse enough to find global bests.

Elitism is often used in conjunction with roulette-wheel selection, rank selection, and tournament selection. The idea is that several elite individuals are selected to reproduce, and the rest of the population is filled with individuals by means of one of the other selection strategies (figure 5.6).

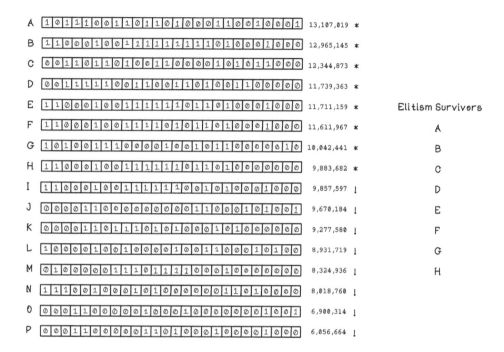

Figure 5.6 Example of elitism selection

Chapter 4 explores a problem in which including items in or excluding items from the knapsack was important. A variety of problem spaces require a different encoding because binary encoding won't make sense. The following three sections describe these scenarios.

Real-value encoding: Working with real numbers

Consider that the Knapsack Problem has changed slightly. The problem remains choosing the most valuable items to fill the weight capacity of the knapsack. But the choice involves more than one unit of each item. As shown in table 5.1, the weights and values remain the same as the original dataset, but a quantity of each item is included. With this slight adjustment, a plethora of new solutions are possible, and one or more of those solutions may be more optimal, because a specific item can be selected more than once. Binary encoding is a poor choice in this scenario. Real-value encoding is better suited to representing the state of potential solutions.

Table 5.1 Knapsack capacity: 6,404,180 kg

Item ID	Item name	Weight (kg)	Value ($)	Quantity
1	Axe	32,252	68,674	19
2	Bronze coin	225,790	471,010	14
3	Crown	468,164	944,620	2
4	Diamond statue	489,494	962,094	9
5	Emerald belt	35,384	78,344	11
6	Fossil	265,590	579,152	6
7	Gold coin	497,911	902,698	4
8	Helmet	800,493	1,686,515	10
9	Ink	823,576	1,688,691	7
10	Jewel box	552,202	1,056,157	3
11	Knife	323,618	677,562	5
12	Long sword	382,846	833,132	13
13	Mask	44,676	99,192	15
14	Necklace	169,738	376,418	8
15	Opal badge	610,876	1,253,986	4
16	Pearls	854,190	1,853,562	9
17	Quiver	671,123	1,320,297	12
18	Ruby ring	698,180	1,301,637	17
19	Silver bracelet	446,517	859,835	16
20	Timepiece	909,620	1,677,534	7
21	Uniform	904,818	1,910,501	6
22	Venom potion	730,061	1,528,646	9
23	Wool scarf	931,932	1,827,477	3
24	Crossbow	952,360	2,068,204	1
25	Yesteryear book	926,023	1,746,556	7
26	Zinc cup	978,724	2,100,851	2

Real-value encoding at its core

Real-value encoding represents a gene in terms of numeric values, strings, or symbols, and expresses potential solutions in the natural state respective to the problem. This encoding is used when potential solutions contain continuous values that cannot be encoded easily with binary encoding. As an example, because more than one item is available to be carried in the knapsack, each item index cannot indicate only whether the item is included; it must indicate the quantity of that item in the knapsack (figure 5.7).

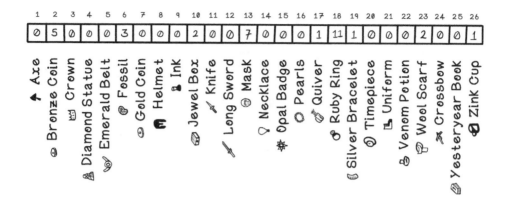

Figure 5.7 Example of real-value encoding

Because the encoding scheme has been changed, new crossover and mutation options become available. The crossover approaches discussed for binary encoding are still valid options to real-value encoding, but mutation should be approached differently.

Arithmetic crossover: Reproduce with math

Arithmetic crossover involves an arithmetic operation to be computed by using each parent as variables in the expression. The result of applying an arithmetic operation using both parents is the new offspring. When we use this strategy with binary encoding, it is important to ensure that the result of the operation is still a valid chromosome. Arithmetic crossover is applicable to binary encoding and real-value encoding (figure 5.8).

> **NOTE** Be wary: this approach can create very diverse offspring, which can be problematic.

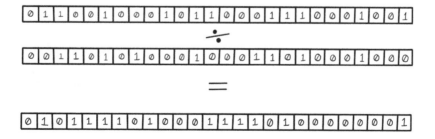

Figure 5.8 Example of arithmetic crossover

Boundary mutation

In boundary mutation, a gene randomly selected from a real-value encoded chromo-some is set randomly to a lower bound value or upper bound value. Given 26 genes in a chromosome, a random index is selected, and the value is set to either a minimum value or a maximum value. In figure 5.9, the original value happens to be 0 and will be adjusted to 6, which is the maximum for that item. The minimum and maximum can be the same for all indexes or set uniquely for each index if knowledge of the problem informs the decision. This approach attempts to evaluate the impact of individual genes on the chromosome.

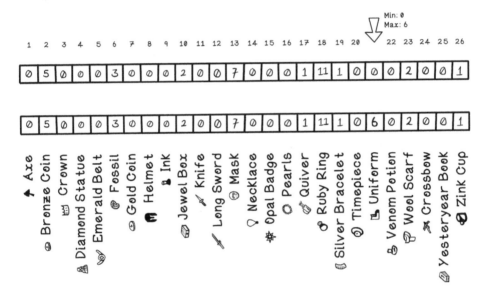

Figure 5.9 Example of boundary mutation

Arithmetic mutation

In arithmetic mutation, a randomly selected gene in a real-value-encoded chromosome is changed by adding or subtracting a small number. Note that although the example in figure 5.10 includes whole numbers, the numbers could be decimal numbers, including fractions.

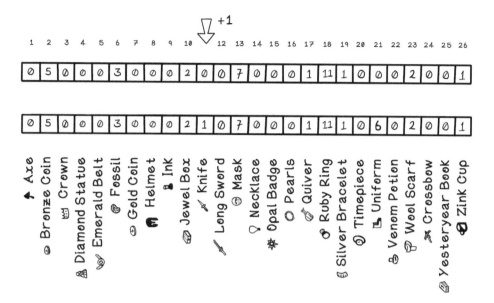

Figure 5.10 Example of arithmetic mutation

Order encoding: Working with sequences

We still have the same items as in the Knapsack Problem. We won't be determining the items that will fit into a knapsack; instead, all the items need to be processed in a refinery in which each item is broken down to extract its source material. Perhaps the gold coin, silver bracelet, and other items are smelted to extract only the source compounds. In this scenario, items are not selected to be included, but all are included.

To make things interesting, the refinery requires a steady rate of extraction, given the extraction time and the value of the item. It's assumed that the value of the refined material is more or less the same as the value of the item. The problem becomes an ordering problem. In what order should the items be processed to maintain a constant rate of value? Table 5.2 describes the items with their respective extraction times.

Table 5.2 Factory value per hour: 600,000

Item ID	Item name	Weight (kg)	Value ($)	Extraction time
1	Axe	32,252	68,674	60
2	Bronze coin	225,790	471,010	30
3	Crown	468,164	944,620	45
4	Diamond statue	489,494	962,094	90
5	Emerald belt	35,384	78,344	70
6	Fossil	265,590	579,152	20
7	Gold coin	497,911	902,698	15
8	Helmet	800,493	1,686,515	20
9	Ink	823,576	1,688,691	10
10	Jewel box	552,202	1,056,157	40
11	Knife	323,618	677,562	15
12	Long sword	382,846	833,132	60
13	Mask	44,676	99,192	10
14	Necklace	169,738	376,418	20
15	Opal badge	610,876	1,253,986	60
16	Pearls	854,190	1,853,562	25
17	Quiver	671,123	1,320,297	30
18	Ruby ring	698,180	1,301,637	70
19	Silver bracelet	446,517	859,835	50
20	Timepiece	909,620	1,677,534	45
21	Uniform	904,818	1,910,501	5
22	Venom potion	730,061	1,528,646	5
23	Wool scarf	931,932	1,827,477	5
24	Crossbow	952,360	2,068,204	25
25	Yesteryear book	926,023	1,746,556	5
26	Zinc cup	978,724	2,100,851	10

Importance of the fitness function

With the change in the Knapsack Problem to the Refinery Problem, a key difference is the measurement of successful solutions. Because the factory requires a constant minimum rate of value per hour, the accuracy of the fitness function used becomes paramount to finding optimal solutions. In the Knapsack Problem, the fitness of a solution is trivial to compute, as it involves only two things: ensuring that the knapsack's weight limit is respected and summing the selected items' value. In the Refinery Problem, the fitness function must calculate the rate of value provided, given the extraction time for each item as well as the value of each item. This calculation is more complex, and an error in the logic of this fitness function directly influences the quality of solutions.

Order encoding at its core

Order encoding, also known as permutation encoding, represents a chromosome as a sequence of elements. Order encoding usually requires all elements to be present in the chromosome, which implies that corrections might need to be made when performing crossover and mutation to ensure that no elements are missing or duplicated. Figure 5.11 depicts how a chromosome represents the order of processing of the available items.

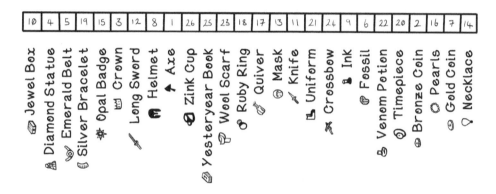

Figure 5.11 Example of order encoding

Another example in which order encoding is sensible is representing potential solutions to route optimization problems. Given a certain number of destinations, each of which must be visited at least once while minimizing the total distance traveled, the route can be represented as a string of the destinations in the order in which they are visited. We will use this example when covering swarm intelligence in chapter 6.

Order mutation: Order/permutation encoding

In order mutation, two randomly selected genes in an order-encoded chromosome swap positions, ensuring that all items remain in the chromosome while introducing diversity (figure 5.12).

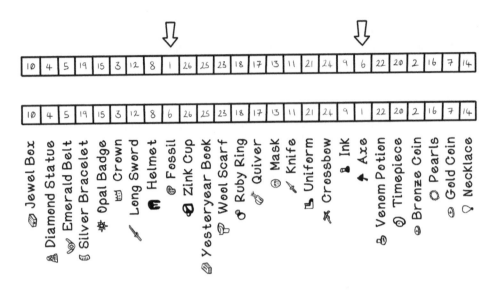

Figure 5.12 Example of order mutation

Tree encoding: Working with hierarchies

The preceding sections show that binary encoding is useful for selecting items from a set, real-value encoding is useful when real numbers are important to the solution, and order encoding is useful for determining priority and sequences. Suppose that the items in the Knapsack Problem are placed in packages to be shipped to homes around the town. Each delivery wagon can hold a specific volume. The requirement is to determine the optimal positioning of packages to minimize empty space in each wagon (table 5.3).

Table 5.3 Wagon capacity: 1000 wide × 1000 high

Item ID	Item name	Weight (kg)	Value ($)	W	H
1	Axe	32,252	68,674	20	60
2	Bronze coin	225,790	471,010	10	10
3	Crown	468,164	944,620	20	20
4	Diamond statue	489,494	962,094	30	70
5	Emerald belt	35,384	78,344	30	20
6	Fossil	265,590	579,152	15	15
7	Gold coin	497,911	902,698	10	10
8	Helmet	800,493	1,686,515	40	50
9	Ink	823,576	1,688,691	5	10
10	Jewel box	552,202	1,056,157	40	30
11	Knife	323,618	677,562	10	30
12	Long sword	382,846	833,132	15	50
13	Mask	44,676	99,192	20	30
14	Necklace	169,738	376,418	15	20
15	Opal badge	610,876	1,253,986	5	5
16	Pearls	854,190	1,853,562	10	5
17	Quiver	671,123	1,320,297	30	70
18	Ruby ring	698,180	1,301,637	5	10
19	Silver bracelet	446,517	859,835	10	20
20	Timepiece	909,620	1,677,534	15	20
21	Uniform	904,818	1,910,501	30	40
22	Venom potion	730,061	1,528,646	15	15
23	Wool scarf	931,932	1,827,477	20	30
24	Crossbow	952,360	2,068,204	50	70
25	Yesteryear book	926,023	1,746,556	25	30
26	Zinc cup	978,724	2,100,851	15	25

In the interest of simplicity, suppose that the wagon's volume is a two-dimensional rectangle and that the packages are rectangular rather than 3D boxes.

Tree encoding at its core

Tree encoding represents a chromosome as a tree of elements. Tree encoding is versatile for representing potential solutions in which the hierarchy of elements is important and/or required. Tree encoding can even represent functions, which consist of a tree of expressions. As a result, tree encoding could be used to evolve program functions in which the function solves a specific problem; the solution may work but look bizarre.

Here is an example in which tree encoding makes sense. We have a wagon with a specific height and width, and a certain number of packages must fit in the wagon. The goal is to fit the packages in the wagon so that empty space is minimized. A tree-encoding approach would work well in representing potential solutions to this problem.

In figure 5.13, the root node, node A, represents the packing of the wagon from top to bottom. Node B represents all packages horizontally, similarly to node C and node D. Node E represents packages packed vertically in its slice of the wagon.

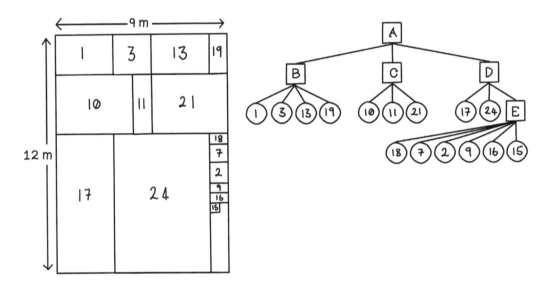

Figure 5.13 Example of a tree used to represent the Wagon Packing Problem

Tree crossover: Inheriting portions of a tree

Tree crossover is similar to single-point crossover (chapter 4) in that a single point in the tree structure is selected and then the parts are exchanged and combined with copies of the parent individuals to create an offspring individual. The inverse process can be used to make a second offspring. The resulting children must be verified to be valid solutions that obey the constraints of the problem. More than one point can be used for crossover if using multiple points makes sense in solving the problem (figure 5.14).

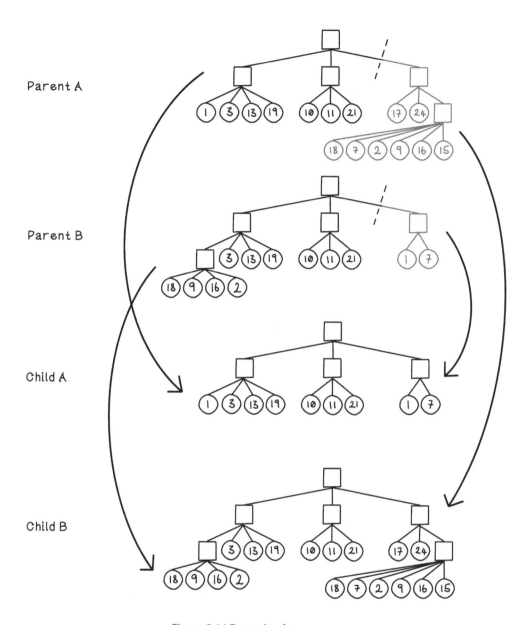

Parent A

Parent B

Child A

Child B

Figure 5.14 Example of tree crossover

Change node mutation: Changing the value of a node

In change node mutation, a randomly selected node in a tree-encoded chromosome is changed to a randomly selected valid object for that node. Given a tree representing an organization of items, we can change an item to another valid item (figure 5.15).

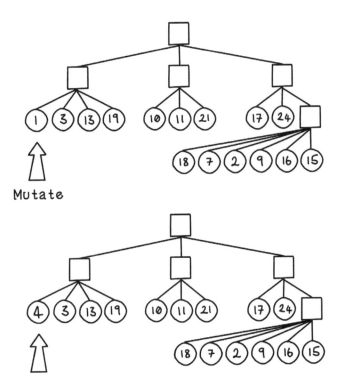

Figure 5.15 Change node mutation in a tree

This chapter and chapter 4 cover several encoding schemes, crossover schemes, and selection strategies. You could substitute your own approaches for these steps in your genetic algorithms if doing so makes sense for the problem you're solving.

Common types of evolutionary algorithms

This chapter focuses on the life cycle and alternative approaches for a genetic algorithm. Variations of the algorithm can be useful for solving different problems. Now that we have a grounding in how a genetic algorithm works, we'll look at these variations and possible use cases for them.

Genetic programming

Genetic programming follows a process similar to that of genetic algorithms but is used primarily to generate computer programs to solve problems. The process described in the previous section also applies here. The fitness of potential solutions in a genetic programming algorithm is how well the generated program solves a computational problem. With this in mind, we see that the tree-encoding method would work well here, because most computer programs are graphs consisting of nodes that indicate operations and processes. These trees of logic can be evolved, so the computer program will be evolved to solve a specific problem. One thing to note: these computer programs usually evolve to look like a mess of code that's difficult for people to understand and debug.

Evolutionary programming

Evolutionary programming is similar to genetic programming, but the potential solution is parameters for a predefined fixed computer program, not a generated computer program. If a program requires finely tuned inputs, and determining a good combination of inputs is difficult, a genetic algorithm can be used to evolve these inputs. The fitness of potential solutions in an evolutionary programming algorithm is determined by how well the fixed computer program performs based on the parameters encoded in an individual. Perhaps an evolutionary programming approach could be used to find good parameters for an artificial neural network (chapter 9).

Glossary of evolutionary algorithm terms

Here is a useful glossary of evolutionary algorithms terms for future research and learning:

- *Allele*—The value of a specific gene in a chromosome

- *Chromosome*—A collection of genes that represents a possible solution

- *Individual*—A single chromosome in a population

- *Population*—A collection of individuals

- *Genotype*—The artificial representation of the potential solution population in the computation space

- *Phenotype*—The actual representation of the potential solution population in the real world

- *Generation*—A single iteration of the algorithm

- *Exploration*—The process of finding a variety of possible solutions, some of which may be good and some of which may be bad

- *Exploitation*—The process of honing in on good solutions and iteratively refining them

- *Fitness function*—A particular type of objective function

- *Objective function*—A function that attempts to maximize or minimize

More use cases for evolutionary algorithms

Some of the use cases for evolutionary algorithms are listed in chapter 4, but many more exist. The following use cases are particularly interesting because they use one or more of the concepts discussed in this chapter:

- *Adjusting weights in artificial neural networks*—Artificial neural networks are discussed later, in chapter 9, but a key concept is adjusting weights in the network to learn patterns and relationships in data. Several mathematical techniques adjust weights, but evolutionary algorithms are more efficient alternatives in the right scenarios.

- *Electronic circuit design*—Electronic circuits with the same components can be designed in many configurations. Some configurations are more efficient than others. If two components that work together often are closer together, this configuration may improve efficiency. Evolutionary algorithms can be used to evolve different circuit configurations to find the most optimal design.

- *Molecular structure simulation and design*—As in electronic circuit design, different molecules behave differently and have their own advantages and disadvantages. Evolutionary algorithms can be used to generate different molecular structures to be simulated and studied to determine their behavioral properties.

Now that we've been through the general genetic algorithm life cycle in chapter 4 and some advanced approaches in this chapter, you should be equipped to apply evolutionary algorithms in your contexts and solutions.

SUMMARY OF ADVANCED EVOLUTIONARY APPROACHES

Genetic algorithms can be used to solve a multitude of problems.

Different selection strategies have different advantages and disadvantages

Real-value encoding is useful in many problem spaces.

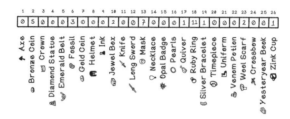

Order encoding is useful when the priority of sequence is important to solving problems.

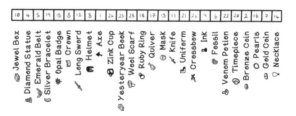

Tree encoding is useful when relationships and hierarchy are important to solving problems.

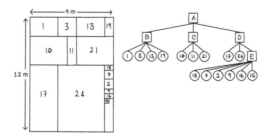

Tweaking all the parameters of the algorithm are important to finding solutions, and finding them efficiently.

This chapter covers

- Seeing and understanding what inspired swarm intelligence algorithms

- Solving problems with swarm intelligence algorithms

- Designing and implementing an ant colony optimization algorithm

What is swarm intelligence?

Swarm intelligence algorithms are a subset of evolutionary algorithms that were discussed in chapter 5 and are also known as nature-inspired algorithms. As with the theory of evolution, the observation of the behavior of life forms in nature is the inspiration for the concepts behind swarm intelligence. When we observe the world around us, we see many life forms that are seemingly primitive and unintelligent as individuals, yet exhibit intelligent emergent behavior when acting in groups.

An example of these life forms is ants. A single ant can carry 10 to 50 times its own body weight and run 700 times its body length per minute.

These are impressive qualities; however, when acting in a group, that single ant can accomplish much more. In a group, ants are able to build colonies; find and retrieve food; and even warn other ants, show recognition to other ants, and use peer pressure to influence others in the colony. They achieve these tasks by means of *pheromones*— essentially, perfumes that ants drop wherever they go. Other ants can sense these perfumes and change their behavior based on them. Ants have access to between 10 and 20 types of pheromones that can be used to communicate different intentions. Because individual ants use pheromones to indicate their intentions and needs, we can observe emergent intelligent behavior in groups of ants.

Figure 6.1 shows an example of ants working as a team to create a bridge between two points to enable other ants to carry out tasks. These tasks may be to retrieve food or materials for their colony.

Figure 6.1 A group of ants working together to cross a chasm

An experiment based on real-life harvesting ants showed that they always converged to the shortest path between the nest and the food source. Figure 6.2 depicts the difference in the colony movement from the start to when ants have walked their paths and increased the pheromone intensity on those paths. This outcome was observed in a classical asymmetric bridge experiment with real ants. Notice that the ants converge to the shortest path after just eight minutes.

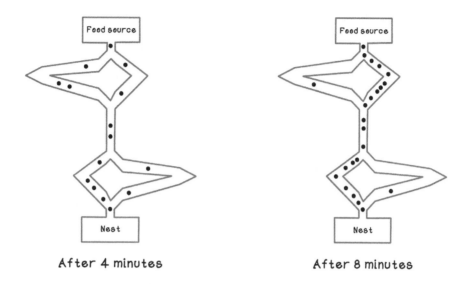

Figure 6.2 Asymmetric bridge experiment

Ant colony optimization (ACO) algorithms simulate the emergent behavior shown in this experiment. In the case of finding the shortest path, the algorithm converges to a similar state, as observed with real ants.

Swarm intelligence algorithms are useful for solving optimization problems when several constraints need to be met in a specific problem space and an absolute best solution is difficult to find due to a vast number of possible solutions—some better and some worse. These problems represent the same class of problems that genetic algorithms aim to solve; the choice of algorithm depends on how the problem can be represented and reasoned about. We dive into the technicalities of optimization problems in particle swarm optimization in chapter 7. Swarm intelligence is useful in several real-world contexts, some of which are represented in figure 6.3.

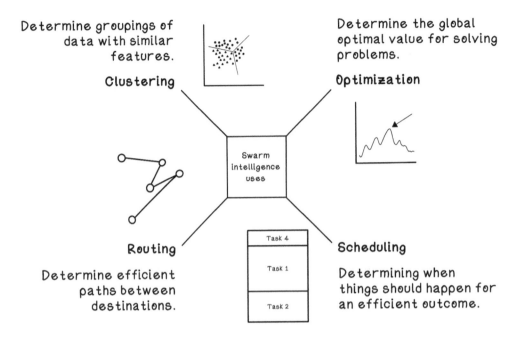

Figure 6.3 Problems addressed by swarm optimization

Given the general understanding of swarm intelligence in ants, the following sections explore specific implementations that are inspired by these concepts. The ant colony optimization algorithm is inspired by the behavior of ants moving between destinations, dropping pheromones, and acting on pheromones that they come across. The emergent behavior is ants converging to paths of least resistance.

Problems applicable to ant colony optimization

Imagine that we are visiting a carnival that has many attractions to experience. Each attraction is located in a different area, with varying distances between attractions. Because we don't feel like wasting time walking too much, we will attempt to find the shortest paths between all the attractions.

Figure 6.4 illustrates the attractions at a small carnival and the distances between them. Notice that taking different paths to the attractions involves different total lengths of travel.

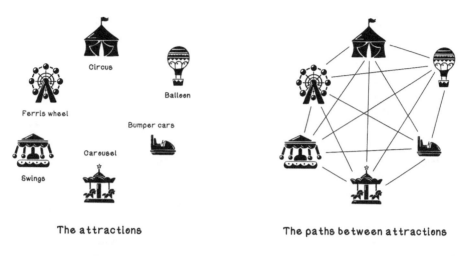

Figure 6.4 Carnival attractions and paths between them

The figure shows six attractions to visit, with 15 paths between them. This example should look familiar. This problem is represented by a fully connected graph, as described in chapter 2. The attractions are vertices or nodes, and the paths between attractions are edges. The following formula is used to calculate the number of edges in a fully connected graph. As the number of attractions gets larger, the number of edges explodes:

$$n(n-1)/2$$

Attractions have different distances between them. Figure 6.5 depicts the distance on each path between every attraction; it also shows a possible path between all attractions. Note that the lines in figure 6.5 showing the distances between the attractions are not drawn to scale.

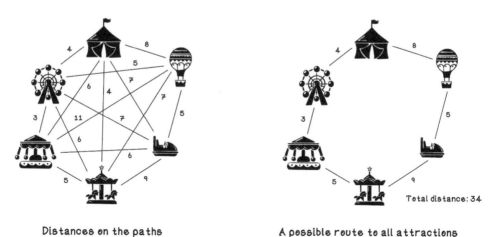

Figure 6.5 Distances between attractions and a possible path

If we spend some time analyzing the distances between all the attractions, we will find that figure 6.6 shows an optimal path between all the attractions. We visit the attractions in this sequence: swings, Ferris wheel, circus, carousel, balloons, and bumper cars.

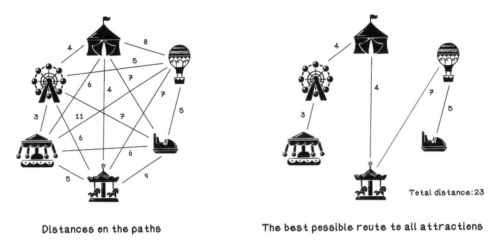

Distances on the paths   The best possible route to all attractions

Figure 6.6 Distances between attractions and an optimal path

The small dataset with six attractions is trivial to solve by hand, but if we increase the number of attractions to 15, the number of possibilities explodes (figure 6.7). Suppose that the attractions are servers, and the paths are network connections. Smart algorithms are needed to solve these problems.

Figure 6.7 A larger dataset of attractions and paths between them

EXERCISE: FIND THE SHORTEST PATH IN THIS CARNIVAL CONFIGURATION BY HAND

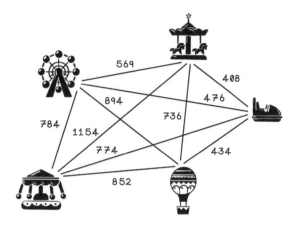

SOLUTION: FIND THE SHORTEST PATH IN THIS CARNIVAL CONFIGURATION BY HAND

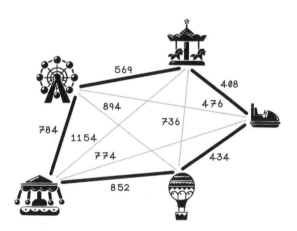

One way to solve this problem computationally is to attempt a brute-force approach: every combination of tours (a tour is a sequence of visits in which every attraction is visited once) of the attractions is generated and evaluated until the shortest total distance is found. Again, this solution may seem to be a reasonable solution, but in a large dataset, this computation is expensive and time-consuming. A brute-force approach with 48 attractions runs for tens of hours before finding an optimal solution.

Representing state: What do paths and ants look like?

Given the Carnival Problem, we need to represent the data of the problem in a way that is suitable to be processed by the ant colony optimization algorithm. Because we have several attractions and all the distances between them, we can use a distance matrix to represent the problem space accurately and simply.

A *distance matrix* is a 2D array in which every index represents an entity; the related set is the distance between that entity and another entity. Similarly, each index in the list denotes a unique entity. This matrix is similar to the adjacency matrix that we dived into in chapter 2 (figure 6.8 and table 6.1).

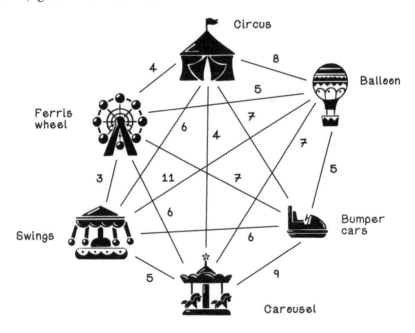

Figure 6.8 An example of the Carnival Problem

Table 6.1 Distances between attractions

	Circus	Balloons	Bumper cars	Carousel	Swings	Ferris wheel
Circus	0	8	7	4	6	4
Balloon	8	0	5	7	11	5
Bumper cars	7	5	0	9	6	7
Carousel	4	7	9	0	5	6
Swings	6	11	6	5	0	3
Ferris wheel	4	5	7	6	3	0

Pseudocode

The distances between attractions can be represented as a distance matrix, an array of arrays in which a reference to x, y in the array references the distance between attractions x and y. Notice that the distance between the same attraction will be 0 because it's in the same position. This array can also be created programmatically by iterating through data from a file and creating each element:

```
let attraction_distances equal
    [
        [0,8,7,4,6,4],
        [8,0,5,7,11,5],
        [7,5,0,9,6,7],
        [4,7,9,0,5,6],
        [6,11,6,5,0,3],
        [4,5,7,6,3,0],
    ]
```

The next element to represent is the ants. Ants move to different attractions and leave pheromones behind. Ants also make a judgment about which attraction to visit next. Finally, ants have knowledge about their respective total distance traveled. Here are the basic properties of an ant (figure 6.9):

- *Memory*—In the ACO algorithm, this is the list of attractions already visited.

- *Best fitness*—This is the shortest total distance traveled across all attractions.

- *Action*—Choose the next destination to visit, and drop pheromones along the way.

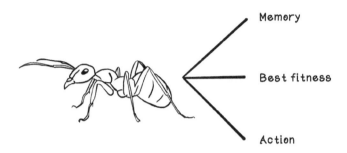

Figure 6.9 Properties of an ant

Although the abstract concept of an ant entails memory, best fitness, and action, specific data and functions are required to solve the Carnival Problem. To encapsulate the logic for an ant, we can use a class. When an instance of the ant class is initialized, an empty array is initialized to represent a list of attractions that the ant will visit. Furthermore, a random attraction will be selected to be the starting point for that specific ant:

```
Ant(attraction_count):
    let ant.visited_attractions equal an empty array
    append a random number between 0 and
        (attraction_count - 1) to ant.visited_attractions
```

The ant class also contains several functions used for ant movement. The `visit_*` functions are used to determine to which attraction the ant moves to next. The `visit_attraction` function generates a random chance of visiting a random attraction. In this case, `visit_random_attraction` is called; otherwise, `roulette_wheel_selection` is used with a calculated list of probabilities. More details are coming up in the next section:

```
Ant functions:
    visit_attraction(pheromone_trails)
    visit_random_attraction()
    visit_probabilistic_attraction(pheromone_trails)
    roulette_wheel_selection(probabilities)
    get_distance_traveled()
```

Last, the `get_distance_traveled` function is used to calculate the total distance traveled by a specific ant, using its list of visited attractions. This distance must be minimized to find the shortest path and is used as the fitness for the ants:

```
get_distance_travelled(ant):
    let total_distance equal 0
    for a in range(1, length of ant.visited_attractions):
        total_distance += distance between ant.visited_attractions[a - 1] and
                                          ant.visited_attractions[a]
    return total_distance
```

The final data structure to design is the concept of pheromone trails. Similarly to the distances between attractions, pheromone intensity on each path can be represented as a distance matrix, but instead of containing distances, the matrix contains pheromone intensities. In figure 6.10, thicker lines indicate more-intense pheromone trails. Table 6.2 describes the pheromone trails between attractions.

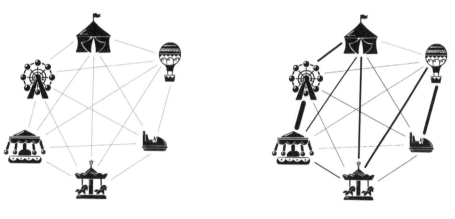

The paths between attractions   Possible pheromone intensity on paths

Figure 6.10 Example pheromone intensity on paths

Table 6.2 Pheromone intensity between attractions

	Circus	Balloons	Bumper cars	Carousel	Swings	Ferris wheel
Circus	0	2	0	8	6	8
Balloon	2	0	10	8	2	2
Bumper cars	2	10	0	0	2	2
Carousel	8	8	2	0	2	2
Swings	6	2	2	2	0	10
Ferris wheel	8	2	2	2	10	0

The ant colony optimization algorithm life cycle

Now that we understand the data structures required, we can dive into the workings of the ant colony optimization algorithm. The approach in designing an ant colony optimization algorithm is based on the problem space being addressed. Each problem has a unique context and a different domain in which data is represented, but the principles remain the same.

That said, let's look into how an ant colony optimization algorithm can be configured to solve the Carnival Problem. The general life cycle of such an algorithm is as follows:

- *Initialize the pheromone trails.* Create the concept of pheromone trails between attractions, and initialize their intensity values.

- *Set up the population of ants.* Create a population of ants in which each ant starts at a different attraction.

- *Choose the next visit for each ant.* Choose the next attraction to visit for each ant until each ant has visited all attractions once.

- *Update the pheromone trails.* Update the intensity of pheromone trails based on the ants' movements on them, as well as factor in evaporation of pheromones.

- *Update the best solution.* Update the best solution, given the total distance covered by each ant.

- *Determine the stopping criteria.* The process of ants visiting attractions repeats for several iterations. One iteration is every ant visiting all attractions once. The stopping criterion determines the total number of iterations to run. More iterations allow ants to make better decisions based on the pheromone trails.

Figure 6.11 describes the general life cycle of the ant colony optimization algorithm.

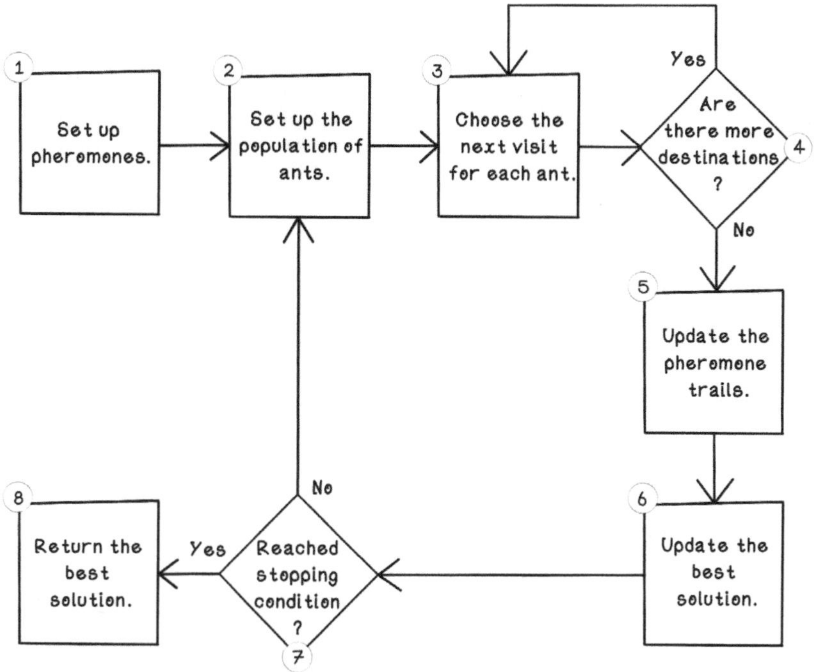

Figure 6.11 The ant colony optimization algorithm life cycle

Initialize the pheromone trails

The first step in the ant colony optimization algorithm is to initialize the pheromone trails. Because no ants have walked on the paths between attractions yet, the pheromone trails will be initialized to 1. When we set all pheromone trails to 1, no trail has any advantage over the others. The important aspect is defining a reliable data structure to contain the pheromone trails, which we look at next (figure 6.12).

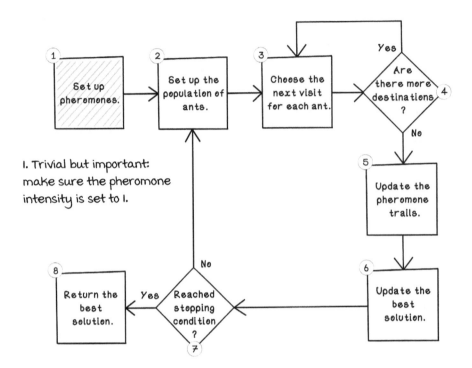

1. Trivial but important:
make sure the pheromone
intensity is set to 1.

Figure 6.12 Set up the pheromones.

This concept can be applied to other problems in which instead of distances between
locations, the pheromone intensity is defined by another heuristic.

In figure 6.13, the heuristic is the distance between two destinations.

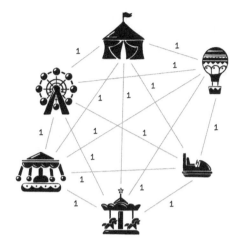

Pheromones initialize at 1

Figure 6.13 Initialization of pheromones

Pseudocode

Similarly to the attraction distances, the pheromone trails can be represented by a distance matrix, but referencing x, y in this array provides the pheromone intensity on the path between attractions x and y. The initial pheromone intensity on every path is initialized to 1. Values for all paths should initialize with the same number to prevent biasing any paths from the start:

```
let pheromone_trails equal
    [
    [1,1,1,1,1,1],
    [1,1,1,1,1,1],
    [1,1,1,1,1,1],
    [1,1,1,1,1,1],
    [1,1,1,1,1,1],
    [1,1,1,1,1,1]
    ]
```

Set up the population of ants

The next step of the ACO algorithm is creating a population of ants that will move between the attractions and leave pheromone trails between them (figure 6.14).

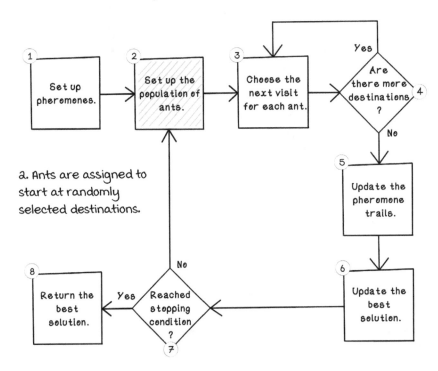

Figure 6.14 Set up the population of ants.

Ants will start at randomly assigned attractions (figure 6.15)—at a random point in a potential sequence because the ant colony optimization algorithm can be applied to problems in which actual distance doesn't exist. After touring all the destinations, ants are set to their respective starting points.

Ants starting at
random attractions

Figure 6.15 Ants start at random attractions.

We can adapt this principle to a different problem. In a task-scheduling problem, each ant starts at a different task.

Pseudocode

Setting up the colony of ants includes initializing several ants and appending them to a list where they can be referenced later. Remember that the initialization function of the ant class chooses a random attraction to start at:

```
setup_ants(attraction_count, number_of_ants_factor):
  let number_of_ants equal round(attraction_count * number_of_ants_factor)
  let ant_colony equal to an empty array
  for i in range(0, number_of_ants):
    append new Ant to ant_colony
  return ant_colony
```

Choose the next visit for each ant

Ants need to select the next attraction to visit. They visit new attractions until they have visited all attractions once, which is called a tour. Ants choose the next destination based on two factors (figure 6.16):

- *Pheromone intensities*—The pheromone intensity on all available paths

- *Heuristic value*—A result from a defined heuristic for all available paths, which is the distance of the path between attractions in the carnival example

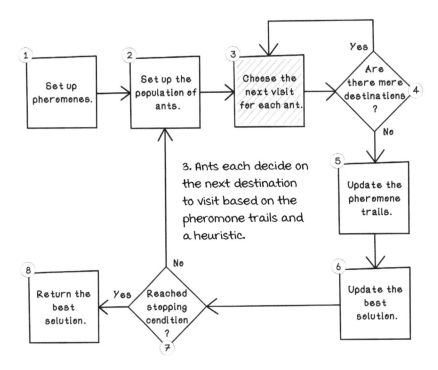

Figure 6.16 Choose the next visit for each ant.

Ants will not travel to destinations they have already visited. If an ant has already visited the bumper cars, it will not travel to that attraction again in the current tour.

The stochastic nature of ants

The ant colony optimization algorithm has an element of randomness. The intention is to allow ants the possibility of exploring less-optimal immediate paths, which might result in a better overall tour distance.

First, an ant has a random probability of deciding to choose a random destination. We could generate a random number between 0 and 1, and if the result is 0.1 or less, the ant will decide to choose a random destination; this is a 10% chance of choosing a random destination. If an ant decides that it will choose a random destination, it needs to randomly select a destination to visit, which is a random selection between all available destinations.

Selecting destination based on a heuristic

When an ant faces the decision of choosing the next destination that is not random, it determines the pheromone intensity on that path and the heuristic value by using the following formula:

$$\frac{(\text{pheromones on path x})^a * (1 \text{ / heuristic for path x})^b}{\underset{\substack{\text{sum of n} \\ \text{available} \\ \text{destinations}}}{} ((\text{pheromones on path n})^a * (1 \text{ / heuristic for path n})^b)}$$

After it applies this function to every possible path toward its respective destination, the ant selects the destination with the best overall value to travel to. Figure 6.17 illustrates the possible paths from the circus with their respective distances and pheromone intensities.

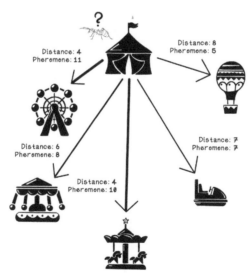

Figure 6.17 Example of possible paths from the circus

Let's work through the formula to demystify the calculations that are happening and how the results affect decision-making (figure 6.18).

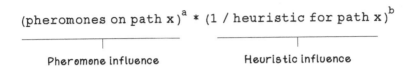

$$\underbrace{(\text{pheromones on path x})^a}_{\text{Pheromone influence}} * \underbrace{(1 \,/\, \text{heuristic for path x})^b}_{\text{Heuristic influence}}$$

Figure 6.18 The pheromone influence and heuristic influence of the formula

The variables *alpha (a)* and *beta (b)* are used to give greater weight to either the pheromone influence or the heuristic influence. These variables can be adjusted to balance the ant's judgment between making a move based on what it knows versus pheromone trails, which represent what the colony knows about that path. These parameters are defined up front and are usually not adjusted while the algorithm runs.

The following example works through each path starting at the circus and calculates the probabilities of moving to each respective attraction.

- *a (alpha)* is set to 1.

- *b (beta)* is set to 2.

Because *b* is greater than *a*, the heuristic influence is favored in this example.

Let's work through an example of the calculations used to determine the probability of choosing a specific path (figure 6.19).

$$\frac{(\text{pheromones on path x})^a * (1\,/\,\text{heuristic for path x})^b}{\sum_{\substack{\text{available} \\ \text{destinations}}} ((\text{pheromones on path n})^a * (1\,/\,\text{heuristic for path n})^b)}$$

$((\text{pheromones on path x})^a * (1\,/\,\text{heuristic for path x})^b)$ ← Apply this to each attraction.

$$
\begin{aligned}
\text{Ferris wheel:} && 11 * (1/4)^2 &= 0.688 \\
\text{Swings:} && 8 * (1/6)^2 &= 0.222 \\
\text{Carousel:} && 10 * (1/4)^2 &= 0.625 \\
\text{Bumper cars:} && 7 * (1/7)^2 &= 0.143 \\
\text{Balloons:} && 5 * (1/8)^2 &= 0.078
\end{aligned}
$$

$\sum_{\substack{\text{available} \\ \text{destinations}}} ((\text{pheromones on path n})^a * (1\,/\,\text{heuristic for path n})^b) = 1.756$ ← Sum of all

Ferris wheel: 0.688 / 1.756 = 0.392 ← Highest probability: 39.2%
Swings: 0.222 / 1.756 = 0.126
Carousel: 0.625 / 1.756 = 0.356 ← High probability: 35.6%
Bumper cars: 0.143 / 1.756 = 0.081
Balloons: 0.078 / 1.756 = 0.044

Figure 6.19 Probability calculations for paths

After applying this calculation, given all the available destinations, the ant is left with the options shown in figure 6.20.

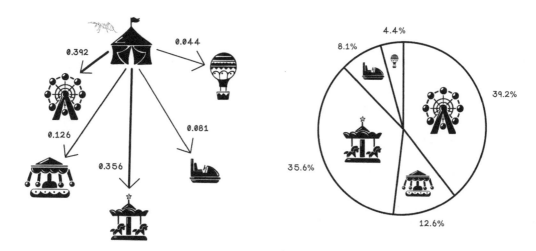

Figure 6.20 The final probability of each attraction being selected

Remember that only the available paths are considered; these paths have not been explored yet. Figure 6.21 illustrates the possible paths from the circus, excluding the Ferris wheel, because it's been visited already. Figure 6.22 shows probability calculations for paths.

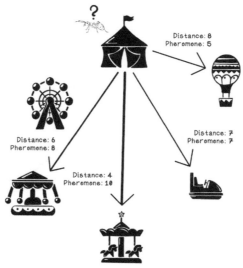

Figure 6.21 Example of possible paths from the circus, excluding visited attractions

$$\frac{(\text{pheromones on path x})^a * (1 / \text{heuristic for path x})^b}{\underset{\substack{\text{sum of n} \\ \text{available} \\ \text{destinations}}}{} ((\text{pheromones on path n})^a * (1 / \text{heuristic for path n})^b)}$$

$((\text{pheromones on path x})^a * (1 / \text{heuristic for path x})^b)$ ⟵ Apply this to each attraction.

$$
\begin{aligned}
\text{Swings:} &\quad 8 * (1/6)^2 &= 0.222 \\
\text{Carousel:} &\quad 10 * (1/4)^2 &= 0.625 \\
\text{Bumper cars:} &\quad 7 * (1/7)^2 &= 0.143 \\
\text{Balloons:} &\quad 5 * (1/8)^2 &= 0.078
\end{aligned}
$$

$\underset{\substack{\text{sum of n} \\ \text{available} \\ \text{destinations}}}{} ((\text{pheromones on path n})^a * (1 / \text{heuristic for path n})^b) = 1.068$ ⟵ Sum of all

$$
\begin{aligned}
\text{Swings:} &\ 0.222 / 1.068 &= 0.208 \\
\textbf{Carousel:} &\ \textbf{0.625 / 1.068} &\mathbf{= 0.585} \\
\text{Bumper cars:} &\ 0.143 / 1.068 &= 0.134 \\
\text{Balloons:} &\ 0.078 / 1.068 &= 0.073
\end{aligned}
$$

⟵ Highest probability: 58.5%

Figure 6.22 Probability calculations for paths

The ant's decision now looks like figure 6.23.

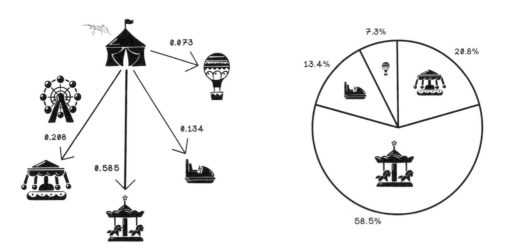

Figure 6.23 The final probability of each attraction being selected

Pseudocode

The pseudocode for calculating the probabilities of visiting the possible attractions is closely aligned with the mathematical functions that we have worked through. Some interesting aspects of this implementation include:

- *Determining the available attractions to visit*—Because the ant would have visited several attractions, it should not return to those attractions. The `possible_attractions` array stores this value by removing `visited_attractions` from the complete list of attractions: `all_attractions`.

- *Using three variables to store the outcome of the probability calculations*— `possible_indexes` stores the attraction indexes; `possible_probabilities` stores the probabilities for the respective index; and `total_probabilities` stores the sum of all probabilities, which should equal 1 when the function is complete. These three data structures could be represented by a class for a cleaner code convention.

```
visit_probabilistic_attraction(pheromone_trails, attraction_count, ant
                                alpha, beta):
  let current_attraction equal ant.visited_attractions[-1]
  let all_attractions equal range(0, attraction_count)
  let possible_attractions equal all_attractions - ant.visited_attractions

  let possible_indexes equal empty array
  let possible_probabilities equal empty array
  let total_probabilities equal 0

  for attraction in possible_attractions:
    append attraction to possible_indexes
    let pheromones_on_path equal
      math.pow(pheromone_trails[current_attraction][attraction], alpha)
    let heuristic_for_path equal
      math.pow(1/attraction_distances[current_attraction][attraction], beta)
    let probability equal pheromones_on_path * heuristic_for_path
    append probability to possible_probabilities
    add probability to total_probabilities
  let possible_probabilities equal [probability / total_probabilities
    for probability in possible_probabilities]
  return [possible_indexes, possible_probabilities]
```

We meet roulette-wheel selection again. The roulette-wheel selection function takes the possible probabilities and attraction indexes as input. It generates a list of slices, each of which includes the index of the attraction in element 0, the start of the slice in index 1, and the end of the slice in index 2. All slices contain a start and end between 0 and 1. A random number between 0 and 1 is generated, and the slices that it falls into is selected as the winner:

```
roulette_wheel_selection(possible_indexes, possible_probabilities,
                         possible_attraction_count):
  let slices equal empty array
  let total equal 0
  for i in range(0, possible_attractions_count):
    append [possible_indexes[i], total, total + possible_probabilities[i]]
      to slices
    total += possible_probabilities[i]
  let spin equal random(0, 1)
  let result equal [slice for slice in slices if slice[1] < spin <= slice[2]]
  return result
```

Now that we have probabilities of selecting the different attractions to visit, we will use roulette-wheel selection.

To recap, roulette-wheel selection (from chapters 3 and 4) gives different possibilities portions of a wheel based on their fitness. Then the wheel is "spun," and an individual is selected. A higher fitness gives an individual a larger slice of the wheel, as shown in figure 6.23 earlier in this chapter. The process of choosing attractions and visiting them continues for every ant until each one has visited all the attractions once.

**EXERCISE: DETERMINE THE PROBABILITIES OF VISITING THE ATTRACTIONS
WITH THE FOLLOWING INFORMATION**

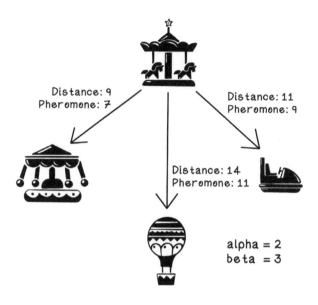

Distance: 9
Pheromone: 7

Distance: 11
Pheromone: 9

Distance: 14
Pheromone: 11

alpha = 2
beta = 3

**SOLUTION: DETERMINE THE PROBABILITIES OF VISITING THE ATTRACTIONS
WITH THE FOLLOWING INFORMATION**

$$\frac{(\text{pheromones on path x})^a * (1 / \text{heuristic for path x})^b}{\underset{\substack{\text{sum of n} \\ \text{available} \\ \text{destinations}}}{} ((\text{pheromones on path n})^a * (1 / \text{heuristic for path n})^b)}$$

$((\text{pheromones on path x})^a * (1 / \text{heuristic for path x})^b)$

$$\text{Swings:} \quad 7^2 * \ (1/9)^3 \ = 0.067$$
$$\text{Bumper cars:} \quad 9^2 * (1/11)^3 \ = 0.061$$
$$\text{Balloons:} \quad 11^2 * (1/14)^3 \ = 0.044$$

$\underset{\substack{\text{sum of n} \\ \text{available} \\ \text{destinations}}}{} ((\text{pheromones on path n})^a * (1 / \text{heuristic for path n})^b) = 0.172$

$$\text{Swings:} \ 0.067 \ / \ 0.172 \ = 0.39$$
$$\text{Bumper cars:} \ 0.061 \ / \ 0.172 \ = 0.355$$
$$\text{Balloons:} \ 0.044 \ / \ 0.172 \ = 0.256$$

Update the pheromone trails

Now that the ants have completed a tour of all the attractions, they have all left pheromones behind, which changes the pheromone trails between the attractions (figure 6.24).

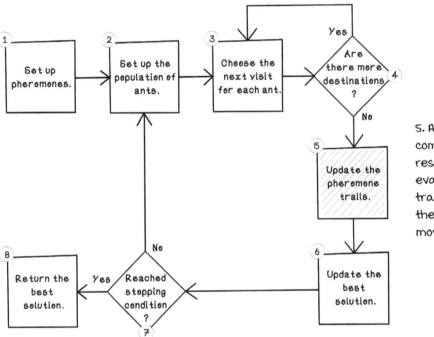

5. After all ants have completed their respective tours, evaporate pheromone trails, and the update them given the ants' movements.

Figure 6.24 Update the pheromone trails.

Two steps are involved in updating the pheromone trails: evaporation and depositing new pheromones.

Updating pheromones due to evaporation

The concept of evaporation is also inspired by nature. Over time, the pheromone trails lose their intensity. Pheromones are updated by multiplying their respective current values by an evaporation factor—a parameter that can be adjusted to tweak the performance of the algorithm in terms of exploration and exploitation. Figure 6.25 illustrates the updated pheromone trails due to evaporation.

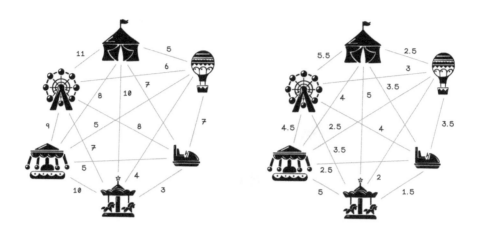

Figure 6.25 Example of updating pheromone trails for evaporation

Updating pheromones based on ant tours

Pheromones are updated based on the ants that have moved along the paths. If more ants move on a specific path, there will be more pheromones on that path.

Each ant contributes its fitness value to the pheromones on every path it has moved on. The effect is that ants with better solutions have a greater influence on the best paths. Figure 6.26 illustrates the updated pheromone trails based on ant movements on the paths.

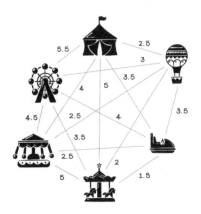

Pheromones on paths after evaporation

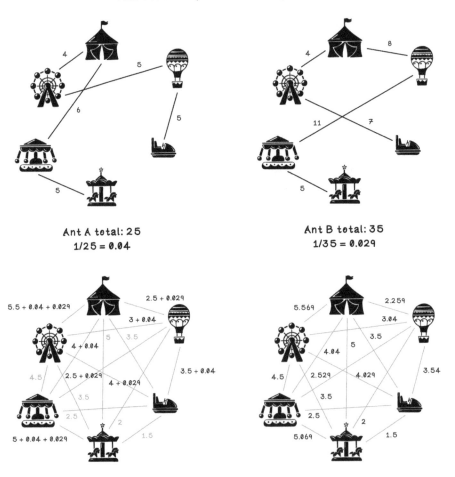

Ant A total: 25
1/25 = 0.04

Ant B total: 35
1/35 = 0.029

Pheromone addition after ant update

Pheromones after ant update

Figure 6.26 Pheromone updates based on ant movements

EXERCISE: CALCULATE THE PHEROMONE UPDATE GIVEN THE FOLLOWING SCENARIO

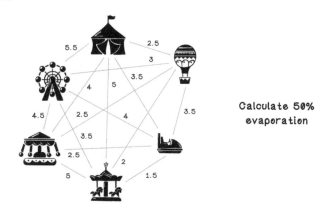

Calculate 50% evaporation

Pheromones on paths

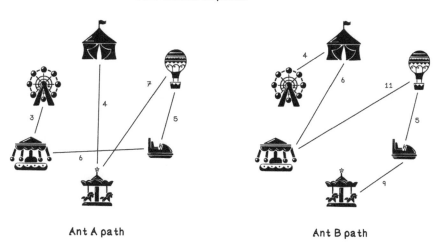

Ant A path   Ant B path

SOLUTION: CALCULATE THE PHEROMONE UPDATE GIVEN THE FOLLOWING SCENARIO

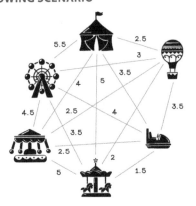

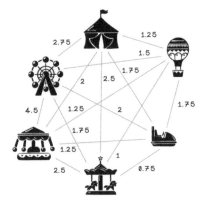

Pheromones on paths

Pheromones on paths after 50% evaporation

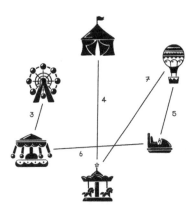

Ant A total: 25
1/25 = 0.04

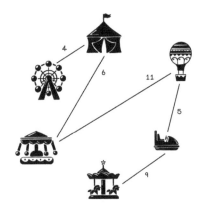

Ant B total: 35
1/35 = 0.029

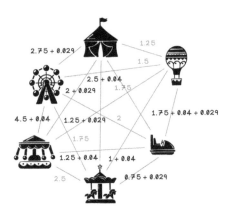

Pheromone addition after ant update

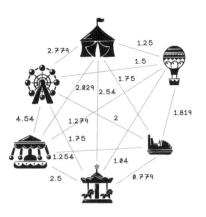

Pheromones after ant update

Pseudocode

The `update_pheromones` function applies two important concepts to the pheromone trails. First, the current pheromone intensity is evaporated based on the evaporation rate. If the evaporation rate is 0.5, for example, the intensity decreases by half. The
second operation adds pheromones based on ant movements on that path. The amount
of pheromones contributed by each ant is determined by the ant's fitness, which in this
case is each respective ant's total distance traveled:

```
update_pheromones(evaporation_rate, pheromone_trails, attraction_count):
    for x in range(0, attraction_count):
        for y in range(0, attraction_count):
            let pheromone_trails[x][y] equal
                pheromone_trails[x][y] * evaporation_rate
            for ant in ant_colony:
                pheromone_trails[x][y] += 1 / ant.get_distance_traveled()
```

Update the best solution

The best solution is described by the sequence of attraction visits that has the lowest total
distance (figure 6.27).

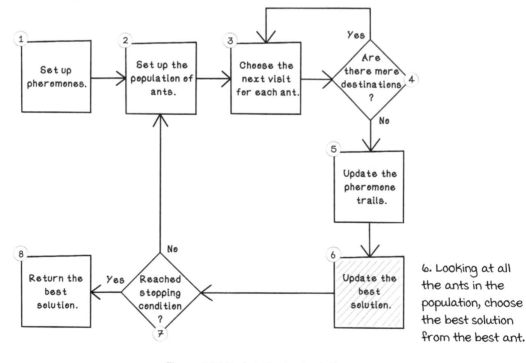

Figure 6.27 Update the best solution.

Pseudocode

After an iteration, after every ant has completed a tour (a tour is complete when an ant visits every attraction), the best ant in the colony must be determined. To make this determination, we find the ant that has the lowest total distance traveled and set it as the new best ant in the colony:

```
get_best(ant_population, previous_best_ant):
  let best_ant equal previous_best_ant
  for ant in ant_population:
    let distance_traveled equal ant.get_distance_traveled()
    if distance_traveled < best_ant.best_distance:
      let best_ant equal ant
  return best_ant
```

Determine the stopping criteria

The algorithm stops after several iterations: conceptually, the number of tours that the group of ants concludes. Ten iterations means that each ant does 10 tours; each ant would visit each attraction once and do that 10 times (figure 6.28).

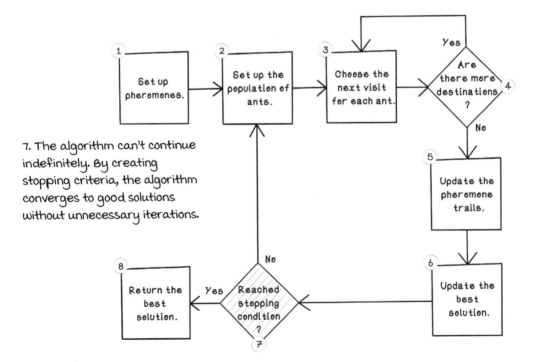

7. The algorithm can't continue indefinitely. By creating stopping criteria, the algorithm converges to good solutions without unnecessary iterations.

Figure 6.28 Reached stopping condition?

The stopping criteria for the ant colony optimization algorithm can differ based on the domain of the problem being solved. In some cases, realistic limits are known, and when they're unknown, the following options are available:

- *Stop when a predefined number of iterations is reached.* In this scenario, we define a total number of iterations for which the algorithm will always run. If 100 iterations are defined, each ant completes 100 tours before the algorithm terminates.

- *Stop when the best solution stagnates.* In this scenario, the best solution after each iteration is compared with the previous best solution. If the solution doesn't improve after a defined number of iterations, the algorithm terminates. If iteration 20 resulted in a solution with fitness 100, and that iteration is repeated up until iteration 30, it is likely (but not guaranteed) that no better solution exists.

Pseudocode

The `solve` function ties everything together and should give you a better idea of the sequence of operations and the overall life cycle of the algorithm. Notice that the algorithm runs for several defined total iterations. The ant colony is also initialized to its starting point at the beginning of each iteration, and a new best ant is determined after each iteration:

```
solve(total_iterations, evaporation_rate, number_of_ants_factor,
        attraction_count):
  let pheromone_trails equal setup_pheromones()
  let best_ant equal Nothing
  for i in range(0, total_iterations):
    let ant_colony equal setup_ants(number_of_ants_factor)
    for r in range(0, attraction_count - 1):
      move_ants(ant_colony)
    update_pheromones(evaporation_rate,
                        pheromone_trails,
                        attraction_count)
    let best_ant equal get_best(ant_colony)
```

We can tweak several parameters to alter the exploration and exploitation of the ant colony optimization algorithm. These parameters influence how long the algorithm will take to find a good solution. Some randomness is good for exploring. Balancing the weighting between heuristics and pheromones influences whether ants attempt a greedy search (when favoring heuristics) or trust pheromones more. The evaporation rate also influences this balance. The number of ants and the total number of iterations they have influences the quality of a solution. When we add more ants and more iterations, more computation is required. Based on the problem at hand, time to compute may influence these parameters (figure 6.29):

```
Set the probability of ants choosing a random attraction to visit (0.0 - 1.0) (0% - 100%)
RANDOM_ATTRACTION_FACTOR = 0.3


Set the weight for pheromones on path for selection by ants.
ALPHA = 4


Set the weight for heuristic of path for selection by ants.
BETA = 7


Set the percentage of ants in the colony based on the total number of attractions.
NUMBER_OF_ANTS_FACTOR = 0.5


Set the number of tours ants must complete.
TOTAL_ITERATIONS = 1000


Set the rate of pheromone evaporation (0.0 - 1.0) (0% - 100%).
EVAPORATION_RATE = 0.4
```

Figure 6.29 Parameters that can be tweaked in the ant colony optimization algorithm

Now you have insight into how ant colony optimization algorithms work and how they can be used to solve the Carnival Problem. The following section describes some other possible use cases. Perhaps these examples may help you find uses for the algorithm in your work.

Use cases for ant colony optimization algorithms

Ant colony optimization algorithms are versatile and useful in several real-world applications. These applications usually center on complex optimization problems such as the following:

- *Route optimization*—Routing problems usually include several destinations that need to be visited with several constraints. In a logistics example, perhaps the distance between destinations, traffic conditions, types of packages being delivered, and times of day are important constraints that need to be considered to optimize the operations of the business. Ant colony optimization algorithms can be used to address this problem. The problem is similar to the carnival problem explored in this chapter, but the heuristic function is likely to be more complex and context specific.

- *Job scheduling*—Job scheduling is present in almost any industry. Nurse shifts are important to ensure that good health care can be provided. Computational jobs on servers must be scheduled in an optimal manner to maximize the use of the hardware without waste. Ant colony optimization algorithms can be used to solve these problems. Instead of looking at the entities that ants visit as locations, we see that ants visit tasks in different sequences. The heuristic function includes constraints and desired rules specific to the context of the jobs being scheduled. Nurses, for example, need days off to prevent fatigue, and jobs with high priorities on a server should be favored.

- *Image processing*—The ant colony optimization algorithm can be used for edge detection in image processing. An image is composed of several adjacent pixels, and the ants move from pixel to pixel, leaving behind pheromone trails. Ants drop stronger pheromones based on the pixel colors' intensity, resulting in pheromone trails along the edges of objects containing the highest density of pheromones. This algorithm essentially traces the outline of the image by performing edge detection. The images may require preprocessing to decolorize the image to grayscale so that the pixel-color values can be compared consistently.

SUMMARY OF ANT COLONY OPTIMIZATION

ACO algorithms use pheromones and heuristics.

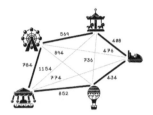

ACO is useful for optimization problems like finding shortest paths or optimal task schedules.

Ants have a concept of memory and performance, and can perform actions.

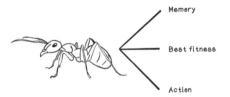

Weightings between a heuristic and the pheromones on paths are used in calculating a probability of selection.

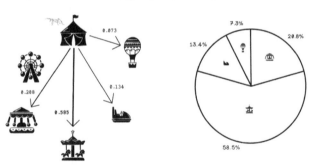

Pheromones are contributed by each ant proportional to its respective performance. Pheromones also evaporate.

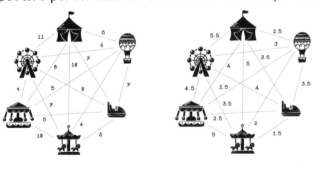

Pheromones on paths   Pheromones on paths after 50% evaporation

This chapter covers

- Understanding the inspiration for particle swarm intelligence algorithms

- Understanding and solving optimization problems

- Designing and implementing a particle swarm optimization algorithm

What is particle swarm optimization?

Particle swarm optimization is another swarm algorithm. Swarm intelligence relies on emergent behavior of many individuals to solve difficult problems as a collective. We saw in chapter 6 how ants can find the shortest paths between destinations through their use of pheromones.

Bird flocks are another ideal example of swarm intelligence in nature. When a single bird is flying, it might attempt several maneuvers and techniques to preserve energy, such as jumping and gliding through the air or leveraging wind currents to carry it in the direction in which it intends to travel. This behavior indicates some primitive level of intelligence in a single individual. But birds also have the need to migrate during different seasons. In winter, there is less availability of insects and other food. Suitable nesting locations also become scarce. Birds tend to flock to warmer areas to take advantage of better weather conditions, which improves their likelihood of survival. Migration is usually not a short trip. It takes thousands of kilometers of movement to arrive at an area with suitable conditions. When birds travel these long distances, they tend to flock. Birds flock because there is strength in numbers when facing predators; additionally, it saves energy. The formation that we observe in bird flocks has several advantages. A large, strong bird will take the lead, and when it flaps its wings, it creates uplift for the birds behind it. These birds can fly while using significantly less energy. Flocks can change leaders if the direction changes or if the leader becomes fatigued. When a specific bird moves out of formation, it experiences more difficulty in flying via air resistance and corrects its movement to get back into formation. Figure 7.1 illustrates a bird flock formation; you may have seen something similar.

Figure 7.1 An example bird flock formation

Craig Reynolds developed a simulator program in 1987 to understand the attributes of emergent behavior in bird flocks and used the following rules to guide the group. These rules are extracted from observation of bird flocks:

- *Alignment*—An individual should steer in the average heading of its neighbors to ensure that the group travels in a similar direction.

- *Cohesion*—An individual should move toward the average position of its neighbors to maintain the formation of the group.

- *Separation*—An individual should avoid crowding or colliding with its neighbors to ensure that individuals do not collide, disrupting the group.

Additional rules are used in different variants of attempting to simulate swarm behavior. Figure 7.2 illustrates the behavior of an individual in different scenarios, as well as the direction in which it is influenced to move to obey the respective rule. Adjusting movement is a balance of these three principles shown in the figure.

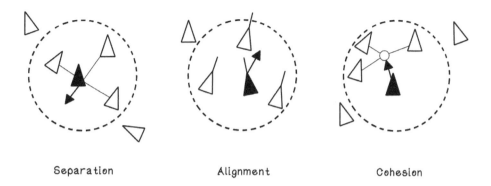

Separation   Alignment   Cohesion

Figure 7.2 Rules that guide a swarm

Particle swarm optimization involves a group of individuals at different points in the solution space, all using real-life swarm concepts to find an optimal solution in the space. This chapter dives into the workings of the particle swarm optimization algorithm and shows how it can be used to solve problems. Imagine a swarm of bees that spreads out looking for flowers and gradually converges on an area that has the most density of flowers. As more bees find the flowers, more are attracted to the flowers. At its core, this example is what particle swarm optimization entails (figure 7.3).

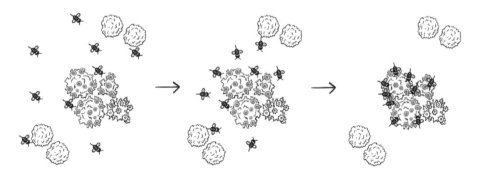

Figure 7.3 A bee swarm converging on its goal

Optimization problems have been mentioned in several chapters. Finding the optimal path through a maze, determining the optimal items for a knapsack, and finding the optimal path between attractions in a carnival are examples of optimization problems. We worked through them without diving into the details behind them. From this chapter on, however, a deeper understanding of optimization problems is important. The next section works through some of the intuition to be able to spot optimization problems when they occur.

Optimization problems: A slightly more technical perspective

Suppose that we have several peppers of different sizes. Usually, small peppers tend to be spicier than large peppers. If we plot all the peppers on a chart based on size and spiciness, it may look like figure 7.4.

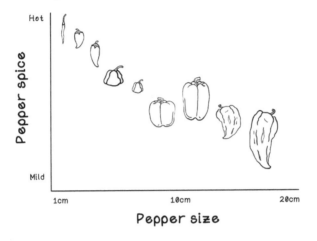

Figure 7.4 Pepper spice vs. pepper size

The figure depicts the size of each pepper and how spicy it is. Now, by removing the imagery of the peppers, plotting the data points, and drawing a possible curve between them, we are left with figure 7.5. If we had more peppers, we would have more data points, and the curve would be more accurate.

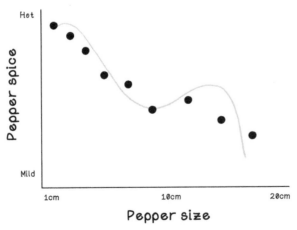

Figure 7.5 Pepper spice vs. pepper size trend

This example could potentially be an optimization problem. If we searched for a minimum from left to right, we would come across several points less than the previous ones, but in the middle, we encounter one that is higher. Should we stop? If we did, we would be missing the actual minimum, which is the last data point, known as the *global minimum.*

The trend line/curve that is approximated can be represented by a function, such as the one shown in figure 7.6. This function can be interpreted as the spiciness of the pepper being equal to the result of this function where the size of the pepper is represented by *x*.

$$f(x) = -(x - 4)(x - 0.2)(x - 2)(x - 3) + 5$$

Figure 7.6 An example function for pepper spice vs. pepper size

Real-world problems typically have thousands of data points, and the minimum output of the function is not as clear as this example. The search spaces are massive and difficult to solve by hand.

Notice that we have used only two properties of the pepper to create the data points, which resulted in a simple curve. If we consider another property of the pepper, such as color, the representation of the data changes significantly. Now the chart has to be represented in 3D, and the trend becomes a surface instead of a curve. A surface is like a warped blanket in three dimensions (figure 7.7). This surface is also represented as a function but is more complex.

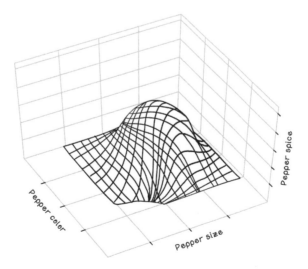

Figure 7.7 Pepper spice vs. pepper size vs. pepper color

Furthermore, a 3D search space could look fairly simple, like figure 7.7, or be so complex that attempting to inspect it visually to find the minimum would be almost impossible (figure 7.8).

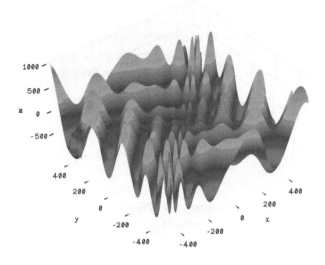

Figure 7.8 A function visualized in the 3D space as a plane

Figure 7.9 shows the function that represents this plane.

$$f(x, y) = -(y + 47) \sin \sqrt{\left| \frac{x}{2} + (y + 47) \right|} - x \sin \sqrt{|x - (y + 47)|}$$

Figure 7.9 The function that represents the surface in figure 7.8

It gets more interesting! We have looked at three attributes of a pepper: its size, its color, and how spicy it is. As a result, we're searching in three dimensions. What if we want to include the location of growth? This attribute would make it even more difficult to visualize and understand the data, because we are searching in four dimensions. If we add the pepper's age and the amount of fertilizer used while growing it, we are left with a massive search space in six dimensions, and we can't imagine what this search might look like. This search too is represented by a function, but again, it is too complex and difficult for a person to solve.

Particle swarm optimization algorithms are particularly good at solving difficult optimization problems. Particles are distributed over the multidimensional search space and work together to find good maximums or minimums.

Particle swarm optimization algorithms are particularly useful in the following scenarios:

- *Large search spaces*—There are many data points and possibilities of combinations.

- *Search spaces with high dimensions*—There is complexity in high dimensions. Many dimensions of a problem are required to find a good solution.

EXERCISE: HOW MANY DIMENSIONS WILL THE SEARCH SPACE FOR THE FOLLOWING SCENARIO BE?

In this scenario, we need to determine a good city to live in based on the average minimum temperature during the year, because we don't like the cold. It is also important that the population be less than 700,000 people, because crowded areas can be inconvenient. The average property price should be as little as possible, and the more trains in the city, the better.

SOLUTION: HOW MANY DIMENSIONS WILL THE SEARCH SPACE FOR THE FOLLOWING SCENARIO BE?

The problem in this scenario consists of five dimensions:

- Average temperature

- Size of population

- Average price of property

- Number of trains

- Result of these attributes, which will inform our decision

Problems applicable to particle swarm optimization

Imagine that we are developing a drone, and several materials are used to create its body and propeller wings (the blades that make it fly). Through many research trials, we have found that different amounts of two specific materials yield different results in terms of optimal performance for lifting the drone and resisting strong winds. These two materials are aluminum, for the chassis, and plastic, for the blades. Too much or too little of either material will result in a poor-performing drone. But several combinations yield a good-performing drone, and only one combination results in an exceptionally well-performing drone.

Figure 7.10 illustrates the components made of plastic and the components made of aluminum. The arrows illustrate the forces that influence the performance of the drone. In simple terms, we want to find a good ratio of plastic to aluminum for a version of the drone that reduces drag during lift and decreases wobble in the wind. So plastic and aluminum are the inputs, and the output is the resulting stability of the drone. Let's describe ideal stability as reducing drag during liftoff and wobble in the wind.

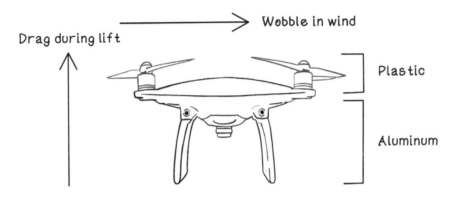

Figure 7.10 The drone optimization example

Precision in the ratio of aluminum and plastic is important, and the range of possibilities is large. In this scenario, researchers have found the function for the ratio of aluminum and plastic. We will use this function in a simulated virtual environment that tests the drag and wobble to find the best values for each material before we manufacture another prototype drone. We also know that the maximum and minimum ratios for the materials are 10 and -10, respectively. This fitness function is similar to a heuristic.

Figure 7.11 shows the fitness function for the ratio between aluminum (*x*) and plastic (*y*). The result is a performance score based on drag and wobble, given the input values for *x* and *y*.

$$f(x, y) = (x + 2y - 7)^2 + (2x + y - 5)^2$$

Figure 7.11 The example function for optimizing aluminum (*x*) and plastic (*y*)

How can we find the amount of aluminum and the amount of plastic required to create a good drone? One possibility is to try every combination of values for aluminum and plastic until we find the best ratio of materials for our drone. Take a step back and imagine the amount of computation required to find this ratio. We could conduct an almost-infinite number of computations before finding a solution if we try every possible number. We need to compute the result for the items in table 7.1. Note that negative numbers for aluminum and plastic are bizarre in reality; however, we're using them in this example to demonstrate the fitness function used to optimize these values.

Table 7.1 Possible values for aluminum and plastic compositions

How many parts aluminum? (x)	How many parts plastic? (y)
-0.1	1.34
-0.134	0.575
-1.1	0.24
-1.1645	1.432
-2.034	-0.65
-2.12	-0.874
0.743	-1.1645
0.3623	-1.87
1.75	-2.7756
...	...
-10 ≥ Aluminum ≥ 10	*-10 ≥ Plastic ≥ 10*

This computation will go on for every possible number between the constraints and is computationally expensive, so it is realistically impossible to brute-force this problem. A better approach is needed.

Particle swarm optimization provides a means to search a large search space without checking every value in each dimension. In the drone problem, aluminum is one dimension of the problem, plastic is the second dimension, and the resulting performance of the drone is the third dimension.

In the next section, we determine the data structures required to represent a particle, including the data about the problem that it will contain.

Representing state: What do particles look like?

Because particles move across the search space, the concept of a particle must be defined (figure 7.12).

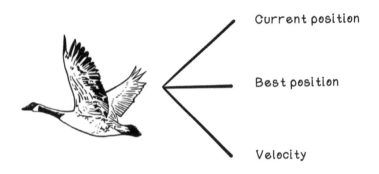

Current position

Best position

Velocity

Figure 7.12 Properties of a particle

The following represent the concept of a particle:

- *Position*—The position of the particle in all dimensions
- *Best position*—The best position found using the fitness function
- *Velocity*—The current velocity of the particle's movement

Pseudocode

To fulfill the three attributes of a particle, including position, best position, and velocity, the following properties are required in a constructor of the particle for the various operations of the particle swarm optimization algorithm. Don't worry about the inertia, cognitive component, and social component right now; they will be explained in upcoming sections:

```
Particle(x, y, inertia, cognitive_constant, social_constant):
    let particle.x equal to x
    let particle.y equal to y
    let particle.fitness equal to infinity
    let particle.velocity equal to 0
    let particle.best_x equal to x
    let particle.best_y equal to y
    let particle.best_fitness equal to infinity
    let particle.inertia equal to inertia
    let particle.cognitive_constant equal to cognitive_constant
    let particle.social_constant equal to social_constant
```

Particle swarm optimization life cycle

The approach to designing a particle swarm optimization algorithm is based on the problem space being addressed. Each problem has a unique context and a different domain in which data is represented. Solutions to different problems are also measured differently. Let's dive into how a particle swarm optimization can be designed to solve the drone construction problem.

The general life cycle of a particle swarm optimization algorithm is as follows (figure 7.13):

1. *Initialize the population of particles.* Determine the number of particles to be used, and initialize each particle to a random position in the search space.

2. *Calculate the fitness of each particle.* Given the position of each particle, determine the fitness of that particle at that position.

3. *Update the position of each particle.* Repetitively update the position of all the particles, using principles of swarm intelligence. Particles will explore the search space and then converge to good solutions.

4. *Determine the stopping criteria.* Determine when the particles stop updating and the algorithm stops.

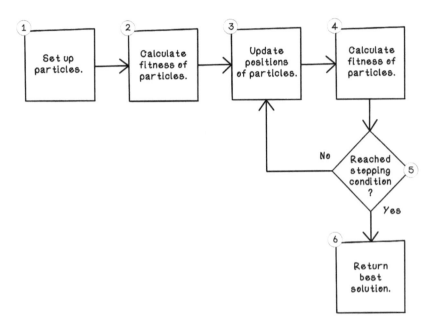

Figure 7.13 The life cycle of a particle swarm optimization algorithm

The particle swarm optimization algorithm is fairly simple, but the details of step 3 are particularly intricate. The following sections look at each step in isolation and uncover the details that make the algorithm work.

Initialize the population of particles

The algorithm starts by creating a specific number of particles, which will remain the same for the lifetime of the algorithm (figure 7.14).

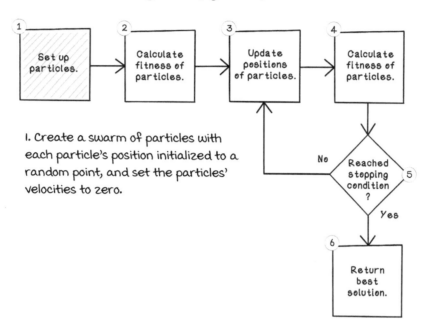

Figure 7.14 Set up the particles.

The three factors that are important in initializing the particles are (figure 7.15):

- *Number of particles*—The number of particles influences computation. The more particles that exist, the more computation is required. Additionally, more particles will likely mean that converging on a global best solution will take longer because more particles are attracted to their local best solutions. The constraints of the problem also affect the number of particles. A larger search space may need more particles to explore it. There could be as many as 1,000 particles or as few as 4. Usually, 50 to 100 particles produce good solutions without being too computationally expensive.

- *Starting position for each particle*—The starting position for each particle should be a random position in all the respective dimensions. It is important that the particles are distributed evenly across the search space. If most of the particles are in a specific region of the search space, they will struggle to find solutions outside that area.

- *Starting velocity for each particle*—The velocity of particles is initialized to 0 because the particles have not been affected yet. A good analogy is that birds begin takeoff for flight from a stationary position.

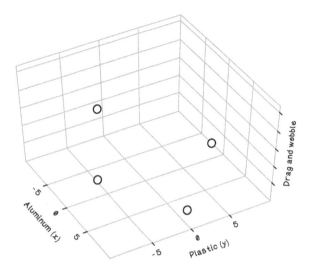

Figure 7.15 A visualization of the initial positions of four particles in a 3D plane

Table 7.2 describes the data encapsulated by each particle at the initialization step of the algorithm. Notice that the velocity is 0; the current fitness and best fitness values are 0 because they have not been calculated yet.

Table 7.2 Data attributes for each particle

Particle	Velocity	Current aluminum (x)	Current plastic (y)	Current fitness	Best aluminum (x)	Best plastic (y)	Best fitness
1	0	7	1	0	7	1	0
2	0	-1	9	0	-1	9	0
3	0	-10	1	0	-10	1	0
4	0	-2	-5	0	-2	-5	0

Pseudocode

The method to generate a swarm consists of creating an empty list and appending new particles to it. The key factors are:

- Ensuring that the number of particles is configurable.

- Ensuring that the random number generation is done uniformly; numbers are distributed across the search space within the constraints. This implementation depends on the features of the random number generator used.

- Ensuring that the constraints of the search space are specified: in this case, -10 and 10 for both *x* and *y* of the particle.

```
generate_swarm(number_of_particles):
  let particles equal an empty list
  for particle in range(number_of_particles):
    append Particle(random(-10, 10), random(-10, 10), INERTIA,
            COGNITIVE_CONSTANT, SOCIAL_CONSTANT) to particles
  return particles
```

Calculate the fitness of each particle

The next step is calculating the fitness of each particle at its current position. The fitness of particles is calculated every time the entire swarm changes position (figure 7.16).

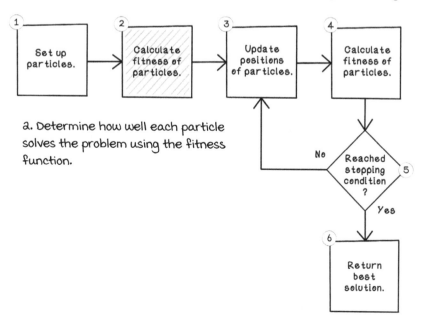

Figure 7.16 Calculate the fitness of the particles.

In the drone scenario, the scientists provided a function in which the result is the amount of drag and wobble given a specific number of aluminum and plastic components. This function is used as the fitness function in the particle swarm optimization algorithm in this example (figure 7.17).

$$f(x, y) = (x + 2y - 7)^2 + (2x + y - 5)^2$$

Figure 7.17 The example function for optimizing aluminum (x) and plastic (y)

If x is aluminum and y is plastic, the calculations in figure 7.18 can be made for each particle to determine its fitness by substituting x and y for the values of aluminum and plastic.

$$f(7,1) = (7 + 2(1) - 7)^2 + (2(7) + 1 - 5)^2 = 104$$

$$f(-1,9) = (-1 + 2(9) - 7)^2 + (2(-1) + 9 - 5)^2 = 104$$

$$f(-10,1) = (-10 + 2(1) - 7)^2 + (2(-10) + 1 - 5)^2 = 801$$

$$f(-2,-5) = (-2 + 2(-5) - 7)^2 + (2(-2) - 5 - 5)^2 = 557$$

Figure 7.18 Fitness calculations for each particle

Now the table of particles represents the calculated fitness for each particle (table 7.3). It is also set as the best fitness for each particle because it is the only known fitness in the first iteration. After the first iteration, the best fitness for each particle is the best fitness in each specific particle's history.

Table 7.3 Data attributes for each particle

Particle	Velocity	Current aluminum (x)	Current plastic (y)	Current fitness	Best aluminum (x)	Best plastic (y)	Best fitness
1	0	7	1	296	7	1	296
2	0	-1	9	104	-1	9	104
3	0	-10	1	80	-10	1	80
4	0	-2	-5	365	-2	-5	365

EXERCISE: WHAT WOULD THE FITNESS BE FOR THE FOLLOWING INPUTS GIVEN THE DRONE FITNESS FUNCTION?

$$f(x, y) = (x + 2y - 7)^2 + (2x + y - 5)^2$$

Particle	Velocity	Current aluminum (x)	Current plastic (y)	Current fitness	Best aluminum (x)	Best plastic (y)	Best fitness
1	0	5	-3	0	5	-3	0
2	0	-6	-1	0	-6	-1	0
3	0	7	3	0	7	3	0
4	0	-1	9	0	-1	9	0

SOLUTION: WHAT WOULD THE FITNESS BE FOR THE FOLLOWING INPUTS GIVEN THE DRONE FITNESS FUNCTION?

$$f(5,-3) = (5 + 2(-3) - 7)^2 + (2(5) - 3 - 5)^2 = 68$$

$$f(-6,-1) = (-6 + 2(-1) - 7)^2 + (2(-6) - 1 - 5)^2 = 549$$

$$f(7,3) = (7 + 2(3) - 7)^2 + (2(7) + 3 - 5)^2 = 180$$

$$f(-1,9) = (-1 + 2(9) - 7)^2 + (2(-1) + 9 - 5)^2 = 104$$

Pseudocode

The fitness function is representing the mathematical function in code. Any math library will contain the operations required, such as a power function and a square-root function:

```
calculate_fitness(x, y):
    return power(x + 2 * y - 7, 2) + power(2 * x + y - 5, 2)
```

The function for updating the fitness of a particle is also trivial, in that it determines whether the new fitness is better than a past best and then stores that information:

```
update_fitness(x, y):
  let particle.fitness equal the result of calculate_fitness(x, y)
  if particle.fitness is less than particle.best_fitness:
    let particle.best_fitness equal particle.fitness
    let particle.best_x equal x
    let particle.best_y equal y
```

The function to determine the best particle in the swarm iterates through all particles, updates their fitness based on their new positions, and finds the particle that yields the smallest value for the fitness function. In this case, we are minimizing, so a smaller value is better:

```
get_best(swarm):
  let best_fitness equal infinity
  let best_particle equal nothing
  for particle in swarm:
    update fitness of particle
    if particle.fitness is less than best_fitness:
      let best_fitness equal particle.fitness
      let best_particle equal particle
  return best_particle
```

Update the position of each particle

The update step of the algorithm is the most intricate, because it is where the magic happens. The update step encompasses the properties of swarm intelligence in nature into a mathematical model that allows the search space to be explored while honing in on good solutions (figure 7.19).

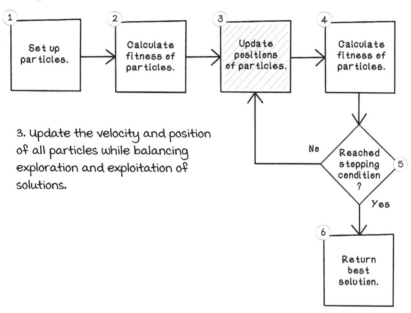

Figure 7.19 Update the positions of the particles.

Particles in the swarm update their position given a cognitive ability and factors in the environment around them, such as inertia and what the swarm is doing. These factors influence the velocity and position of each particle. The first step is understanding how velocity is updated. The velocity determines the direction and speed of movement of the particle.

The particles in the swarm move to different points in the search space to find better solutions. Each particle relies on its memory of a good solution and the knowledge of the swarm's best solution. Figure 7.20 illustrates the movement of the particles in the swarm as their positions are updated.

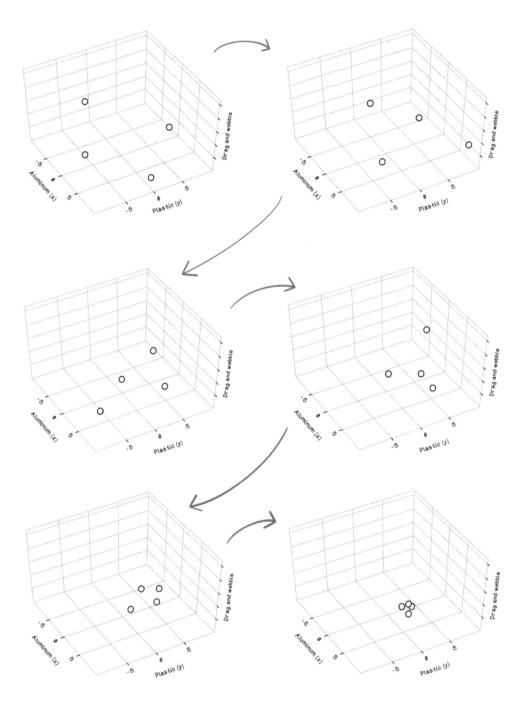

Figure 7.20 The movement of particles over five iterations

The components of updating velocity

Three components are used to calculate the new velocity of each particle: inertia, cognitive, and social. Each component influences the movement of the particle. We will look at each of the components in isolation before diving into how they are combined to update the velocity and, ultimately, the position of a particle:

- *Inertia*—The inertia component represents the resistance to movement or change in direction for a specific particle that influences its velocity. The inertia component consists of two values: the inertia magnitude and the current velocity of the particle. The inertia value is a number between 0 and 1.

  Inertia component:

  `inertia * current velocity`

  - ° A value closer to 0 translates to exploration, potentially taking more iterations.
  - ° A value closer to 1 translates to more exploration for particles in fewer iterations.

- *Cognitive*—The cognitive component represents the internal cognitive ability of a specific particle. The cognitive ability is a sense of a particle knowing its best position and using that position to influence its movement. The cognitive constant is a number greater than 0 and less than 2. A greater cognitive constant means more exploitation by the particles.

  Cognitive component:

  `cognitive acceleration` `* (particle best position - current position)`

  `cognitive acceleration = cognitive constant * random cognitive number`

- *Social*—The social component represents the ability of a particle to interact with the swarm. A particle knows the best position in the swarm and uses this information to influence its movement. Social acceleration is determined by using a constant and scaling it with a random number. The social constant remains the same for the lifetime of the algorithm, and the random factor encourages diversity in favoring the social factor.

  Social component:

  `social acceleration` `* (swarm best position - current position)`

  `social acceleration = social constant * random social number`

The greater the social constant, the more exploration there will be, because the particle favors its social component more. The social constant is a number between 0 and 2. A greater social constant means more exploration.

Updating velocity
Now that we understand the inertia component, cognitive component, and social component, let's look at how they can be combined to update a new velocity for the particles (figure 7.21).

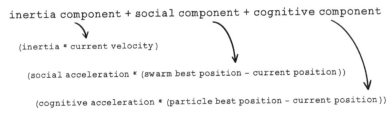

New velocity:

inertia component + social component + cognitive component

(inertia * current velocity)

(social acceleration * (swarm best position – current position))

(cognitive acceleration * (particle best position – current position))

Figure 7.21 Formula to calculate velocity

By looking at the math, we may find it difficult to understand how the different components in the function affect the velocity of the particles. Figure 7.22 depicts how the different factors influence a particle.

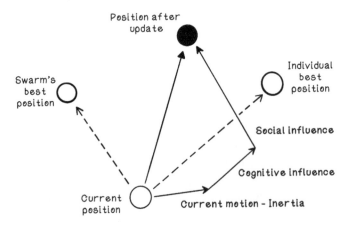

Figure 7.22 The intuition of the factors influencing velocity updates

Table 7.4 shows the attributes of each particle after the fitness of each is calculated.

Table 7.4 Data attributes for each particle

Particle	Velocity	Current aluminum	Current plastic	Current fitness	Best aluminum	Best plastic	Best fitness
1	0	7	1	296	2	4	296
2	0	-1	9	104	-1	9	104
3	0	-10	1	80	-10	1	80
4	0	-2	-5	365	-2	-5	365

Next, we will dive into the velocity update calculations for a particle, given the formulas that we have worked through.

Here are the constant configurations that have been set for this scenario:

- *Inertia is set to 0.2.* This setting favors slower exploration.

- *Cognitive constant is set to 0.35.* Because this constant is less than the social constant, the social component is favored over an individual particle's cognitive component.

- *Social constant is set to 0.45.* Because this constant is more than the cognitive constant, the social component is favored. Particles put more weight on the best values found by the swarm.

Figure 7.23 describes the calculations of the inertia component, cognitive component, and social component for the velocity update formula.

Inertia component:

inertia * current velocity

= 0.2 * 0

= 0

Cognitive component:

cognitive acceleration = cognitive constant * random cognitive number

= 0.35 * 0.2

= 0.07

cognitive acceleration * (particle best position - current position)

= 0.07 * ([7,1] - [7,1])

= 0.07 * 0

= 0

Social component:

social acceleration = social constant * random social number

= 0.45 * 0.3

= 0.135

social acceleration * (swarm best position - current position)

= 0.135 * ([-10,1] - [7,1])

= 0.135 * $sqrt((-10 - 7)^2 + (1 - 1)^2)$ Distance formula: $sqrt((x1 - x2)^2 + (y1 - y2)^2)$

= 0.135 * 17

= 2.295

New velocity:

inertia component + cognitive component + social component

= 0 + 0 + 2.295

= 2.295

Figure 7.23 Particle velocity calculation walkthrough

After these calculations have been completed for all particles, the velocity of each particle is updated, as represented in table 7.5.

Table 7.5 Data attributes for each particle

Particle	Velocity	Current aluminum	Current plastic	Current fitness	Best aluminum	Best plastic	Best fitness
1	2.295	7	1	296	7	1	296
2	1.626	-1	9	104	-1	9	104
3	2.043	-10	1	80	-10	1	80
4	1.35	-2	-5	365	-2	-5	365

Position update

Now that we understand how velocity is updated, we can update the current position of each particle, using the new velocity (figure 7.24).

```
Position:

current position + new velocity


New position:

current position + new velocity
= ([7,1]) + 2.295
= [9.295, 3.295]
```

Figure 7.24 Calculating the new position of a particle

By adding the current position and new velocity, we can determine the new position of each particle and update the table of particle attributes with the new velocities. Then the fitness of each particle is calculated again, given its new position, and its best position is remembered (table 7.6).

Table 7.6 Data attributes for each particle

Particle	Velocity	Current aluminum	Current plastic	Current fitness	Best aluminum	Best plastic	Best fitness
1	2.295	9.925	3.325	721.286	7	1	296
2	1.626	0.626	10	73.538	0.626	10	73.538
3	2.043	7.043	1.043	302.214	-10	1	80
4	1.35	-0.65	-3.65	179.105	-0.65	-3.65	179.105

Calculating the initial velocity for each particle in the first iteration is fairly simple because there was no previous best position for each particle—only a swarm best position that affected only the social component.

Let's examine what the velocity update calculation will look like with the new information for each particle's best position and the swarm's new best position. Figure 7.25 describes the calculation for particle 1 in the list.

Inertia component:

inertia * current velocity

= 0.2 * 2.295

= 0.59

Cognitive component:

cognitive acceleration = cognitive constant * random cognitive number

= 0.35 * 0.2   Note: We're not adjusting the random numbers for ease of understanding only.

= 0.07

cognitive acceleration * (particle best position - current position)

= 0.07 * ([7,1] – [9.925,3.325])

= 0.07 * sqrt((7 – 9.925)^2+ (1 – 3.325)^2)

= 0.07 * 3.736

= 0.266

Social component:

social acceleration = social constant * random social number

= 0.45 * 0.3

= 0.135

social acceleration * (swarm best position - current position)

= 0.135 * ([0.626,10] – [9.925,3.325])

= 0.135 * sqrt((0.626 – 9.925)^2+ (10 – 3.325)^2)

= 0.135 * 11.447

= 1.545

New velocity:

inertia component + cognitive component + social component

= 0.59 + 0.266 + 1.545

= 2.401

Figure 7.25 Particle velocity calculation walkthrough

In this scenario, the cognitive component and the social component both play a role in updating the velocity, whereas the scenario described in figure 7.23 is influenced by the social component, due to it being the first iteration.

Particles move to different positions over several iterations. Figure 7.26 depicts the particles' movement and their convergence on a solution.

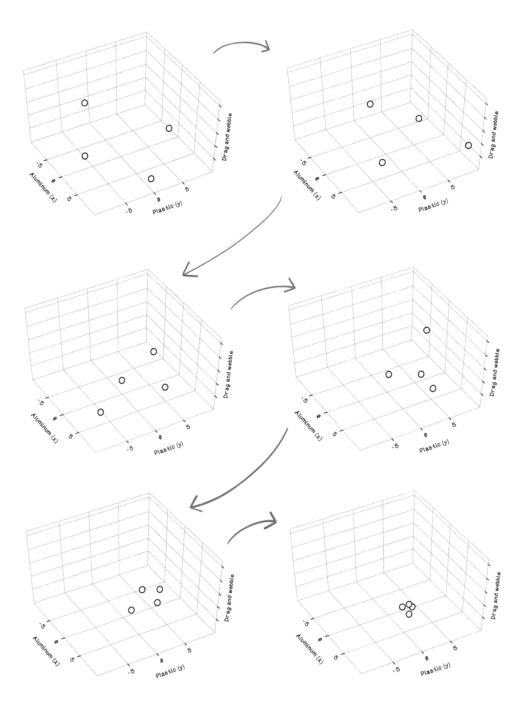

Figure 7.26 A visualization of the movement of particles in the search space

In the last frame of figure 7.26, all the particles have converged in a specific region in the search space. The best solution from the swarm will be used as the final solution. In real-world optimization problems, it is not possible to visualize the entire search space (which would make optimization algorithms unnecessary). But the function that we used for the drone example is a known function called the Booth function. By mapping it to the 3D Cartesian plane, we can see that the particles indeed converge on the minimum point in the search space (figure 7.27).

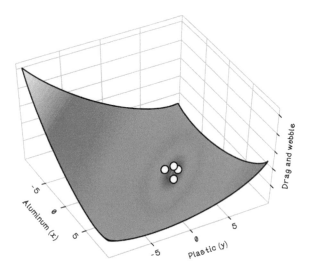

Figure 7.27 Visualization of convergence of particles and a known surface

After using the particle swarm optimization algorithm for the drone example, we find that the optimal ratio of aluminum and plastic to minimize drag and wobble is 1:3—that is, 1 part aluminum and 3 parts plastic. When we feed these values into the fitness function, the result is 0, which is the minimum value for the function.

Pseudocode

The update step can seem to be daunting, but if the components are broken into simple focused functions, the code becomes simpler and easier to write, use, and understand. The first functions are the inertia calculation function, the cognitive acceleration function, and the social acceleration function. We also need a function to measure the distance between two points, which is represented by root squaring the sum of the square of the difference in x values summed with the square of the difference in the y values:

```
calculate_inertia(inertia_constant, velocity):
  return inertia_constant * current_velocity


calculate_cognitive_acceleration(cognitive_constant):
  return cognitive_constant * random number between 0 and 1


calculate_social_acceleration(social_constant):
  return social_constant * random number between 0 and 1


calculate_distance(best_x, best_y, current_x, current_y):
  return square_root(
            power(best_x - current_x), 2) + power(best_y - current_y), 2)
          )
```

The cognitive component is calculated by finding the cognitive acceleration, using the function that we defined in an earlier section, and the distance between the particle's best position and its current position:

```
calculate_cognitive(cognitive_constant,
                    particle_best_x, particle_best_y
                    particle_current_x, particle_current_y):
  let acceleration equal cognative_acceleration(cognitive_constant)
  let distance equal calculate_distance(particle_best_x,
                                        particle_best_y
                                        particle_current_x,
                                        particle_current_y)
  return acceleration * distance
```

The social component is calculated by finding the social acceleration, using the function that we defined earlier, and the distance between the swarm's best position and the particle's current position:

```
calculate_social(social_constant,
                 swarm_best_x,swarm_best_y
                 particle_current_x,particle_current_y):
   let acceleration equal social_acceleration(social_constant)
   let distance equal calculate_distance(swarm_best_x,
                                          swarm_best_y
                                          particle_current_x,
                                          particle_current_y)
return acceleration * distance
```

The update function wraps everything that we have defined to carry out the actual update of a particle's velocity and position. The velocity is calculated by using the inertia component, cognitive component, and social component. The position is calculated by adding the new velocity to the particle's current position:

```
update_particle(cognitive_constant,social_constant,particle_velocity,
                particle_best_x,particle_best_y,
                swarm_best_x,swarm_best_y,
                particle_current_x,particle_current_y)
   let inertia equal calculate_inertia(inertia_constant,
                                        particle_constant)
   let cognitive equal calculate_cognitive(cognitive_constant,
                                            particle_best_x,particle_best_y
                                            particle_current_x,particle_current_y)
   let social equal calculate_social(social_constant,
                                      swarm_best_x,swarm_best_y
                                      particle_current_x,particle_current_y)
   let particle.velocity equal inertia + cognitive + social
   let particle.x equal particle.x + velocity
   let particle.y equal particle.y + velocity
```

EXERCISE: CALCULATE THE NEW VELOCITY AND POSITION FOR PARTICLE 1 GIVEN THE FOLLOWING INFORMATION ABOUT THE PARTICLES

- Inertia is set to 0.1.

- The cognitive constant is set to 0.5, and the cognitive random number is 0.2.

- The social constant is set to 0.5, and the social random number is 0.5.

Particle	Velocity	Current aluminum	Current plastic	Current fitness	Best aluminum	Best plastic	Best fitness
1	3	4	8	721.286	7	1	296
2	4	3	3	73.538	0.626	10	73.538
3	1	6	2	302.214	-10	1	80
4	2	2	5	179.105	-0.65	-3.65	179.105

SOLUTION: CALCULATE THE NEW VELOCITY AND POSITION FOR PARTICLE 1 GIVEN THE FOLLOWING INFORMATION ABOUT THE PARTICLES

Inertia component:

inertia * current velocity

= 0.1 * 3

= 0.3

Cognitive component:

cognitive acceleration = cognitive constant * random cognitive number

= 0.5 * 0.2

= 0.1

cognitive acceleration * (particle best position – current position)

= 0.1 * ([7,1] – [4,8])

= 0.1 * sqrt $((7 - 4)^2 + (1 - 8)^2)$

= 0.1 * 7.616

= 0.7616

Social component:

social acceleration = social constant * random social number

= 0.5 * 0.5

= 0.25

social acceleration * (swarm best position – current position)

= 0.25 * ([0.626,10] – [4,8])

= 0.25 * sqrt $((0.626 - 4)^2 + (10 - 8)^2)$

= 0.25 * 3.922

= 0.981

New velocity:

inertia component + cognitive component + social component

= 0.3 + 0.7616 + 0.981

= 2.0426

Determine the stopping criteria

The particles in the swarm cannot keep updating and searching indefinitely. A stopping criterion needs to be determined to allow the algorithm to run for a reasonable number of iterations to find a suitable solution (figure 7.28).

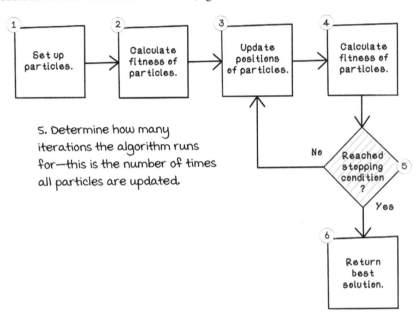

Figure 7.28 Has the algorithm reached a stopping condition?

The number of iterations influences several aspects of finding solutions, including:

- *Exploration*—Particles require time to explore the search space to find areas with better solutions. Exploration is also influenced by the constants defined in the update velocity function.

- *Exploitation*—Particles should converge on a good solution after reasonable exploration occurs.

A strategy to stop the algorithm is to examine the best solution in the swarm and determine whether it is stagnating. Stagnation occurs when the value of the best solution doesn't change or doesn't change by a significant amount. Running more iterations in this scenario will not help find better solutions. When the best solution stagnates, the parameters in the update function can be adjusted to favor more exploration. If more exploration is desired, this adjustment usually means more iterations. Stagnation could mean that a good solution was found or that that the swarm is stuck on a local best solution. If enough exploration occurred at the start, and the swarm gradually stagnates, the swarm has converged on a good solution (figure 7.29).

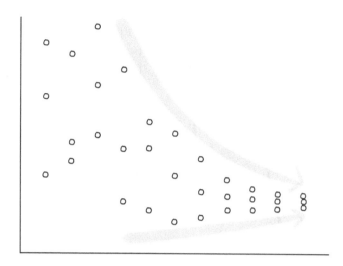

Figure 7.29 Exploration converging and exploiting

Use cases for particle swarm optimization algorithms

Particle swarm optimization algorithms are interesting because they simulate a natural phenomenon, which makes them easier to understand, but they can be applied to a range of problems at different levels of abstraction. This chapter looked at an optimization problem for drone manufacturing, but particle swarm optimization algorithms can be used in conjunction with other algorithms, such as artificial neural networks, playing a small but critical role in finding good solutions.

One interesting application of a particle swarm optimization algorithm is deep brain stimulation. The concept involves installing probes with electrodes into the human brain to stimulate it to treat conditions such as Parkinson's disease. Each probe contains electrodes that can be configured in different directions to treat the condition correctly per patient. Researchers at the University of Minnesota have developed a particle swarm optimization algorithm to optimize the direction of each electrode to maximize the region of interest, minimize the region of avoidance, and minimize energy use. Because particles are effective in searching these multidimensional problem spaces, the particle swarm optimization algorithm is effective for finding optimal configurations for electrodes on the probes (figure 7.30).

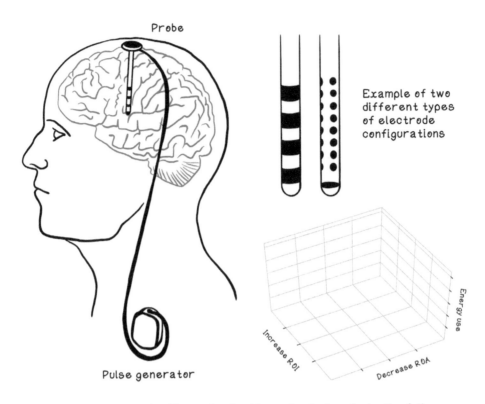

Figure 7.30 Example of factors involved for probes in deep brain stimulation

Here are some other real-world applications of particle swarm optimization algorithms:

- *Optimizing weights in an artificial neural network*—Artificial neural networks are modeled on an idea of how the human brain works. Neurons pass signals to other neurons, and each neuron adjusts the signal before passing it on. An artificial neural network uses weights to adjust each signal. The power of the network is finding the right balance of weights to form patterns in relationships of the data. Adjusting weights is computationally expensive, as the search space is massive. Imagine having to brute-force every possible decimal number combination for 10 weights. That process would take years.

  Don't panic if this concept sounds confusing. We explore how artificial neural networks operate in chapter 9. Particle swarm optimization can be used to adjust the weights of neural networks faster, because it seeks optimal values in the search space without exhaustively attempting each one.

- *Motion tracking in videos*—Motion tracking of people is a challenging task in computer vision. The goal is to identify the poses of people and imply a motion by using the information from the images in the video alone. People move differently, even though their joints move similarly. Because the images contain many aspects, the search space becomes large, with many dimensions to predict the motion for a person. Particle swarm optimization works well in high-dimension search spaces and can be used to improve the performance of motion tracking and prediction.

- *Speech enhancement in audio*—Audio recordings are nuanced. There is always background noise that may interfere with what someone is saying in the recording. A solution is to remove the noise from recorded speech audio clips. A technique used for this purpose is filtering the audio clip with noise and comparing similar sounds to remove the noise in the audio clip. This solution is still complex, as reduction of certain frequencies may be good for parts of the audio clip but may deteriorate other parts of it. Fine searching and matching must be done for good noise removal. Traditional methods are slow, as the search space is large. Particle swarm optimization works well in large search spaces and can be used to speed the process of removing noise from audio clips.

SUMMARY OF PARTICLE SWARM OPTIMIZATION

PSOs find good solutions in large search spaces.

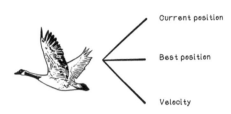

Current position

Best position

Velocity

Particles use their best position and the swarm's best position to move through the search space.

Adjusting the particles' velocity is the critical step of the PSO algorithm using inertia, cognitive, and social influence.

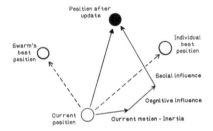

New velocity:

inertia component + social component + cognitive component

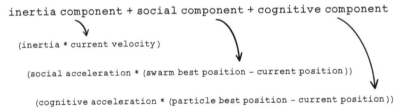

(inertia * current velocity)

(social acceleration * (swarm best position − current position))

(cognitive acceleration * (particle best position − current position))

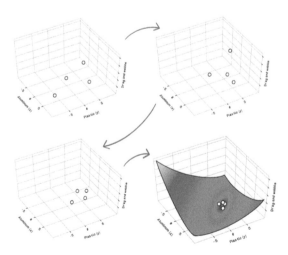

Particles move through the search space while finding different good solutions and ideally converging on a global best solution.

This chapter covers

- Solving problems with machine learning algorithms

- Grasping a machine learning life cycle, preparing data, and selecting algorithms

- Understanding and implementing a linear-regression algorithm for predictions

- Understanding and implementing a decision-tree learning algorithm for classification

- Gaining intuition about other machine learning algorithms and their usefulness

What is machine learning?

Machine learning can seem like a daunting concept to learn and apply, but with the right framing and understanding of the process and algorithms, it can be interesting and fun.

Suppose that you're looking for a new apartment. You speak to friends and family, and do some online searches for apartments in the city. You notice that apartments in different areas are priced differently. Here are some of your observations from all your research:

- A one-bedroom apartment in the city center (close to work) costs $5,000 per month.

- A two-bedroom apartment in the city center costs $7,000 per month.

- A one-bedroom apartment in the city center with a garage costs $6,000 per month.

- A one-bedroom apartment outside the city center, where you will need to travel to work, costs $3,000 per month.

- A two-bedroom apartment outside the city center costs $4,500 per month.

- A one-bedroom apartment outside the city center with a garage costs $3,800 per month.

You notice some patterns. Apartments in the city center are most expensive and are usually between $5,000 and $7,000 per month. Apartments outside the city are cheaper. Increasing the number of rooms adds between $1,500 and $2,000 per month, and access to a garage adds between $800 and $1,000 per month (figure 8.1).

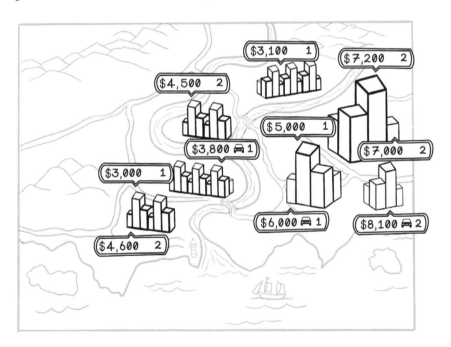

Figure 8.1 An illustration of property prices and features in different regions

This example shows how we use data to find patterns and make decisions. If you encounter a two-bedroom apartment in the city center with a garage, it's reasonable to assume that the price would be approximately $8,000 per month.

Machine learning aims to find patterns in data for useful applications in the real world. We could spot the pattern in this small dataset, but machine learning spots them for us in large, complex datasets. Figure 8.2 depicts the relationships among different attributes of the data. Each dot represents an individual property.

Notice that there are more dots closer to the city center and that there is a clear pattern related to price per month: the price gradually drops as distance to the city center increases. There is also a pattern in the price per month related to the number of rooms; the gap between the bottom cluster of dots and the top cluster shows that the price jumps significantly. We could naïvely assume that this effect may be related to the distance from the city center. Machine learning algorithms can help us validate or invalidate this assumption. We dive into how this process works throughout this chapter.

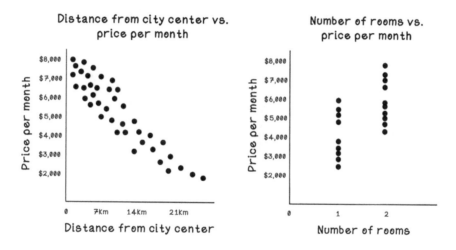

Figure 8.2 Example visualization of relationships among data

Typically, data is represented in tables. The columns are referred to as *features* of the data, and the rows are referred to as *examples*. When we compare two features, the feature being measured is sometimes represented as *y*, and the features being changed are grouped as *x*. We will gain a better intuition for this terminology as we work through some problems.

Problems applicable to machine learning

Machine learning is useful only if you have data and have questions to ask that the data might answer. Machine learning algorithms find patterns in data but cannot do useful things magically. Different categories of machine learning algorithms use different approaches for different scenarios to answer different questions. These broad categories are supervised learning, unsupervised learning, and reinforcement learning (figure 8.3).

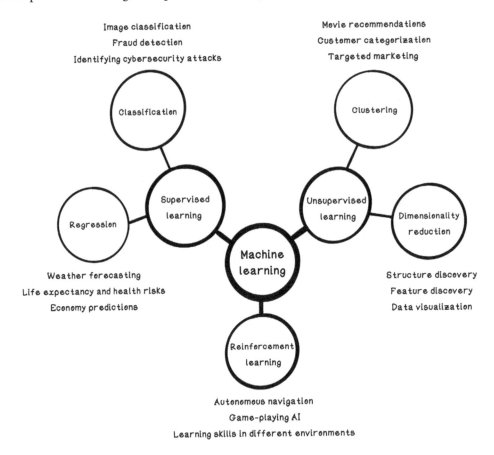

Figure 8.3 Categorization of machine learning and uses

Supervised learning

One of the most common techniques in traditional machine learning is *supervised learning*. We want to look at data, understand the patterns and relationships among the data, and predict the results if we are given new examples of different data in the same format. The apartment-finding problem is an example of supervised learning to find the pattern. We also see this example in action when we type a search that autocompletes or when music applications suggest new songs to listen to based on our activity and preference. Supervised learning has two subcategories: regression and classification.

Regression involves drawing a line through a set of data points to most closely fit the overall shape of the data. Regression can be used for applications such as trends between marketing initiatives and sales. (Is there a direct relationship between marketing through online ads and actual sales of a product?) It can also be used to determine factors that affect something. (Is there a direct relationship between time and the value of cryptocurrency, and will cryptocurrency increase exponentially in value as time passes?)

Classification aims to predict categories of examples based on their features. (Can we determine whether something is a car or a truck based on its number of wheels, weight, and top speed?)

Unsupervised learning

Unsupervised learning involves finding underlying patterns in data that may be difficult to find by inspecting the data manually. Unsupervised learning is useful for clustering data that has similar features and uncovering features that are important in the data. On an e-commerce site, for example, products might be clustered based on customer purchase behavior. If many customers purchase soap, sponges, and towels together, it is likely that more customers would want that combination of products, so soap, sponges, and towels would be clustered and recommended to new customers.

Reinforcement learning

Reinforcement learning is inspired by behavioral psychology and operates by rewarding or punishing an algorithm based on its actions in an environment. It has similarities to supervised learning and unsupervised learning, as well as many differences. Reinforcement learning aims to train an agent in an environment based on rewards and penalties. Imagine rewarding a pet for good behavior with treats; the more it is rewarded for a specific behavior, the more it will exhibit that behavior. We discuss reinforcement learning in chapter 10.

A machine learning workflow

Machine learning isn't just about algorithms. In fact, it is often about the context of the data, the preparation of the data, and the questions that are asked.

We can find questions in two ways:

- A problem can be solved with machine learning, and the right data needs to be collected to help solve it. Suppose that a bank has a vast amount of transaction data for legitimate and fraudulent transactions, and it wants to train a model with this question: "Can we detect fraudulent transactions in real time?"

- We have data in a specific context and want to determine how it can be used to solve several problems. An agriculture company, for example, might have data about the weather in different locations, nutrition required for different plants, and the soil content in different locations. The question might be "What correlations and relationships can we find among the different types of data?" These relationships may inform a more concrete question, such as "Can we determine the best location for growing a specific plant based on the weather and soil in that location?"

Figure 8.4 is a simplified view of the steps involved in a typical machine learning endeavor.

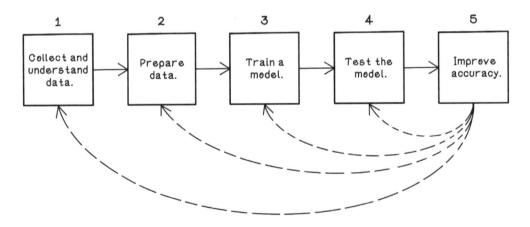

Figure 8.4 A workflow for machine learning experiments and projects

Collecting and understanding data: Know your context

Collecting and understanding the data you're working with is paramount to a successful machine learning endeavor. If you're working in a specific area in the finance industry, knowledge of the terminology and workings of the processes and data in that area is important for sourcing the data that is best to help answer questions for the goal you're trying to achieve. If you want to build a fraud detection system, understanding what data is stored about transactions and what it means is critical to identifying fraudulent transactions. Data may also need to be sourced from various systems and combined to be effective. Sometimes, the data we use is augmented with data from outside the organization to enhance accuracy. In this section, we use an example dataset about diamond measurements to understand the machine learning workflow and explore various algorithms (figure 8.5).

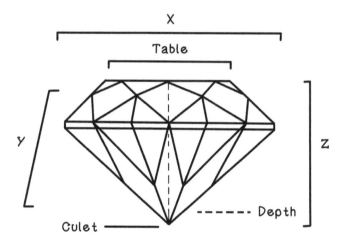

Figure 8.5 Terminology of diamond measurements

Table 8.1 describes several diamonds and their properties. X, Y, and Z describe the size of a diamond in the three spatial dimensions. Only a subset of data is used in the examples.

Table 8.1 The diamond dataset

	Carat	Cut	Color	Clarity	Depth	Table	Price	X	Y	Z
1	0.30	Good	J	SI1	64.0	55	339	4.25	4.28	2.73
2	0.41	Ideal	I	SI1	61.7	55	561	4.77	4.80	2.95
3	0.75	Very Good	D	SI1	63.2	56	2,760	5.80	5.75	3.65
4	0.91	Fair	H	SI2	65.7	60	2,763	6.03	5.99	3.95
5	1.20	Fair	F	I1	64.6	56	2,809	6.73	6.66	4.33
6	1.31	Premium	J	SI2	59.7	59	3,697	7.06	7.01	4.20
7	1.50	Premium	H	I1	62.9	60	4,022	7.31	7.22	4.57
8	1.74	Very Good	H	I1	63.2	55	4,677	7.62	7.59	4.80
9	1.96	Fair	I	I1	66.8	55	6,147	7.62	7.60	5.08
10	2.21	Premium	H	I1	62.2	58	6,535	8.31	8.27	5.16

The diamond dataset consists of 10 columns of data, which are referred to as *features*. The full dataset has more than 50,000 rows. Here's what each feature means:

- *Carat*—The weight of the diamond. Out of interest: 1 carat equals 200 mg.
- *Cut*—The quality of the diamond, by increasing quality: fair, good, very good, premium, and ideal.
- *Color*—The color of the diamond, ranging from D to J, where D is the best color and J is the worst color. D indicates a clear diamond, and J indicates a foggy one.
- *Clarity*—The imperfections of the diamond, by decreasing quality: FL, IF, VVS1, VVS2, VS1, VS2, SI1, SI2, I1, I2, and I3. (Don't worry about understanding these code names; they simply represent different levels of perfection.)
- *Depth*—The percentage of depth, which is measured from the culet to the table of the diamond. Typically, the table-to-depth ratio is important for the "sparkle" aesthetic of a diamond.
- *Table*—The percentage of the flat end of the diamond relative to the X dimension.
- *Price*—The price of the diamond when it was sold.
- *X*—The x dimension of the diamond, in millimeters.
- *Y*—The y dimension of the diamond, in millimeters.
- *Z*—The z dimension of the diamond, in millimeters.

Keep this dataset in mind; we will be using it to see how data is prepared and processed by machine learning algorithms.

Preparing data: Clean and wrangle

Real-world data is never ideal to work with. Data might be sourced from different systems and different organizations, which may have different standards and rules for data integrity. There are always missing data, inconsistent data, and data in a format that is difficult to work with for the algorithms that we want to use.

In the sample diamond dataset in table 8.2, again, it is important to understand that the columns are referred to as the *features* of the data and that each row is an *example*.

Table 8.2 The diamond dataset with missing data

	Carat	Cut	Color	Clarity	Depth	Table	Price	X	Y	Z
1	0.30	Good	J	SI1	64.0	55	339	4.25	4.28	2.73
2	0.41	Ideal	I	si1	61.7	55	561	4.77	4.80	2.95
3	0.75	Very Good	D	SI1	63.2	56	2,760	5.80	5.75	3.65
4	0.91	-	H	SI2	-	60	2,763	6.03	5.99	3.95
5	1.20	Fair	F	I1	64.6	56	2,809	6.73	6.66	4.33
6	1.21	Good	E	I1	57.2	62	3,144	7.01	6.96	3.99
7	1.31	Premium	J	SI2	59.7	59	3,697	7.06	7.01	4.20
8	1.50	Premium	H	I1	62.9	60	4,022	7.31	7.22	4.57
9	1.74	Very Good	H	i1	63.2	55	4,677	7.62	7.59	4.80
10	1.83	fair	J	I1	70.0	58	5,083	7.34	7.28	5.12
11	1.96	Fair	I	I1	66.8	55	6,147	7.62	7.60	5.08
12	-	Premium	H	i1	62.2	-	6,535	8.31	-	5.16

Missing data

In table 8.2, example 4 is missing values for the Cut and Depth features, and example 12 is missing values for Carat, Table, and Y. To compare examples, we need complete understanding of the data, and missing values make this difficult. A goal for a machine learning project might be to estimate these values; we cover estimations in the upcoming material. Assume that missing data will be problematic in our goal to use it for something useful. Here are some ways to deal with missing data:

- *Remove*—Remove the examples that have missing values for features—in this case, examples 4 and 12 (table 8.3). The benefit of this approach is that the data is more reliable because nothing is assumed; however, the removed examples may have been important to the goal we're trying to achieve.

Table 8.3 The diamond dataset with missing data: removing examples

	Carat	Cut	Color	Clarity	Depth	Table	Price	X	Y	Z
1	0.30	Good	J	SI1	64.0	55	339	4.25	4.28	2.73
2	0.41	Ideal	I	si1	61.7	55	561	4.77	4.80	2.95
3	0.75	Very Good	D	SI1	63.2	56	2,760	5.80	5.75	3.65
4	0.91	-	H	SI2	-	60	2,763	6.03	5.99	3.95
5	1.20	Fair	F	I1	64.6	56	2,809	6.73	6.66	4.33
6	1.21	Good	E	I1	57.2	62	3,144	7.01	6.96	3.99
7	1.31	Premium	J	SI2	59.7	59	3,697	7.06	7.01	4.20
8	1.50	Premium	H	I1	62.9	60	4,022	7.31	7.22	4.57
9	1.74	Very Good	H	i1	63.2	55	4,677	7.62	7.59	4.80
10	1.83	fair	J	I1	70.0	58	5,083	7.34	7.28	5.12
11	1.96	Fair	I	I1	66.8	55	6,147	7.62	7.60	5.08
12	-	Premium	H	i1	62.2	-	6,535	8.31	-	5.16

- *Mean or median*—Another option is to replace the missing values with the mean
  or median for the respective feature.

  The *mean* is the average calculated by adding all the values and dividing by the
  number of examples. The *median* is calculated by ordering the examples by value
  ascending and choosing the value in the middle.

  Using the mean is easy and efficient to do but doesn't take into account
  possible correlations between features. This approach cannot be used with
  categorical features such as the Cut, Clarity, and Depth features in the diamond
  dataset (table 8.4).

Table 8.4 The diamond dataset with missing data: using mean values

	Carat	Cut	Color	Clarity	Depth	Table	Price	X	Y	Z
1	0.30	Good	J	SI1	64.0	55	339	4.25	4.28	2.73
2	0.41	Ideal	I	si1	61.7	55	561	4.77	4.80	2.95
3	0.75	Very Good	D	SI1	63.2	56	2,760	5.80	5.75	3.65
4	0.91	-	H	SI2	-	60	2,763	6.03	5.99	3.95
5	1.20	Fair	F	I1	64.6	56	2,809	6.73	6.66	4.33
6	1.21	Good	E	I1	57.2	62	3,144	7.01	6.96	3.99
7	1.31	Premium	J	SI2	59.7	59	3,697	7.06	7.01	4.20
8	1.50	Premium	H	I1	62.9	60	4,022	7.31	7.22	4.57
9	1.74	Very Good	H	i1	63.2	55	4,677	7.62	7.59	4.80
10	1.83	fair	J	I1	70.0	58	5,083	7.34	7.28	5.12
11	1.96	Fair	I	I1	66.8	55	6,147	7.62	7.60	5.08
12	**1.19**	Premium	H	i1	62.2	**57**	6,535	8.31	-	5.16

To calculate the mean of the Table feature, we add every available value and divide the total by the number of values used:

```
Table mean = (55 + 55 + 56 + 60 + 56 + 62 + 59 + 60 + 55 + 58 + 55) / 11
Table mean = 631 / 11
Table mean = 57.364
```

Using the Table mean for the missing values seems to make sense, because the table size doesn't seem to differ radically among different examples of data. But there could be correlations that we do not see, such as the relationship between the table size and the width of the diamond (X dimension).

On the other hand, using the Carat mean does not make sense, because we can see a correlation between the Carat feature and the Price feature if we plot the data on a graph. The price seems to increase as the Carat value increases.

- *Most frequent*—Replace the missing values with the value that occurs most often for that feature, which is known as the *mode* of the data. This approach works well with categorical features but doesn't take into account possible correlations among features, and it can introduce bias by using the most frequent values.

- *(Advanced) Statistical approaches*—Use k-nearest neighbor, or neural networks. K-nearest neighbor uses many features of the data to find an estimated value. Similar to k-nearest neighbor, a neural network can predict the missing values accurately, given enough data. Both algorithms are computationally expensive for the purpose of handling missing data.

- *(Advanced) Do nothing*—Some algorithms handle missing data without any preparation, such as XGBoost, but the algorithms that we will be exploring will fail.

Ambiguous values

Another problem is values that mean the same thing but are represented differently. Examples in the diamond dataset are rows 2, 9, 10, and 12. The values for the Cut and Clarity features are lowercase instead of uppercase. Note that we know this only because we understand these features and the possible values for them. Without this knowledge, we might see Fair and fair as different categories. To fix this problem, we can standardize these values to uppercase or lowercase to maintain consistency (table 8.5).

Table 8.5 The diamond dataset with ambiguous data: standardizing values

	Carat	Cut	Color	Clarity	Depth	Table	Price	X	Y	Z
1	0.30	Good	J	SI1	64.0	55	339	4.25	4.28	2.73
2	0.41	Ideal	I	si1	61.7	55	561	4.77	4.80	2.95
3	0.75	Very Good	D	SI1	63.2	56	2,760	5.80	5.75	3.65
4	0.91	-	H	SI2	-	60	2,763	6.03	5.99	3.95
5	1.20	Fair	F	I1	64.6	56	2,809	6.73	6.66	4.33
6	1.21	Good	E	I1	57.2	62	3,144	7.01	6.96	3.99
7	1.31	Premium	J	SI2	59.7	59	3,697	7.06	7.01	4.20
8	1.50	Premium	H	I1	62.9	60	4,022	7.31	7.22	4.57
9	1.74	Very Good	H	i1	63.2	55	4,677	7.62	7.59	4.80
10	1.83	fair	J	I1	70.0	58	5,083	7.34	7.28	5.12
11	1.96	Fair	I	I1	66.8	55	6,147	7.62	7.60	5.08
12	1.19	Premium	H	i1	62.2	57	6,535	8.31	-	5.16

Encoding categorical data

Because computers and statistical models work with numeric values, there will be a problem with modeling string values and categorical values such as Fair, Good, SI1, and I1. We need to represent these categorical values as numerical values. Here are ways to accomplish this task:

- *One-hot encoding*—Think about one-hot encoding as switches, all of which are off except one. The one that is on represents the presence of the feature at that position. If we were to represent Cut with one-hot encoding, the Cut feature becomes five different features, and each value is 0 except for the one that represents the Cut value for each respective example. Note that the other features have been removed in the interest of space in table 8.6.

Table 8.6 The diamond dataset with encoded values

	Carat	Cut: Fair	Cut: Good	Cut: Very Good	Cut: Premium	Cut: Ideal
1	0.30	0	1	0	0	0
2	0.41	0	0	0	0	1
3	0.75	0	0	1	0	0
4	0.91	0	0	0	0	0
5	1.20	1	0	0	0	0
6	1.21	0	1	0	0	0
7	1.31	0	0	0	1	0
8	1.50	0	0	0	1	0
9	1.74	0	0	1	0	0
10	1.83	1	0	0	0	0
11	1.96	1	0	0	0	0
12	1.19	0	0	0	1	0

- *Label encoding*—Represent each category as a number between 0 and the number of categories. This approach should be used only for ratings or rating-related labels; otherwise, the model that we will be training will assume that the number carries weight for the example and can introduce unintended bias.

EXERCISE: IDENTIFY AND FIX THE PROBLEM DATA IN THIS EXAMPLE

Decide which data preparation techniques can be used to fix the following dataset. Decide which rows to delete, what values to use the mean for, and how categorical values will be encoded. Note that the dataset is slightly different from what we've been working with thus far.

	Carat	Origin	Depth	Table	Price	X	Y	Z
1	0.35	South Africa	64.0	55	450	4.25		2.73
2	0.42	Canada	61.7	55	680		4.80	2.95
3	0.87	Canada	63.2	56	2,689	5.80	5.75	3.65
4	0.99	Botswana	65.7		2,734	6.03	5.99	3.95
5	1.34	Botswana	64.6	56	2,901	6.73	6.66	
6	1.45	South Africa	59.7	59	3,723	7.06	7.01	4.20
7	1.65	Botswana	62.9	60	4,245	7.31	7.22	4.57
8	1.79		63.2	55	4,734	7.62	7.59	4.80
9	1.81	Botswana	66.8	55	6,093	7.62	7.60	5.08
10	2.01	South Africa	62.2	58	7,452	8.31	8.27	5.16

SOLUTION: IDENTIFY AND FIX THE PROBLEM DATA IN THIS EXAMPLE

One approach for fixing this dataset involves the following three tasks:

- *Remove row 8 due to missing Origin.* We don't know what the dataset will be used for. If the Origin feature is important, this row will be missing and it may cause issues. Alternatively, the value for this feature could be estimated if it has a relationship with other features.

- *Use one-hot encoding to encode the Origin column value.* In the example explored thus far in the chapter, we used label encoding to convert string values to numeric values. This approach worked because the values indicated more superior cut, clarity, or color. In the case of Origin, the value identifies where the diamond was sourced. By using label encoding, we introduce bias to the dataset, because no Origin location is better than another in this dataset.

- *Find the mean for missing values.* Row 1, 2, 4, and 5 are missing values for Y, X, Table, and Z, respectively. Using a mean value should be a good technique because, as we know about diamonds, the dimensions and table features are related.

Testing and training data

Before we jump into training a linear regression model, we need to ensure that we have data to teach (or train) the model, as well as some data to test how well it does in predicting new examples. Think back to the property-price example. After gaining a feel for the attributes that affect price, we could make a price prediction by looking at the distance and number of rooms. For this example, we will use table 8.7 as the training data because we have more real-world data to use for training later.

Training a model: Predict with linear regression

Choosing an algorithm to use is based largely on two factors: the question that is being asked and the nature of the data that is available. If the question is to make a prediction about the price of a diamond with a specific carat weight, regression algorithms can be useful. The algorithm choice also depends on the number of features in the dataset and the relationships among those features. If the data has many dimensions (there are many features to consider to make a prediction), we can consider several algorithms and approaches.

Regression means predicting a continuous value, such as the price or carat of the diamond. Continuous means that the values can be any number in a range. The price of $2,271, for example, is a continuous value between 0 and the maximum price of any diamond that regression can help predict.

Linear regression is one of the simplest machine learning algorithms; it finds relationships between two variables and allows us to predict one variable given the other. An example is predicting the price of a diamond based on its carat value. By looking at many examples of known diamonds, including their price and carat values, we can teach a model the relationship and ask it to estimate predictions.

Fitting a line to the data

Let's start trying to find a trend in the data and attempt to make some predictions. For exploring linear regression, the question we're asking is "Is there a correlation between the carats of a diamond and its price, and if there is, can we make accurate predictions?"

We start by isolating the carat and price features and plotting the data on a graph. Because we want to find the price based on carat value, we will treat carats as *x* and price as *y*. Why did we choose this approach?

- *Carat as the independent variable (x)*—An *independent variable* is one that is changed in an experiment to determine the effect on a dependent variable. In this example, the value for carats will be adjusted to determine the price of a diamond with that value.

- *Price as the dependent variable (y)*—A *dependent variable* is one that is being tested. It is affected by the independent variable and changes based on the independent variable value changes. In our example, we are interested in the price given a specific carat value.

Figure 8.6 shows the carat and price data plotted on a graph, and table 8.7 describes the actual data.

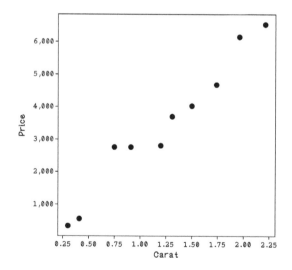

Table 8.7 Carat and price data

	Carat (x)	Price (y)
1	0.30	339
2	0.41	561
3	0.75	2,760
4	0.91	2,763
5	1.20	2,809
6	1.31	3,697
7	1.50	4,022
8	1.74	4,677
9	1.96	6,147
10	2.21	6,535

Figure 8.6 A scatterplot of carat and price data

Notice that compared with Price, the Carat values are tiny. The price goes into the thousands, and carats are in the range of decimals. To make the calculations easier to understand for the purposes of learning in this chapter, we can scale the Carat values to be comparable to the Price values. By multiplying every Carat value by 1,000, we get numbers that are easier to compute by hand in the upcoming walkthroughs. Note that by scaling all the rows, we are not affecting the relationships in the data, because every example has the same operation applied to it. The resulting data (figure 8.7) is represented in table 8.8.

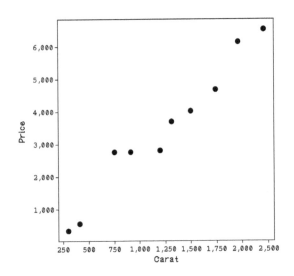

Figure 8.7 A scatterplot of carat and price data

Table 8.8 Data with adjusted carat values

	Carat (x)	Price (y)
1	300	339
2	410	561
3	750	2,760
4	910	2,763
5	1,200	2,809
6	1,310	3,697
7	1,500	4,022
8	1,740	4,677
9	1,960	6,147
10	2,210	6,535

Finding the mean of the features
The first thing we need to do to find a regression line is find the mean for each feature. The mean is the sum of all values divided by the number of values. The mean is 1,229 for carats, represented by the vertical line on the x axis. The mean is $3,431 for price, represented by the horizontal line on the y axis (figure 8.8).

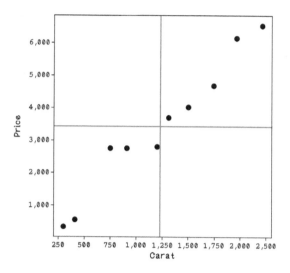

Figure 8.8 The means of *x* and *y* represented by vertical and horizontal lines

The mean is important because mathematically, any regression line we find will pass through the intersection of the mean of *x* and the mean of *y*. Many lines may pass through this point. Some regression lines might be better than others at fitting the data. The *method of least squares* aims to create a line that minimizes the distances between the line and among all the points in the dataset. The method of least squares is a popular method for finding regression lines. Figure 8.9 illustrates examples of regression lines.

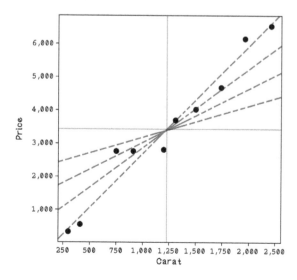

Figure 8.9 Possible regression lines

Finding regression lines with the least-squares method
But what is the regression line's purpose? Suppose that we're building a subway that tries to be as close as possible to all major office buildings. It will not be feasible to have a subway line that visits every building; there will be too many stations and it will cost a lot. So, we will try to create a straight-line route that minimizes the distance to each building. Some commuters may have to walk farther than others, but the straight line is optimized for everyone's office. This goal is exactly what a regression line aims to achieve; the buildings are data points, and the line is the straight subway path (figure 8.10).

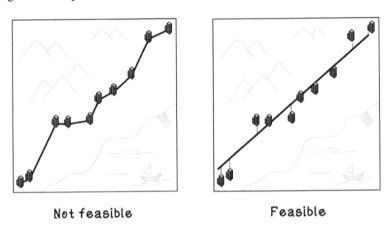

Figure 8.10 Intuition of regression lines

Linear regression will always find a straight line that fits the data to minimize distance among points overall. Understanding the equation for a line is important because we will be learning how to find the values for the variables that describe a line.

A straight line is represented by the equation $y = c + mx$ (figure 8.11):

- y: The dependent variable

- x: The independent variable

- m: The slope of the line

- c: The y-value where the line intercepts the y axis

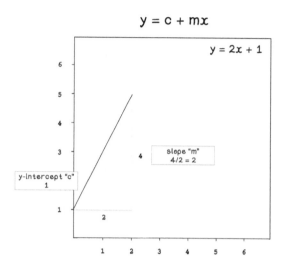

Figure 8.11 Intuition of the equation that represents a line

The method of least squares is used to find the regression line. At a high level, the process involves the steps depicted in figure 8.12. To find the line that's closest to the data, we find the difference between the actual data values and the predicted data values. The differences for data points will vary. Some differences will be large, and some will be small. Some differences will be negative values, and some will be positive values. By squaring the differences and summing them, we take into consideration all differences for all data points. Minimizing the total difference is getting the least square difference to achieve a good regression line. Don't worry if figure 8.12 looks a bit daunting; we will work through each step.

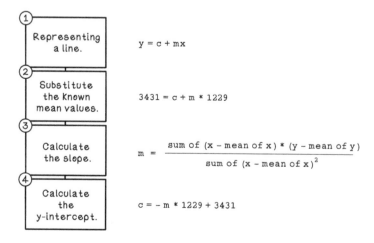

Figure 8.12 The basic workflow for calculating a regression line

Thus far, our line has some known variables. We know that an x value is 1,229 and a y value is 3,431, as shown in step 2.

Next, we calculate the difference between every Carat value and the Carat mean, as well as the difference between every Price value and the Price mean, to find (x – mean of x) and (y – mean of y), which is used in step 3 (table 8.9).

Table 8.9 The diamond dataset and calculations

	Carat (x)	Price (y)	x – mean of x		y – mean of y	
1	300	339	300 – 1,229	-929	339 – 3,431	-3,092
2	410	561	410 – 1,229	-819	561 – 3,431	-2,870
3	750	2,760	750 – 1,229	-479	2,760 – 3,431	-671
4	910	2,763	910 – 1,229	-319	2,763 – 3,431	-668
5	1,200	2,809	2,100 – 1,229	-29	2,809 – 3,431	-622
6	1,310	3,697	1,310 – 1,229	81	3,697 – 3,431	266
7	1,500	4,022	1,500 – 1,229	271	4,022 – 3,431	591
8	1,740	4,677	1,740 – 1,229	511	4,677 – 3,431	1,246
9	1,960	6,147	1,960 – 1,229	731	6,147 – 3,431	2,716
10	2,210	6,535	2,210 – 1,229	981	6,535 – 3,431	3,104
	1,229	3,431				
	Means					

For step 3, we also need to calculate the square of the difference between every carat and the carat mean to find (x – mean of x)^2. We also need to sum these values to minimize, which equals 3,703,690 (table 8.10).

Table 8.10 The diamond dataset and calculations, part 2

	Carat (x)	Price (y)	x – mean of x		y – mean of y		(x – mean of x)^2
1	300	339	300 – 1,229	-929	339 – 3,431	-3,092	863,041
2	410	561	410 – 1,229	-819	561 – 3,431	-2,870	670,761
3	750	2,760	750 – 1,229	-479	2,760 – 3,431	-671	229,441
4	910	2,763	910 – 1,229	-319	2,763 – 3,431	-668	101,761
5	1,200	2,809	2,100 – 1,229	-29	2,809 – 3,431	-622	841
6	1,310	3,697	1,310 – 1,229	81	3,697 – 3,431	266	6,561
7	1,500	4,022	1,500 – 1,229	271	4,022 – 3,431	591	73,441
8	1,740	4,677	1,740 – 1,229	511	4,677 – 3,431	1,246	261,121
9	1,960	6,147	1,960 – 1,229	731	6,147 – 3,431	2,716	534,361
10	2,210	6,535	2,210 – 1,229	981	6,535 – 3,431	3,104	962,361
	1,229	3,431					3,703,690
	Means						Sums

The last missing value for the equation in step 3 is the value for $(x - \text{mean of } x) * (y - \text{mean of } y)$. Again, the sum of the values is required. The sum equals 11,624,370 (table 8.11).

Table 8.11 The diamond dataset and calculations, part 3

	Carat (x)	Price (y)	x – mean of x		y – mean of y		(x – mean of x)^2	(x – mean of x) * (y – mean of y)
1	300	339	300 – 1,229	-929	339 – 3,431	-3,092	863,041	2,872,468
2	410	561	410 – 1,229	-819	561 – 3,431	-2,870	670,761	2,350,530
3	750	2,760	750 – 1,229	-479	2,760 – 3,431	-671	229,441	321,409
4	910	2,763	910 – 1,229	-319	2,763 – 3,431	-668	101,761	213,092
5	1,200	2,809	2,100 – 1,229	-29	2,809 – 3,431	-622	841	18,038
6	1,310	3,697	1,310 – 1,229	81	3,697 – 3,431	266	6,561	21,546
7	1,500	4,022	1,500 – 1,229	271	4,022 – 3,431	591	73,441	160,161
8	1,740	4,677	1,740 – 1,229	511	4,677 – 3,431	1,246	261,121	636,706
9	1,960	6,147	1,960 – 1,229	731	6,147 – 3,431	2,716	534,361	1,985,396
10	2,210	6,535	2,210 – 1,229	981	6,535 – 3,431	3,104	962,361	3,045,024
	1,229	3,431					3,703,690	11,624,370
	Means						Sums	

Now we can plug in the calculated values to the least-squares equation to calculate *m*:

```
m = 11624370 / 3703690
m = 3.139
```

Now that we have a value for *m*, we can calculate *c* by substituting the mean values for *x* and *y*. Remember that all regression lines will pass this point, so it is a known point within the regression line:

```
y = c + mx

3431 = c + 3.139x
3431 = c + 391.5594
3431 - 391.5594 = c
c = 3,039.4406
```

Complete regression line:

```
y = 3039.4406 + 0.3186x
```

Finally, we can plot the line by generating some values for carats between the minimum value and maximum value, plugging them into the equation that represents the regression line, and then plotting it (figure 8.13):

```
x (Carat) minimum = 300
x (Carat) maximum = 2210
```

Sample between the minimum and maximum at intervals of 500:
```
x = [300, 2210]
```

Plug the values for x into the regression line:
```
y = [-426 + 3.139(300) = 515.7,
     -426 + 3.139(2210) = 6511.19]
```

Complete x and y samples:
```
x = [300, 2210]
y = [3981, 9975]
```

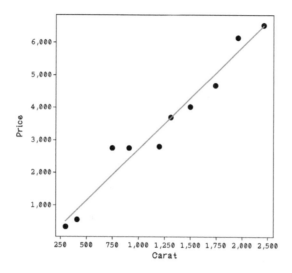

Figure 8.13 A regression line plotted with the data points

We've trained a linear regression line based on our dataset that accurately fits the data, so we've done some machine learning by hand.

EXERCISE: CALCULATE A REGRESSION LINE USING THE LEAST-SQUARES METHOD

Following the steps described and using the following dataset, calculate the regression line with the least-squares method.

	Carat (x)	Price (y)
1	320	350
2	460	560
3	800	2,760
4	910	2,800
5	1,350	2,900
6	1,390	3,600
7	1,650	4,000
8	1,700	4,650
9	1,950	6,100
10	2,000	6,500

SOLUTION: CALCULATE A REGRESSION LINE USING THE LEAST-SQUARES METHOD

The means for each dimension need to be calculated. The means are 1,253 for *x* and 3,422 for *y*. The next step is calculating the difference between each value and its mean. Next, the square of the difference between *x* and the mean of *x* is calculated and summed, which results in 3,251,610. Finally, the difference between *x* and the mean of *x* is multiplied by the difference between *y* and the mean of *y* and summed, resulting in 10,566,940.

	Carat (x)	Price (y)	x – mean of x	y – mean of y	(x – mean of x)^2	(x – mean of x) * (y – mean of y)
1	320	350	-933	-3,072	870,489	2,866,176
2	460	560	-793	-2,862	628,849	2,269,566
3	800	2,760	-453	-662	205,209	299,886
4	910	2,800	-343	-622	117,649	213,346
5	1,350	2,900	97	-522	9,409	-50,634
6	1,390	3,600	137	178	18,769	24,386
7	1,650	4,000	397	578	157,609	229,466
8	1,700	4,650	447	1,228	199,809	548,916
9	1,950	6,100	697	2,678	485,809	1,866,566
10	2,000	6,500	747	3,078	558,009	2,299,266
	1,253	3,422			3,251,610	10,566,940

The values can be used to calculate the slope, *m*:

```
m = 10566940 / 3251610
m = 3.25
```

Remember the equation for a line:

```
y = c + mx
```

Substitute the mean values for *x* and *y* and the newly calculated *m*:

```
3422 = c + 3.35 * 1253
c = -775.55
```

Substitute the minimum and maximum values for *x* to calculate points to plot a line:

```
Point 1, we use the minimum value for Carat: x = 320
y = 775.55 + 3.25 * 320
y = 1 815.55

Point 2, we use the maximum value for Carat: x = 2000
y = 775.55 + 3.25 * 2000
y = 7 275.55
```

Now that we have an intuition about how to use linear regression and how regression lines are calculated, let's take a look at the pseudocode.

Pseudocode

The code is similar to the steps that we walked through. The only interesting aspects are the two `for` loops used to calculate summed values by iterating over every element in the dataset:

```
fit_regression_line(carats, prices):
  let mean_X equal mean(carats)
  let mean_Y equal mean(price)
  let sum_x_squared equal 0
  for i in range(n):
    let ans equal (carats[i] - mean_X) ** 2
    sum_x_squared equal sum_x_squared + ans
  let sum_multiple equal 0
  for i in range(n):
    let ans equal (carats[i] - mean_X) * (price[i] - mean_Y)
    sum_multiple equal sum_multiple + ans
  let b1 equal sum_multiple / sum_x_squared
  let b0 equal mean_Y - (b1 * mean_X)
  let min_x equal min(carats)
  let max_x equal max(carats)
  let y1 equal b0 + b1 * min_x
  let y2 equal b0 + b1 * max_x
```

Express the first point of the regression line by $y = c + mx$

Express the second point of the regression line by $y = c + mx$

Testing the model: Determine the accuracy of the model

Now that we have determined a regression line, we can use it to make price predictions for other Carat values. We can measure the performance of the regression line with new examples in which we know the actual price and determine how accurate the linear regression model is.

We can't test the model with the same data that we used to train it. This approach would result in high accuracy and be meaningless. The trained model must be tested with real data that it hasn't been trained with.

Separating training and testing data

Training and testing data are usually split 80/20, with 80% of the available data used as training data and 20% used to test the model. Percentages are used because the number of examples needed to train a model accurately is difficult to know; different contexts and questions being asked may need more or less data.

Figure 8.14 and table 8.12 represent a set of testing data for the diamond example. Remember that we scaled the Carat values to be similar-size numbers to the Price values (all Carat values have been multiplied by 1,000) to make them easier to read and work with. The dots represent the testing data points, and the line represents the trained regression line.

Table 8.12 The carat and price data

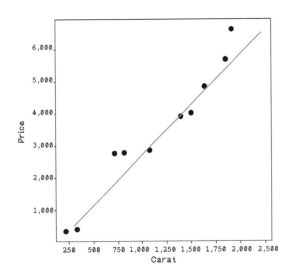

	Carat (x)	Price (y)
1	220	342
2	330	403
3	710	2,772
4	810	2,789
5	1,080	2,869
6	1,390	3,914
7	1,500	4,022
8	1,640	4,849
9	1,850	5,688
10	1,910	6,632

Figure 8.14 A regression line plotted with the data points

Testing a model involves making predictions with unseen training data and then comparing the accuracy of the model's prediction with the actual values. In the diamond example, we have the actual Price values, so we will determine what the model predicts and compare the difference.

Measuring the performance of the line

In linear regression, a common method of measuring the accuracy of the model is calculating R^2 (R squared). R^2 is used to determine the variance between the actual value and a predicted value. The following equation is used to calculate the R^2 score:

$$R^2 \; = \; \frac{\text{sum of (predicted y - mean of actual y)}^2}{\text{sum of (actual y - mean of actual y)}^2}$$

The first things we need to do, similar to the training step, are calculate the mean of the actual Price values, calculate the distances between the actual Price values and the mean of the prices, and then calculate the square of those values. We are using the values plotted as dots in figure 8.14 (table 8.13).

Table 8.13 The diamond dataset and calculations

	Carat (x)	Price (y)	y – mean of y	(y – mean of y)^2
1	220	342	-3,086	9,523,396
2	330	403	-3,025	9,150,625
3	710	2,772	-656	430,336
4	810	2,789	-639	408,321
5	1,080	2,869	-559	312,481
6	1,390	3,914	486	236,196
7	1,500	4,022	594	352,836
8	1,640	4,849	1,421	2,019,241
9	1,850	5,688	2,260	5,107,600
10	1,910	6,632	3,204	10,265,616
		3,428		37,806,648
		Mean		Sum

The next step is calculating the predicted Price value for every Carat value, squaring the values, and calculating the sum of all those values (table 8.14).

Table 8.14 The diamond dataset and calculations, part 2

	Carat (x)	Price (y)	y – mean of y	(y – mean of y)^2	Predicted y	Predicted y – mean of y	(Predicted y – mean of y)^2
1	220	342	-3,086	9,523,396	264	-3,164	10,009,876
2	330	403	-3,025	9,150,625	609	-2,819	7,944,471
3	710	2,772	-656	430,336	1,802	-1,626	2,643,645
4	810	2,789	-639	408,321	2,116	-1,312	1,721,527
5	1,080	2,869	-559	312,481	2,963	-465	215,900
6	1,390	3,914	486	236,196	3,936	508	258,382
7	1,500	4,022	594	352,836	4,282	854	728,562
8	1,640	4,849	1,421	2,019,241	4,721	1,293	1,671,748
9	1,850	5,688	2,260	5,107,600	5,380	1,952	3,810,559
10	1,910	6,632	3,204	10,265,616	5,568	2,140	4,581,230
		3,428		3,7806,648			33,585,901
		Mean		Sum			Sum

Using the sum of the square of the difference between the predicted price and mean, and the sum of the square of the difference between the actual price and mean, we can calculate the R^2 score:

$$R^2 = \frac{\text{sum of (predicted y - mean of actual y)}^2}{\text{sum of (actual y - mean of actual y)}^2}$$

$$R^2 = 33585901 / 37806648$$
$$R^2 = 0.88$$

The result—0.88—means that the model is 88% accurate to the new unseen data. This result is a fairly good one, showing that the linear regression model is fairly accurate. For the diamond example, this result is satisfactory. Determining whether the accuracy is satisfactory for the problem we're trying to solve depends on the domain of the problem. We will be exploring performance of machine learning models in the next section.

Additional information: For a gentle introduction to fitting lines to data, reference http://mng.bz/Ed5q—a chapter from *Math for Programmers* by Manning Publications. Linear regression can be applied to more dimensions. We can determine the relationship among Carat values, prices, and cut of diamonds, for example, through a process called *multiple regression*. This process adds some complexity to the calculations, but the fundamental principles remain the same.

Improving accuracy

After training a model on data and measuring how well it performs on new testing data, we have an idea of how well the model performs. Often, models don't perform as well as desired, and additional work needs to be done to improve the model, if possible. This improvement involves iterating on the various steps in the machine learning life cycle (figure 8.15).

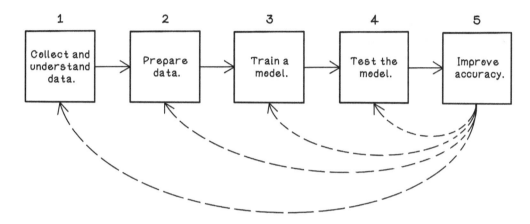

Figure 8.15 A refresher on the machine learning life cycle

The results may require us to pay attention to one or more of the following areas. Machine learning is experimental work in which different tactics at different stages are tested before settling on the best-performing approach. In the diamond example, if the model that used Carat values to predict Price performed poorly, we might use the dimensions of the diamond that indicate size, coupled with the Carat value, to try to predict the price more accurately. Here are some ways to improve the accuracy of the model:

- *Collect more data.* One solution may be to collect more data related to the dataset that is being explored, perhaps augmenting the data with relevant external data or including data that previously was not considered.

- *Prepare the data differently.* The data used for training may need to be prepared in a different way. Referring to the techniques used to fix data earlier in this chapter, there may be errors in the approach. We may need to use different techniques to find values for missing data, replace ambiguous data, and encode categorical data.

- *Choose different features in the data.* Other features in the dataset may be better suited to predicting the dependent variable. The X dimension value might be a good choice to predict the Table value, for example, because it has a physical relationship with it, as shown in the diamond terminology figure (figure 8.5), whereas predicting Clarity with the X dimension is meaningless.

- *Use a different algorithm to train the model.* Sometimes, the selected algorithm is not suited to the problem being solved or the nature of the data. We can use a different algorithm to accomplish different goals, as discussed in the next section.

- *Dealing with false-positive tests.* Tests can be deceiving. A good test score may show that the model performs well, but when the model is presented with unseen data, it might perform poorly. This problem can be due to overfitting the data. *Overfitting* is when the model is too closely aligned with the training data and is not flexible for dealing with new data with more variance. This approach is usually applicable to classification problems, which we also dive into in the next section.

If linear regression didn't provide useful results, or if we have a different question to ask, we can try a range of other algorithms. The next two sections will explore algorithms to use when the question is different in its nature.

Classification with decision trees

Simply put, classification problems involve assigning a label to an example based on its attributes. These problems are different from regression, in which a value is estimated. Let's dive into classification problems and see how to solve them.

Classification problems: Either this or that

We have learned that regression involves predicting a value based on one or more other variables, such as predicting the price of a diamond given its Carat value. Classification is similar in that it aims to predict a value but predicts discrete classes instead of continuous values. Discrete values are categorical features of a dataset such as Cut, Color, or Clarity in the diamond dataset, as opposed to continuous values such as Price or Depth.

Here's another example. Suppose that we have several vehicles that are cars and trucks. We will measure the weight of each vehicle and the number of wheels of each vehicle. We also forget for now that cars and trucks look different. Almost all cars have four wheels, and many large trucks have more than four wheels. Trucks are usually heavier than cars, but a large sport-utility vehicle may be as heavy as a small truck. We could find relationships between the weight and number of wheels of vehicles to predict whether a vehicle is a car or a truck (figure 8.16).

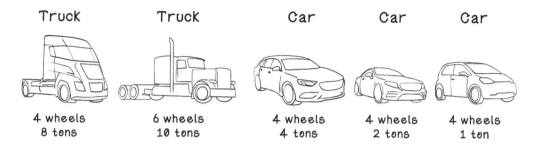

Figure 8.16 Example vehicles for potential classification based
on the number of wheels and weight

EXERCISE: REGRESSION VS. CLASSIFICATION

Consider the following scenarios, and determine whether each one is a regression or classification problem:

1. Based on data about rats, we have a life-expectancy feature and an obesity feature. We're trying to find a correlation between the two features.

2. Based on data about animals, we have the weight of each animal and whether or not it has wings. We're trying to determine which animals are birds.

3. Based on data about computing devices, we have the screen size, weight, and operating system of several devices. We want to determine which devices are tablets, laptops, or phones.

4. Based on data about weather, we have the amount of rainfall and a humidity value. We want to determine the humidity in different rainfall seasons.

SOLUTION: REGRESSION VS. CLASSIFICATION

1. *Regression*—The relationship between two variables is being explored. Life expectancy is the dependent variable, and obesity is the independent variable.

2. *Classification*—We are classifying an example as a bird or not a bird, using the weight and the wing characteristic of the examples.

3. *Classification*—An example is being classified as a tablet, laptop, or phone by using its other characteristics.

4. *Regression*—The relationship between rainfall and humidity is being explored. Humidity is the dependent variable, and rainfall is the independent variable.

The basics of decision trees

Different algorithms are used for regression and classification problems. Some popular algorithms include support vector machines, decision trees, and random forests. In this section, we will be looking at a decision-tree algorithm to learn classification.

Decision trees are structures that describe a series of decisions that are made to find a solution to a problem (figure 8.17). If we're deciding whether to wear shorts for the day, we might make a series of decisions to inform the outcome. Will it be cold during the day? If not, will we be out late in the evening, when it does get cold? We might decide to wear shorts on a warm day, but not if we will be out when it gets cold.

Should I wear shorts today?

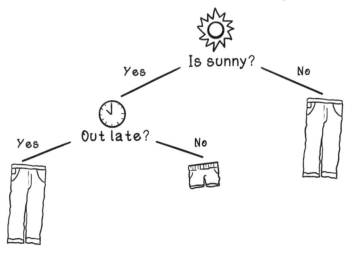

Figure 8.17 Example of a basic decision tree

For the diamond example, we will try to predict the cut of a diamond based on the Carat and Price values by using a decision tree. To simplify this example, assume that we're a diamond dealer who doesn't care about each specific cut. We will group the different cuts into two broader categories. Fair and Good cuts will be grouped into a category called Okay, and Very Good, Premium, and Ideal cuts will be grouped into a category called Perfect.

1	Fair	1	Okay
2	Good		
3	Very Good	2	Perfect
4	Premium		
5	Ideal		

Our sample dataset now looks like table 8.15.

Table 8.15 The dataset used for the classification example

	Carat	Price	Cut
1	0.21	327	Okay
2	0.39	897	Perfect
3	0.50	1,122	Perfect
4	0.76	907	Okay
5	0.87	2,757	Okay
6	0.98	2,865	Okay
7	1.13	3,045	Perfect
8	1.34	3,914	Perfect
9	1.67	4,849	Perfect
10	1.81	5,688	Perfect

By looking at the values in this small example and intuitively looking for patterns, we might notice something. The price seems to spike significantly after 0.98 carats, and the increased price seems to correlate with the diamonds that are Perfect, whereas diamonds with smaller Carat values tend to be Average. But example 3, which is Perfect, has a small Carat value. Figure 8.18 shows what would happen if we were to create questions to filter the data and categorize it by hand. Notice that decision nodes contain our questions, and leaf nodes contain examples that have been categorized.

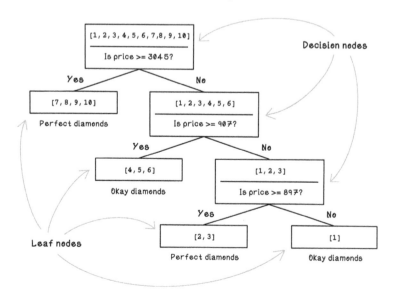

Figure 8.18 Example of a decision tree designed through human intuition

With the small dataset, we could easily categorize the diamonds by hand. In real-world datasets, however, there are thousands of examples to work through, with possibly thousands of features, making it close to impossible for a person to create a decision tree by hand. This is where decision tree algorithms come in. Decision trees can create the questions that filter the examples. A decision tree finds the patterns that we might miss and is more accurate in its filtering.

Training decision trees

To create a tree that is intelligent in making the right decisions to classify diamonds, we need a training algorithm to learn from the data. There is a family of algorithms for decision tree learning, and we will use a specific one named CART (Classification and Regression Tree). The foundation of CART and the other tree learning algorithms is this: decide what questions to ask and when to ask those questions to best filter the examples into their respective categories. In the diamond example, the algorithm must learn the best questions to ask about the Carat and Price values, and when to ask them, to best segment Average and Perfect diamonds.

Data structures for decision trees

To help us understand how the decisions of the tree will be structured, we can review the following data structures, which organize logic and data in a way that's suitable for the decision tree learning algorithm:

- *Map of classes/label groupings*—A *map* is a key-value pair of elements that cannot have two keys that are the same. This structure is useful for storing the number of examples that match a specific label and will be useful to store the values required for calculating entropy, also known as *uncertainty*. We'll learn about entropy soon.

- *Tree of nodes*—As depicted in the previous tree figure (figure 8.18), several nodes are linked to compose a tree. This example may be familiar from some of the earlier chapters. The nodes in the tree are important for filtering/partitioning the examples into categories:

  ◦ *Decision node*—A node in which the dataset is being split or filtered.

    - Question: What question is being asked? (See the Question point coming up).

    - True examples: The examples that satisfy the question.

    - False examples: The examples that don't satisfy the question.

  ◦ *Examples node/leaf node*—A node containing a list of examples only. All examples in this list would have been categorized correctly.

- *Question*—A question can be represented differently depending on how flexible it can be. We could ask, "Is the Carat value > 0.5 and < 1.13?" To keep this example simple to understand, the question is a variable feature, a variable value, and the >= operator: "Is Carat >= 0.5?" or "Is Price >=3,045?"

- ° *Feature*—The feature that is being interrogated

- ° *Value*—The constant value that the comparing value must be greater than or equal to

Decision-tree learning life cycle

This section discusses how a decision-tree algorithm filters data with decisions to classify a dataset correctly. Figure 8.19 shows the steps involved in training a decision tree. The flow described in figure 8.19 is covered throughout the rest of this section.

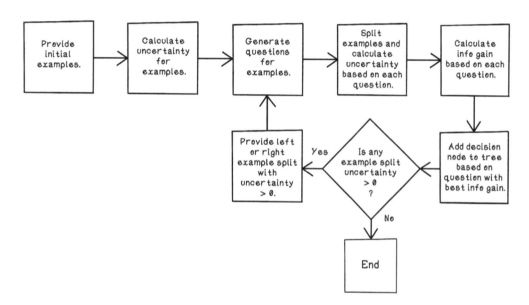

Figure 8.19 A basic flow for building a decision tree

In building a decision tree, we test all possible questions to determine which one is the best question to ask at a specific point in the decision tree. To test a question, we use the concept of *entropy*—the measurement of uncertainty of a dataset. If we had 5 Perfect diamonds and 5 Okay diamonds, and tried to pick a Perfect diamond by randomly selecting a diamond from the 10, what are the chances that the diamond would be Perfect (figure 8.20)?

Figure 8.20 Example of uncertainty

Given an initial dataset of diamonds with the Carat, Price, and Cut features, we can determine the uncertainty of the dataset by using the Gini index. A Gini index of 0 means that the dataset has no uncertainty and is pure; it might have 10 Perfect diamonds, for example. Figure 8.21 describes how the Gini index is calculated.

	Carat	Price	Cut
1	0.21	327	Okay
2	0.39	897	Perfect
3	0.50	1,122	Perfect
4	0.76	907	Okay
5	0.87	2,757	Okay
6	0.98	2,865	Okay
7	1.13	3,045	Okay
8	1.34	3,914	Perfect
9	1.67	4,849	Perfect
10	1.81	5,688	Perfect

$$\text{Gini} = 1 - (\text{Okay count} / \text{total})^2 - (\text{Perfect count} / \text{total})^2$$

$$\text{Gini} = 1 - (5 / 10)^2 + (5 / 10)^2$$
$$\text{Gini} = 1 - (0.5)^2 - (0.5)^2$$
$$\text{Gini} = 1 - 0.5$$
$$\text{Gini} = 0.5$$

Figure 8.21 The Gini index calculation

The Gini index is 0.5, so there's a 50% chance of choosing an incorrectly labeled example if one is randomly selected, as shown in figure 8.20 earlier.

The next step is creating a decision node to split the data. The decision node includes a question that can be used to split the data in a sensible way and decrease the uncertainty. Remember that 0 means no uncertainty. We aim to partition the dataset into subsets with zero uncertainty.

Many questions are generated based on every feature of each example to split the data and determine the best split outcome. Because we have 2 features and 10 examples, the total number of questions generated would be 20. Figure 8.22 depicts some of the questions asked—simple questions about whether the value of a feature is greater than or equal to a specific value.

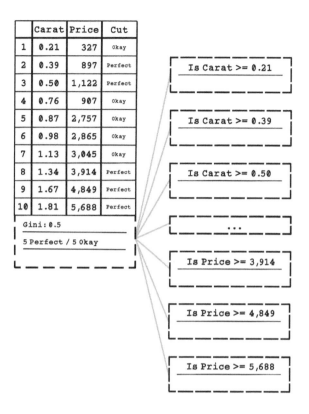

Figure 8.22 An example of questions asked to split the data with a decision node

Uncertainty in a dataset is determined by the *Gini index,* and questions aim to reduce uncertainty. *Entropy* is another concept that measures disorder using the Gini index for a specific split of data based on a question asked. We must have a way to determine how well a question reduced uncertainty, and we accomplish this task by measuring information gain. *Information gain* describes the amount of information gained by asking a specific question. If a lot of information is gained, the uncertainty is smaller.

Information gain is calculated by the subtracting entropy before the question is asked by the entropy after the question is asked, following these steps:

1. Split the dataset by asking a question.

2. Measure the Gini index for the left split.

3. Measure the entropy for the left split compared with the dataset before the split.

4. Measure the Gini index for the right split.

5. Measure the entropy for the right split compared with the dataset before the split.

6. Calculate the total entropy after by adding the left entropy and right entropy.

7. Calculate the information gain by subtracting the total entropy after from the total entropy before.

Figure 8.23 illustrates the data split and information gain for the question "Is Price >= 3914?"

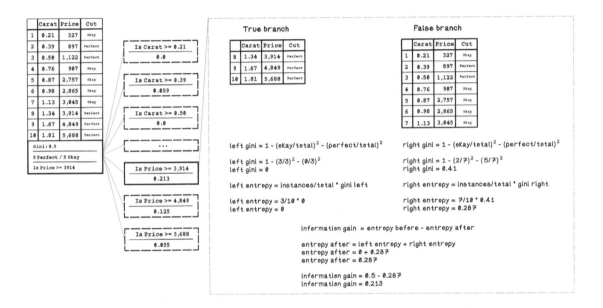

Figure 8.23 Illustration of data split and information gain based on a question

In the example in figure 8.23, the information gain for all questions is calculated, and the question with the highest information gain is selected as the best question to ask at that point in the tree. Then the original dataset is split based on the decision node with the question "Is Price >= 3,914?" A decision node containing this question is added to the decision tree, and the left and right splits stem from that node.

In figure 8.24, after the dataset is split, the left side contains a pure dataset of Perfect diamonds only, and the right side contains a dataset with mixed diamond classifications, including two Perfect diamonds and five Okay diamonds. Another question must be asked on the right side of the dataset to split the dataset further. Again, several questions are generated by using the features of each example in the dataset.

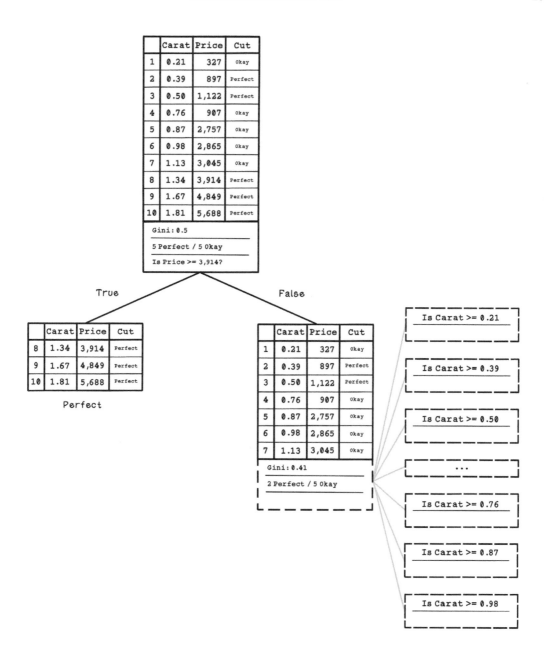

Figure 8.24 The resulting decision tree after the first decision node and possible questions

EXERCISE: CALCULATING UNCERTAINTY AND INFORMATION GAIN FOR A QUESTION

Using the knowledge gained and figure 8.23 as a guide, calculate the information gain for the question "Is Carat >= 0.76?"

SOLUTION: CALCULATING UNCERTAINTY AND INFORMATION GAIN FOR A QUESTION

The solution depicted in figure 8.25 highlights the reuse of the pattern of calculations that determine the entropy and information gain, given a question. Feel free to practice more questions and compare the results with the information-gain values in the figure.

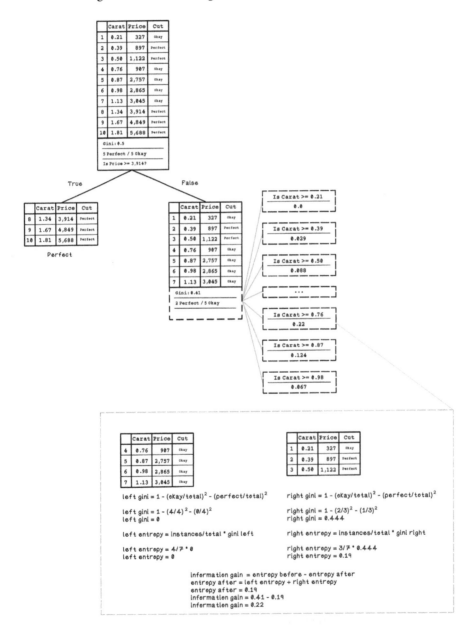

Figure 8.25 Illustration of data split and information gain based on a question at the second level

The process of splitting, generating questions, and determining information gained happens recursively until the dataset is completely categorized by questions. Figure 8.26 shows the complete decision tree, including all the questions asked and the resulting splits.

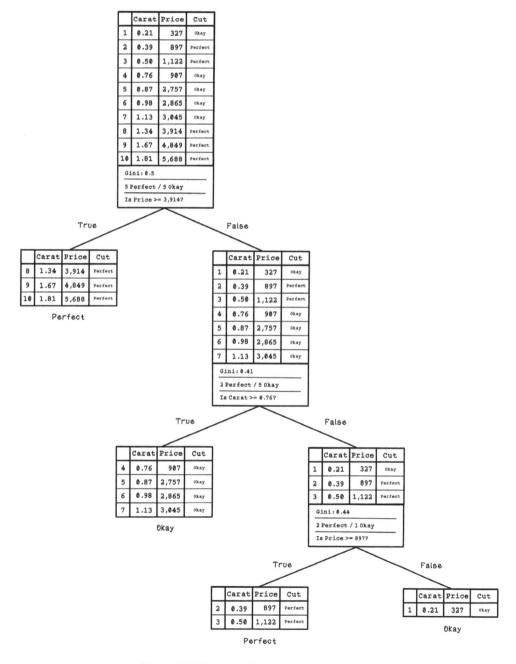

Figure 8.26 The complete trained decision tree

It is important to note that decision trees are usually trained with a much larger sample of data. The questions asked need to be more general to accommodate a wider variety of data and, thus, would need a variety of examples to learn from.

Pseudocode

When programming a decision tree from scratch, the first step is counting the number of examples of each class—in this case, the number of Okay diamonds and the number of Perfect diamonds:

```
find_unique_label_counts(examples):
  let class_count equal empty map
  for example in examples:
    let label equal example['quality']
    if label not in class_count:
      let class_count[label] equal 0
    class_count[label] equal class_count[label] + 1
  return class_count
```

Next, examples are split based on a question. Examples that satisfy the question are stored in examples_true, and the rest are stored in examples_false:

```
split_examples(examples, question):
  let examples_true equal empty array
  let examples_false equal empty array
  for example in examples:
    if question.filter(example):
      append example to examples_true
    else:
      append example to examples_false
  return examples_true, examples_false
```

We need a function that calculates the Gini index for a set of examples. The next function calculates the Gini index by using the method described in figure 8.23:

```
calculate_gini(examples):
  let label_counts equal find_unique_label_counts(examples)
  let uncertainty equal 1
  for label in label_counts:
    let probability_of_label equal label_counts[label] / length(examples))
    uncertainty equals uncertainty - probability_of_label ^ 2
  return uncertainty
```

information_gain uses the left and right splits and the current uncertainty to determine the information gain:

```
calculate_information_gain(left, right, current_uncertainty):
  let total equal length(left) + length(right)
  let left_gini equal calculate_gini(left)
  let left_entropy equal length(left) / total * left_gini
  let right_gini equal calculate_gini(right)
  let right_entropy equal length(right) / total * right_gini
  let uncertainty_after equal left_entropy + right_entropy
  let information_gain equal current_uncertainty - uncertainty_after
  return information_gain
```

The next function may look daunting, but it's iterating over all the features and their values in the dataset, and finding the best information gain to determine the best question to ask:

```
find_best_split(examples, number_of_features):
  let best_gain equal 0
  let best_question equal None
  let current_uncertainty equal calculate_gini(examples)
  for feature_index in range(number_of_features):
    let values equal [example[feature_index] for example in examples]
    for value in values:
      let question equal Question(feature_index, value)
      let true_examples, false_examples equal
        split_examples(examples, question)
      if length(true_examples) != 0 or length(false_examples) != 0:
        let gain equal calculate_information_gain
            (true_examples, false_examples, current_uncertainty)
        if gain >= best_gain:
          best_gain, best_question equal gain, question
  return best_gain, best_question
```

The next function ties everything together, using the functions defined previously to build a decision tree:

```
build_tree(examples, number_of_features):
  let gain, question equal find_best_split(examples, number_of_features)
  if gain == 0:
    return ExamplesNode(examples)
  let true_examples, false_examples equal split_examples(examples, question)
  let true_branch equal build_tree(true_examples)
  let false_branch equal build_tree(false_examples)
  return DecisionNode(question, true_branch, false_branch)
```

Note that this function is recursive. It splits the data and recursively splits the resulting dataset until there is no information gain, indicating that the examples cannot be split any further. As a reminder, decision nodes are used to split the examples, and example nodes are used to store split sets of examples.

We've now learned how to build a decision-tree classifier. Remember that the trained decision-tree model will be tested with unseen data, similar to the linear regression approach explored earlier.

One problem with decision trees is overfitting, which occurs when the model is trained too well on several examples but performs poorly for new examples. Overfitting happens when the model learns the patterns of the training data but new real-world data is slightly different and doesn't meet the splitting criteria of the trained model. A model with 100% accuracy is usually overfitted to the data. Some examples are classified incorrectly in an ideal model as a consequence of the model being more general to support different cases. Overfitting can happen with any machine learning model, not just decision trees.

Figure 8.27 illustrates the concept of overfitting. Underfitting includes too many incorrect classifications, and overfitting includes too few or no incorrect classifications; the ideal is somewhere in between.

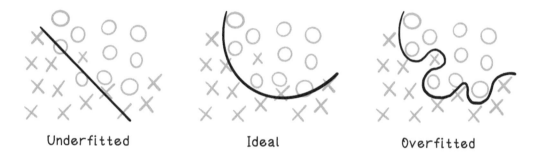

Figure 8.27 Underfitting, ideal, and overfitting

Classifying examples with decision trees

Now that a decision tree has been trained and the right questions have been determined, we can test it by providing it new data to classify. The model that we're referring to is the decision tree of questions that was created by the training step.

To test the model, we provide several new examples of data and measure whether they have been classified correctly, so we need to know the labeling of the testing data. In the diamond example, we need more diamond data, including the Cut feature, to test the decision tree (table 8.16).

Table 8.16 The diamond dataset for classification

	Carat	Price	Cut
1	0.26	689	Perfect
2	0.41	967	Perfect
3	0.52	1,012	Perfect
4	0.76	907	Okay
5	0.81	2,650	Okay
6	0.90	2,634	Okay
7	1.24	2,999	Perfect
8	1.42	3850	Perfect
9	1.61	4,345	Perfect
10	1.78	3,100	Okay

Figure 8.28 illustrates the decision-tree model that we trained, which will be used to process the new examples. Each example is fed through the tree and classified.

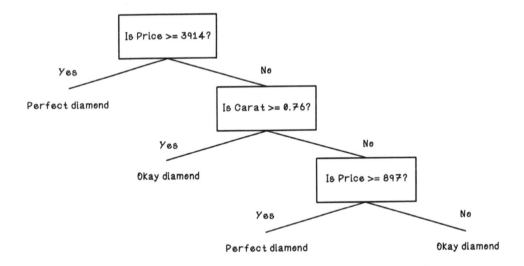

Figure 8.28 The decision tree model that will process new examples

The resulting predicted classifications are detailed in table 8.17. Assume that we're trying to predict Okay diamonds. Notice that three examples are incorrect. That result is 3 of 10, which means that the model predicted 7 of 10, or 70% of the testing data correctly. This performance isn't terrible, but it illustrates how examples can be misclassified.

Table 8.17 The diamond dataset for classification and predictions

	Carat	Price	Cut	Prediction	
1	0.26	689	Okay	Okay	✓
2	0.41	880	Perfect	Perfect	✓
3	0.52	1,012	Perfect	Perfect	✓
4	0.76	907	Okay	Okay	✓
5	0.81	2,650	Okay	Okay	✓
6	0.90	2,634	Okay	Okay	✓
7	1.24	2,999	**Perfect**	**Okay**	†
8	1.42	3,850	**Perfect**	**Okay**	†
9	1.61	4,345	Perfect	Perfect	✓
10	1.78	3,100	**Okay**	**Perfect**	†

A confusion matrix is often used to measure the performance of a model with testing data. A *confusion matrix* describes the performance using the following metrics (figure 8.29):

- *True positive (TP)*—Correctly classified examples as Okay
- *True negative (TN)*—Correctly classified examples as Perfect
- *False positive (FP)*—Perfect examples classified as Okay
- *False negative (FN)*—Okay examples classified as Perfect

	Predicted positive	Predicted negative	
Actual positive	True positive TP	False negative FN	Sensitivity TP / TP + FN
Actual negative	False positive FP	True negative TN	Specificity TN / TN + FP
	Precision TP / TP + FP	Negative precision TN / TN + FN	Accuracy $\dfrac{TP + TN}{TP + TN + FP + FN}$

Figure 8.29 A confusion matrix

The outcomes of testing the model with unseen examples can be used to deduce several measurements:

- *Precision*—How often Okay examples are classified correctly

- *Negative precision*—How often Perfect examples are classified correctly

- *Sensitivity or recall*—Also known as the *true-positive rate*; the ratio of correctly classified Okay diamonds to all the actual Okay diamonds in the training set

- *Specificity*—Also known as the *true-negative rate*; the ratio of correctly classified Perfect diamonds to all actual Perfect diamonds in the training set

- *Accuracy*—How often the classifier is correct overall between classes

Figure 8.30 shows the resulting confusion matrix, with the results of the diamond example listed as input. Accuracy is important, but the other measurements can unveil additional useful information about the model's performance.

	Predicted positive	Predicted negative	
Actual positive	True positive 4	False negative 1	Sensitivity $4 / 4 + 1 = 0.8$
Actual negative	False positive 2	True negative 3	Specificity $3 / 3 + 2 = 0.6$
	Precision $4 / 6 = 0.67$	Negative precision $3 / 4 = 0.75$	Accuracy $\frac{7}{10} = 0.7$

Figure 8.30 Confusion matrix for the diamond test example

By using these measurements, we can make more-informed decisions in a machine learning life cycle to improve the performance of the model. As mentioned throughout this chapter, machine learning is an experimental exercise involving some trial and error. These metrics are guides in this process.

Other popular machine learning algorithms

This chapter explores two popular and fundamental machine learning algorithms. The linear-regression algorithm is used for regression problems in which the relationships between features are discovered. The decision-tree algorithm is used for classification problems in which the relationships between features and categories of examples are discovered. But many other machine learning algorithms are suitable in different contexts and for solving different problems. Figure 8.31 illustrates some popular algorithms and shows how they fit into the machine learning landscape.

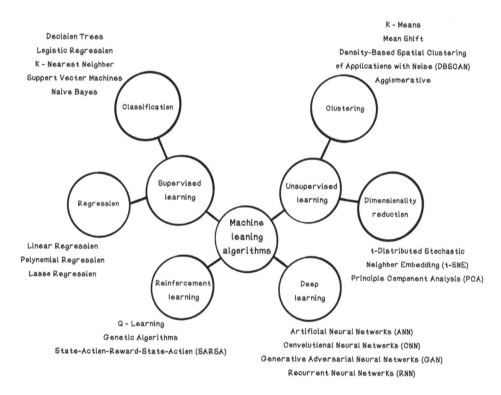

Figure 8.31 A map of popular machine learning algorithms

The classification and regression algorithms satisfy problems similar to the ones explored in this chapter. Unsupervised learning contains algorithms that can help with some of the data preparation steps, find hidden underlying relationships in data, and inform what questions can be asked in a machine learning experiment.

Notice the introduction of deep learning in figure 8.31. Chapter 9 covers artificial neural networks—a key concept in deep learning. This chapter will give us a better understanding of the types of problems that can be solved with these approaches and how the algorithms are implemented.

Use cases for machine learning algorithms

Machine learning can be applied in almost every industry to solve a plethora of problems in different domains. Given the right data and the right questions, the possibilities are potentially endless. We have all interacted with a product or service that uses some aspect of machine learning and data modeling in our everyday lives. This section highlights some of the popular ways machine learning can be used to solve real-world problems at scale:

- *Fraud and threat detection*—Machine learning has been used to detect and prevent fraudulent transactions in the finance industry. Financial institutions have gained a wealth of transactional information over the years, including fraudulent transaction reports from their customers. These fraud reports are an input to labeling and characterizing fraudulent transactions. The models might consider the location of the transaction, the amount, the merchant, and so on to classify transactions, saving consumers from potential losses and the financial institution from insurance losses. The same model can be applied to network threat detection to detect and prevent attacks based on known network use and reported unusual behavior.

- *Product and content recommendations*—Many of us use e-commerce sites to purchase goods or media streaming services for audio and video consumption. Products may be recommended to us based on what we're purchasing, or content may be recommended based on our interests. This functionality is usually enabled by machine learning, in which patterns in purchase or viewing behavior is derived from people's interactions. Recommender systems are being used in more and more industries and applications to enable more sales or provide a better user experience.

- *Dynamic product and service pricing*—Products and services are often priced based on what someone is willing to pay for them or based on risk. For a ride-sharing system, it might make sense to hike the price if there are fewer available cars than the demand for a ride, sometimes referred to as *surge pricing*. In the insurance industry, a price might be hiked if a person is categorized as high-risk. Machine learning is used to find the attributes and relationships between the attributes that influence pricing based on dynamic conditions and details about a unique individual.

- *Health-condition risk prediction*—The medical industry requires health professionals to acquire an abundance of knowledge so that they can diagnose and treat patients. Over the years, they have gained a vast amount of data about patients: blood types, DNA, family-illness history, geographic location, lifestyle, and more. This data can be used to find potential patterns that can guide the diagnosis of illness. The power of using data to find diagnoses is that we can treat conditions before they mature. Additionally, by feeding the outcomes back into the machine learning system, we can strengthen its reliability in making predictions.

SUMMARY OF MACHINE LEARNING

Machine learning is more about context, understanding data, and asking the right questions than algorithms.

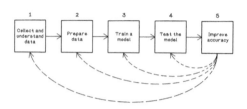

The life cycle of ML projects is iterative and experimental.

Linear regression involves finding the best line to fit the data, which means minimizing the error to each data point.

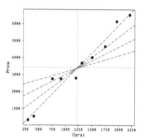

Possible regression lines

Decision trees split data using questions until the dataset is perfectly split into categories. The key concept is reducing uncertainty in the dataset.

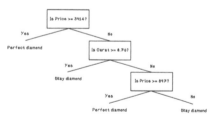

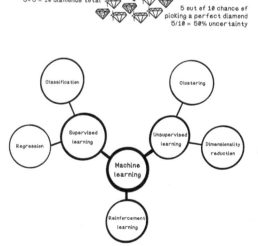

Different ML algorithms are used to answer different types of questions and achieve different goals in different contexts.

This chapter covers

- Understanding the inspiration and intuition of artificial neural networks

- Identifying problems that can be solved with artificial neural networks

- Understanding and implementing forward propagation using a trained network

- Understanding and implementing backpropagation to train a network

- Designing artificial neural network architectures to tackle different problems

What are artificial neural networks?

Artificial neural networks (ANNs) are powerful tools in the machine learning toolkit, used in a variety of ways to accomplish objectives such as image recognition, natural language processing, and game playing. ANNs learn in a similar way to other machine learning algorithms: by using training data. They are best suited to unstructured data where it's difficult to understand how features relate to one another. This chapter covers the inspiration of ANNs; it also shows how the algorithm works and how ANNs are designed to solve different problems.

To gain a clear understanding of how ANNs fit into the bigger machine learning landscape, we should review the composition and categorization of machine learning algorithms. *Deep learning* is the name given to algorithms that use ANNs in varying architectures to accomplish an objective. Deep learning, including ANNs, can be used to solve supervised learning, unsupervised learning, and reinforcement learning problems. Figure 9.1 shows how deep learning relates to ANNs and other machine learning concepts.

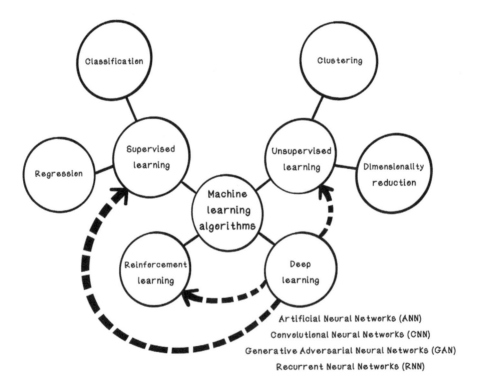

Figure 9.1 A map describing the flexibility of deep learning and ANNs

ANNs can be seen as just another model in the machine learning life cycle (chapter 8). Figure 9.2 recaps that life cycle. A problem needs to be identified; that data needs to be collected, understood, and prepared; and the ANN model will be tested and improved if necessary.

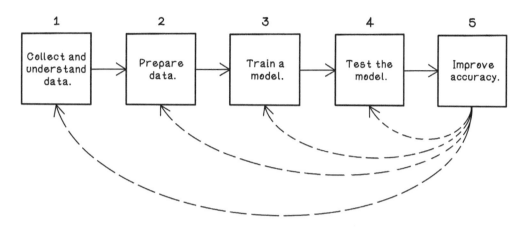

Figure 9.2 A workflow for machine learning experiments and projects

Now that we have an idea of how ANNs fit into the abstract machine learning landscape and know that an ANN is another model that is trained in the life cycle, let's explore the intuition and workings of ANNs. Like genetic algorithms and swarm-intelligence algorithms, ANNs are inspired by natural phenomena—in this case, the brain and nervous system. The nervous system is a biological structure that allows us to feel sensations and is the basis of how our brains operate. We have nerves across our entire bodies and neurons that behave similarly in our brains.

Neural networks consist of interconnected neurons that pass information by using electrical and chemical signals. Neurons pass information to other neurons and adjust information to accomplish a specific function. When you grab a cup and take a sip of water, millions of neurons process the intention of what you want to do, the physical action to accomplish it, and the feedback to determine whether you were successful. Think about little children learning to drink from a cup. They usually start out poorly, dropping the cup a lot. Then they learn to grab it with two hands. Gradually, they learn to grab the cup with a single hand and take a sip without any problems. This process takes months. What's happening is that their brains and nervous systems are learning through practice or training. Figure 9.3 depicts a simplified model of receiving inputs (stimuli), processing them in a neural network, and providing outputs (response).

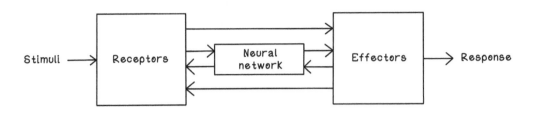

Figure 9.3 A simplified model of a biological neural system

Simplified, a *neuron* (figure 9.4) consists of dendrites that receive signals from other neurons; a cell body and a nucleus that activates and adjusts the signal; an axon that passes the signal to other neurons; and synapses that carry, and in the process adjust, the signal before it is passed to the next neuron's dendrites. Through approximately 90 billion neurons working together, our brains can function at the high level of intelligence that we know.

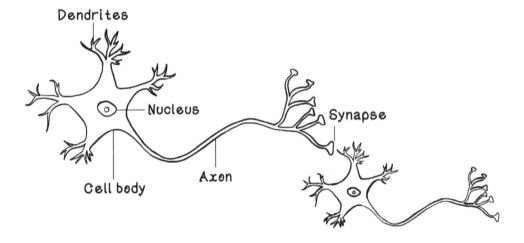

Figure 9.4 The general composition of neurons

Although ANNs are inspired by biological neural networks and use many of the concepts that are observed in these systems, ANNs are not identical representations of biological neural systems. We still have a lot to learn about the brain and nervous system.

The Perceptron: A representation of a neuron

The neuron is the fundamental concept that makes up the brain and nervous system. As mentioned earlier, it accepts many inputs from other neurons, processes those inputs, and transfers the result to other connected neurons. ANNs are based on the fundamental concept of the *Perceptron*—a logical representation of a single biological neuron.

Like neurons, the Perceptron receives inputs (like dendrites), alters these inputs by using weights (like synapses), processes the weighted inputs (like the cell body and nucleus), and outputs a result (like axons). The Perceptron is loosely based on a neuron. You may notice that the synapses are depicted after the dendrites, representing the influence of synapses on incoming inputs. Figure 9.5 depicts the logical architecture of the Perceptron.

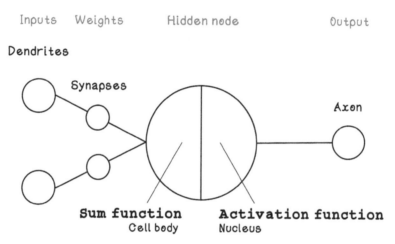

Figure 9.5 Logical architecture of the Perceptron

The components of the Perceptron are described by variables that are useful in calculating the output. Weights modify the inputs; that value is processed by a hidden node; and finally, the result is provided as the output.

Here is a brief description of the components of the Perceptron:

- *Inputs*—Describe the input values. In a neuron, these values would be an input signal.

- *Weights*—Describe the weights on each connection between an input and the hidden node. Weights influence the intensity of an input and result in a weighted input. In a neuron, these connections would be the synapses.

- *Hidden node (sum and activation)*—Sums the weighted input values and then applies an activation function to the summed result. An activation function determines the activation/output of the hidden node/neuron.

- *Output*—Describes the final output of the Perceptron.

To understand the workings of the Perceptron, we will examine the use of one by revisiting the apartment-hunting example from chapter 8. Suppose that we are real estate agents trying to determine whether a specific apartment will be rented within a month, based on the size of the apartment and the price of the apartment. Assume that a Perceptron has already been trained, meaning that the weights for the Perceptron have already been adjusted. We explore the way Perceptions and ANNs are trained later in this chapter; for now, understand that the weights encode relationships among the inputs by adjusting the strength of inputs.

Figure 9.6 shows how we can use a pretrained Perceptron to classify whether an apartment will be rented. The inputs represent the price of a specific apartment and the size of that apartment. We're also using the maximum price and size to scale the inputs ($8,000 for maximum price and 80 square meters for maximum size). For more about scaling data, see the next section.

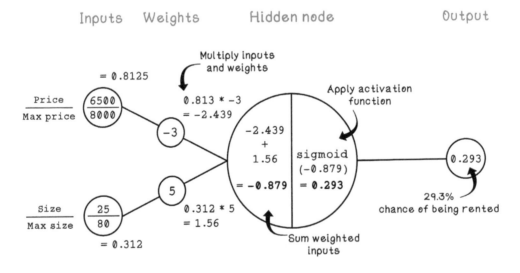

Figure 9.6 An example of using a trained Perceptron

Notice that the price and size are the inputs and that the predicted chance of the apartment being rented is the output. The weights are key to achieving the prediction. Weights are the variables in the network that learn relationships among inputs. The summation and activation functions are used to process the inputs multiplied by the weights to make a prediction.

Notice that we're using an activation function called the sigmoid function. Activation functions play a critical role in the Perceptron and ANNs. In this case, the activation function is helping us solve a linear problem. But when we look at ANNs in the next section, we will see how activation functions are useful for receiving inputs to solve non-linear problems. Figure 9.7 describes the basics of linear problems.

The sigmoid function results in an S curve between 0 and 1, given inputs between 0 and 1. Because the sigmoid function allows changes in *x* to result in small changes in *y*, it allows for gradual learning. When we get to the deeper workings of ANNs later in this chapter, we will see how this function helps solve nonlinear problems as well.

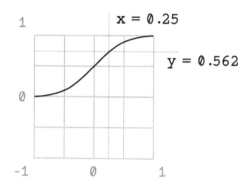

Figure 9.7 The sigmoid function

Let's take a step back and look at the data that we're using for the Perceptron. Understanding the data related to whether an apartment was sold is important for understanding what the Perceptron is doing. Figure 9.8 illustrates the examples in the dataset, including the price and size of each apartment. Each apartment is labeled as one of two classes: rented or not rented. The line separating the two classes is the function described by the Perceptron.

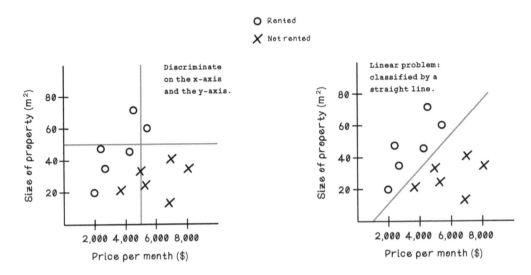

Figure 9.8 Example of a linear classification problem

Although the Perceptron is useful for solving linear problems, it cannot solve nonlinear problems. If a dataset cannot be classified by a straight line, the Perceptron will fail.

ANNs use the concept of the Perceptron at scale. Many neurons similar to the Perceptron work together to solve nonlinear problems in many dimensions. Note that the activation function used influences the learning capabilities of the ANN.

EXERCISE: CALCULATE THE OUTPUT OF THE FOLLOWING INPUT FOR THE PERCEPTRON

Using your knowledge of how the Perceptron works, calculate the output for the following:

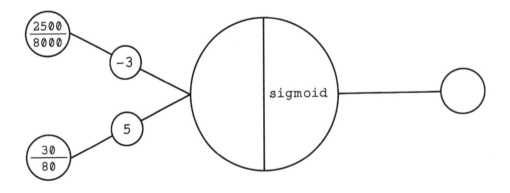

SOLUTION: CALCULATE THE OUTPUT OF THE FOLLOWING INPUT FOR THE PERCEPTRON

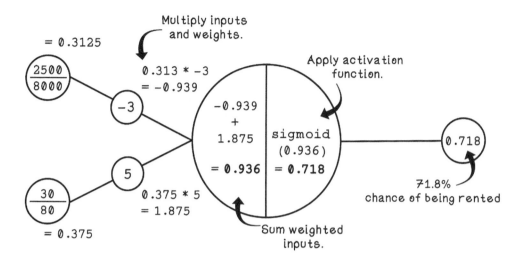

Defining artificial neural networks

The Perceptron is useful for solving simple problems, but as the dimensions of the data increases, it becomes less feasible. ANNs use the principles of the Perceptron and apply them to many hidden nodes as opposed to a single one.

To explore the workings of multi-node ANNs, consider an example dataset related to car collisions. Suppose that we have data from several cars at the moment that an unforeseen object enters the path of their movement. The dataset contains features related to the conditions and whether a collision occurred, including the following:

- *Speed*—The speed at which the car was traveling before encountering the object

- *Terrain quality*—The quality of the road on which the car was traveling before encountering the object

- *Degree of vision*—The driver's degree of vision before the car encountered the object

- *Total experience*—The total driving experience of the driver of the car

- *Collision occurred?*—Whether a collision occurred or not

Given this data, we want to train a machine learning model—namely, an ANN—to learn the relationship between the features that contribute to a collision, as shown in table 9.1.

Table 9.1 Car collision dataset

	Speed	Terrain quality	Degree of vision	Total experience	Collision occurred?
1	65 km/h	5/10	180°	80,000 km	No
2	120 km/h	1/10	72°	110,000 km	Yes
3	8 km/h	6/10	288°	50,000 km	No
4	50 km/h	2/10	324°	1,600 km	Yes
5	25 km/h	9/10	36°	160,000 km	No
6	80 km/h	3/10	120°	6,000 km	Yes
7	40 km/h	3/10	360°	400,000 km	No

An example ANN architecture can be used to classify whether a collision will occur based on the features we have. The features in the dataset must be mapped as inputs to the ANN, and the class that we are trying to predict is mapped as the output of the ANN. In this example, the input nodes are speed, terrain quality, degree of vision, and total experience; the output node is whether a collision happened (figure 9.9).

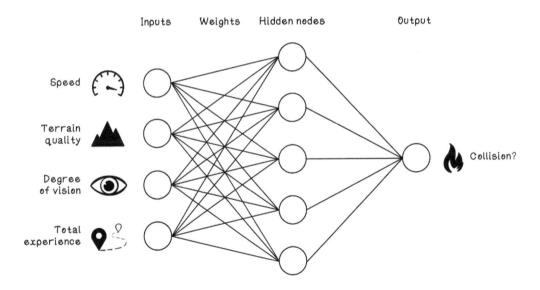

Figure 9.9 Example ANN architecture for the car-collision example

As with the other machine learning algorithms that we've worked through, preparing data is important for making an ANN classify data successfully. The primary concern is representing data in comparable ways. As humans, we understand the concept of speed and degree of vision, but the ANN doesn't have this context. Directly comparing

65 km/h and 36-degree vision doesn't make sense for the ANN, but comparing the ratio of speed with the degree of vision is useful. To accomplish this task, we need to scale our data.

A common way to scale data so that it can be compared is to use the *min-max* scaling approach, which aims to scale data to values between 0 and 1. By scaling all the data in a dataset to be consistent in format, we make the different features comparable. Because ANNs do not have any context about the raw features, we also remove bias with large input values. As an example, 1,000 seems to be much larger than 65, but 1,000 in the context of total driving experience is poor, and 65 in the context of driving speed is significant. Min-max scaling represents these pieces of data with the correct context by taking into account the minimum and maximum possible values for each feature.

Here are the minimum and maximum values selected for the features in the car-collision data:

- *Speed*—The minimum speed is 0, which means that the car is not moving. We will use the maximum speed of 120, because 120 km/h is the maximum legal speed limit in most places around the world. We will assume that the driver follows the rules.

- *Terrain quality*—Because the data is already in a rating system, the minimum value is 0, and the maximum value is 10.

- *Degree of vision*—We know that the total field of view in degrees is 360. So the minimum value is 0, and the maximum value is 360.

- *Total experience*—The minimum value is 0 if the driver has no experience. We will subjectively make the maximum value 400,000 for driving experience. The rationale is that if a driver has 400,000 km of driving experience, we consider that driver to be highly competent, and any further experience doesn't matter.

Min-max scaling uses the minimum and maximum values for a feature and finds the percentage of the actual value for the feature. The formula is simple: subtract the minimum from the value, and divide the result by the minimum subtracted from the maximum. Figure 9.10 illustrates the min-max scaling calculation for the first row of data in the car-collision example:

	Speed	Terrain quality	Degree of vision	Total experience	Collision occurred?
1	65 km/h	5/10	180°	80,000 km	No

	Speed	Terrain quality	Degree of vision	Total experience
	65 km/h	5/10	180°	80,000
	Min: 0 Max: 120	Min: 0 Max: 10	Min: 0 Max: 360	Min: 0 Max: 400,000
$\dfrac{value - min}{max - min}$	$\dfrac{65 - 0}{120 - 0}$	$\dfrac{5 - 0}{10 - 0}$	$\dfrac{180 - 0}{360 - 0}$	$\dfrac{80000 - 0}{400000 - 0}$
Scaled value	0.542	0.5	0.5	0.2

Figure 9.10 Min-max scaling example with car collision data

Notice that all the values are between 0 and 1 and can be compared equally. The same formula is applied to all the rows in the dataset to ensure that every value is scaled. Note that for the value for the "Collision occurred?" feature, Yes is replaced with 1, and No is replaced with 0. Table 9.2 depicts the scaled car-collision data.

Table 9.2 Car collision dataset scaled

	Speed	Terrain quality	Degree of vision	Total experience	Collision occurred?
1	0.542	0.5	0.5	0.200	0
2	1.000	0.1	0.2	0.275	1
3	0.067	0.6	0.8	0.125	0
4	0.417	0.2	0.9	0.004	1
5	0.208	0.9	0.1	0.400	0
6	0.667	0.3	0.3	0.015	1
7	0.333	0.3	1.0	1.000	0

Pseudocode

The code for scaling the data follows the logic and calculations for min-max scaling identically. We need the minimums and maximums for each feature, as well as the total number of features in our dataset. The scale_dataset function uses these parameters to iterate over every example in the dataset and scale the value by using the scale_data_feature function:

```
FEATURE_MIN = [0, 0, 0, 0]
FEATURE_MAX = [120, 10, 360, 400000]
FEATURE_COUNT = 4


scale_dataset(dataset, feature_count, feature_min, feature_max):
  let scaled_data equal empty array
  for data in dataset:
    let example equal empty array
    for i in range(0, feature_count):
      append scale_data_feature(data[i], feature_min[i], feature_max[i])
        to example
    append example to scaled_data
  return scaled_data


scale_data_feature(data, feature_min, feature_max):
  return (data - feature_min) / (feature_max - feature_min)
```

Now that we have prepared the data in a way that is suitable for an ANN to process, let's explore the architecture of a simple ANN. Remember that the features used to predict a class are the input nodes, and the class that is being predicted is the output node.

Figure 9.11 shows an ANN with one hidden layer, which is the single vertical layer in the figure, with five hidden nodes. These layers are called *hidden layers* because they are not directly observed from outside the network. Only the inputs and outputs are interacted with, which leads to the perception of ANNs as being black boxes. Each hidden node is similar to the Perceptron. A hidden node takes inputs and weights and then computes the sum and an activation function. Then the results of each hidden node are processed by a single output node.

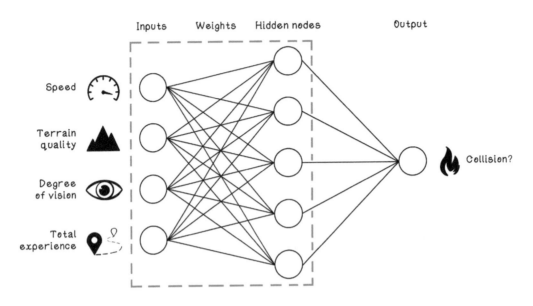

Figure 9.11 Example ANN architecture for the car-collision problem

Before we consider the calculations and computation of an ANN, let's try to dig intuitively into what the network weights are doing at a high level. Because a single hidden node is connected to every input node but every connection has a different weight, independent hidden nodes might be concerned with specific relationships among two or more input nodes.

Figure 9.12 depicts a scenario in which the first hidden node has strong weightings on the connections to terrain quality and degree of vision but weak weightings on the connections to speed and total experience. This specific hidden node is concerned with the relationship between terrain quality and degree of vision. It might gain an understanding of the relationship between these two features and how it influences whether collisions happen; poor terrain quality and poor degree of vision, for example, might influence the likelihood of collisions more than good terrain quality and an average degree of vision. These relationships are usually more intricate than this simple example.

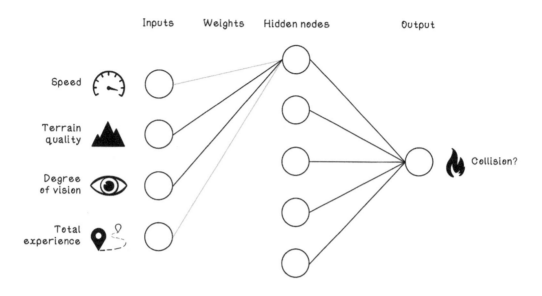

Figure 9.12 Example of a hidden node comparing terrain quality and degree of vision

In figure 9.13, the second hidden node might have strong weightings on the connections to terrain quality and total experience. Perhaps there is a relationship among different terrain qualities and variance in total driving experience that contributes to collisions.

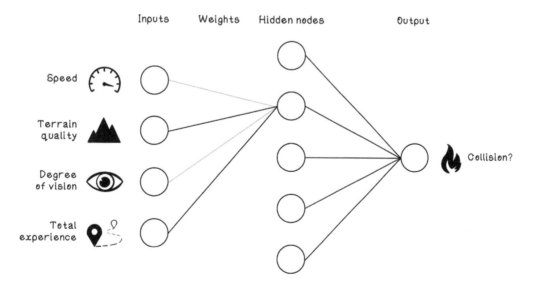

Figure 9.13 Example of a hidden node comparing terrain quality and total experience

The nodes in a hidden layer can be conceptually compared with the analogy of ants discussed in chapter 6. Individual ants fulfill small tasks that are seemingly insignificant, but when the ants act as a colony, intelligent behavior emerges. Similarly, individual hidden nodes contribute to a greater goal in the ANN.

By analyzing the figure of the car-collision ANN and the operations within it, we can describe the data structures required for the algorithm:

- *Input nodes*—The input nodes can be represented by a single array that stores the values for a specific example. The array size is the number of features in the dataset that are being used to predict a class. In the car-collision example, we have four inputs, so the array size is 4.

- *Weights*—The weights can be represented by a matrix (a 2D array), because each input node has a connection to each hidden node and each input node has five connections. Because there are 4 input nodes with 5 connections each, the ANN has 20 weights toward the hidden layer and 5 toward the output layer, because there are 5 hidden nodes and 1 output node.

- *Hidden nodes*—The hidden nodes can be represented by a single array that stores the results of activation of each respective node.

- *Output node*—The output node is a single value representing the predicted class of a specific example or the chance that the example will be in a specific class. The output might be 1 or 0, indicating whether a collision occurred; or it could be something like 0.65, indicating a 65% chance that the example resulted in a collision.

Pseudocode

The next piece of pseudocode describes a class that represents a neural network. Notice that the layers are represented as properties of the class and that all the properties are arrays, with the exception of the weights, which are matrices. An `output` property represents the predictions for the given examples, and an `expected_output` property is used during the training process:

```
NeuralNetwork(features, labels, hidden_node_count):
  let input equal features
  let weights_input equal a random matrix, size: features * hidden_node_count
  let hidden equal zero array, size: hidden_node_count
  let weights_hidden equal a random matrix, size: hidden_node_count
  let expected_output equal labels
  let output equal zero array, size: length of labels


let nn equal NeuralNetwork(scaled_feature_data,
                           scaled_label_data,
                           hidden_node_count)
```

Forward propagation: Using a trained ANN

A trained ANN is a network that has learned from examples and adjusted its weights to best predict the class of new examples. Don't panic about how the training happens and how the weights are adjusted; we will tackle this topic in the next section. Understanding forward propagation will assist us in grasping backpropagation (how weights are trained).

Now that we have a grounding in the general architecture of ANNs and the intuition of what nodes in the network might be doing, let's walk through the algorithm for using a trained ANN (figure 9.14).

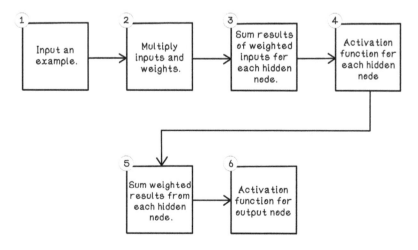

Figure 9.14 Life cycle of forward propagation in an ANN

As mentioned previously, the steps involved in calculating the results for the nodes in an ANN are similar to the Perceptron. Similar operations are performed on many nodes that work together; this addresses the Perceptron's flaws and is used to solve problems that have more dimensions. The general flow of forward propagation includes the following steps:

1. *Input an example*—Provide a single example from the dataset for which we want to predict the class.

2. *Multiply inputs and weights*—Multiply every input by each weight of its connection to hidden nodes.

3. *Sum results of weighted inputs for each hidden node*—Sum the results of the weighted inputs.

4. *Activation function for each hidden node*—Apply an activation function to the summed weighted inputs.

5. *Sum results of weighted outputs of hidden nodes to the output node*—Sum the weighted results of the activation function from all hidden nodes.

6. *Activation function for output node*—Apply an activation function to the summed weighted hidden nodes.

For the purpose of exploring forward propagation, we will assume that the ANN has been trained and the optimal weights in the network have been found. Figure 9.15 depicts the weights on each connection. The first box next to the first hidden node, for example, has the weight 3.35, which is related to the Speed input node; the weight -5.82 is related to the Terrain Quality input node; and so on.

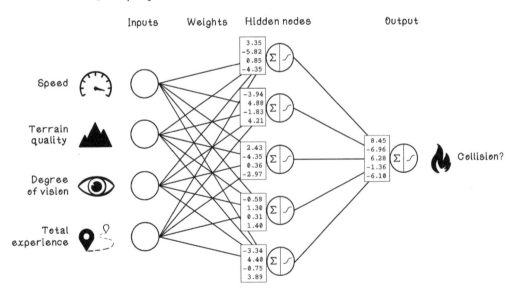

Figure 9.15 Example of weights in a pretrained ANN

Because the neural network has been trained, we can use it to predict the chance of collisions by providing it with a single example. Table 9.3 serves as a reminder of the scaled dataset that we are using.

Table 9.3 Car collision dataset scaled

	Speed	Terrain quality	Degree of vision	Total experience	Collision occurred?
1	0.542	0.5	0.5	0.200	0
2	1.000	0.1	0.2	0.275	1
3	0.067	0.6	0.8	0.125	0
4	0.417	0.2	0.9	0.004	1
5	0.208	0.9	0.1	0.400	0
6	0.667	0.3	0.3	0.015	1
7	0.333	0.3	1.0	1.000	0

If you've ever looked into ANNs, you may have noticed some potentially frightening mathematical notations. Let's break down some of the concepts that can be represented mathematically.

The inputs of the ANN are denoted by X. Every input variable will be X subscripted by a number. Speed is X_0, Terrain Quality is X_1, and so on. The output of the network is denoted by y, and the weights of the network are denoted by W. Because we have two layers in the ANN—a hidden layer and an output layer—there are two groups of weights. The first group is superscripted by W_0, and the second group is W_1. Then each weight is denoted by the nodes to which it is connected. The weight between the Speed node and the first hidden node is $W_{00,0}$, and the weight between the Terrain Quality node and the first hidden node is $W_{01,0}$. These denotations aren't necessarily important for this example, but understanding them now will support future learning.

Figure 9.16 shows how the following data is represented in an ANN:

	Speed	Terrain quality	Degree of vision	Total experience	Collision occurred?
1	0.542	0.5	0.5	0.200	0

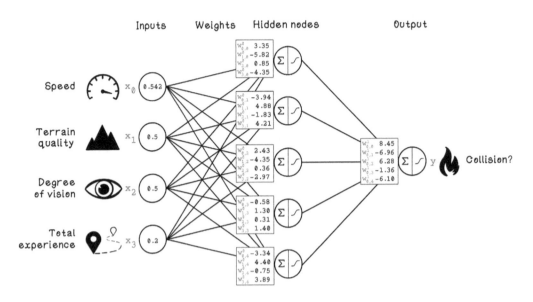

Figure 9.16 Mathematical denotation of an ANN

As with the Perceptron, the first step is calculating the weighted sum of the inputs and the weight of each hidden node. In figure 9.17, each input is multiplied by each weight and summed for every hidden node.

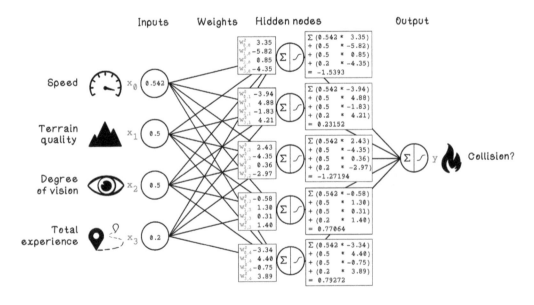

Figure 9.17 Weighted sum calculation for each hidden node

The next step is calculating the activation of each hidden node. We are using the sigmoid function, and the input for the function is the weighted sum of the inputs calculated for each hidden node (figure 9.18).

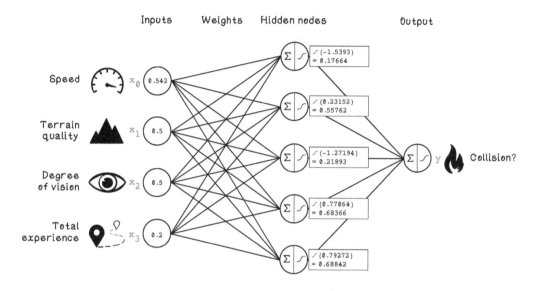

Figure 9.18 Activation function calculation for each hidden node

Now we have the activation results for each hidden node. When we mirror this result back to neurons, the activation results represent the activation intensity of each neuron. Because different hidden nodes may be concerned with different relationships in the data through the weights, the activations can be used in conjunction to determine an overall activation that represents the chance of a collision, given the inputs.

Figure 9.19 depicts the activations for each hidden node and the weights from each hidden node to the output node. To calculate the final output, we repeat the process of calculating the weighted sum of the results from each hidden node and applying the sigmoid activation function to that result.

> **NOTE** The sigma symbol (Σ) in the hidden nodes depicts the sum operation.

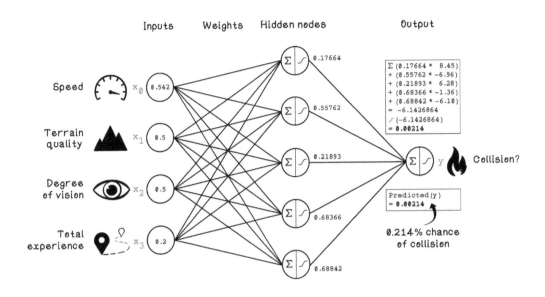

Figure 9.19 Final activation calculation for the output node

We have calculated the output prediction for our example. The result is 0.00214, but what does this number mean? The output is a value between 0 and 1 that represents the probability that a collision will occur. In this case, the output is 0.214 percent (0.00214 × 100), indicating that the chance of a collision is almost 0.

The following exercise uses another example from the dataset.

EXERCISE: CALCULATE THE PREDICTION FOR THE EXAMPLE BY USING FORWARD PROPAGATION WITH THE FOLLOWING ANN

	Speed	Terrain quality	Degree of vision	Total experience	Collision occurred?
2	1.000	0.1	0.2	0.275	1

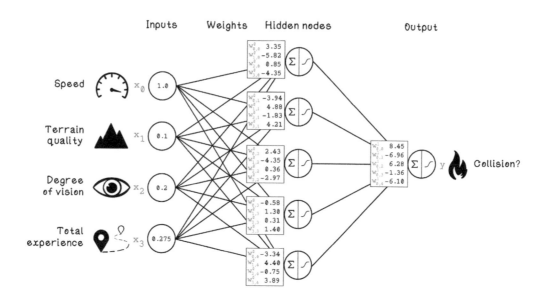

SOLUTION: CALCULATE THE PREDICTION FOR THE EXAMPLE BY USING FORWARD PROPAGATION WITH THE FOLLOWING ANN

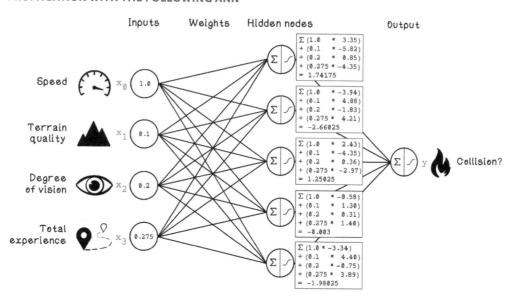

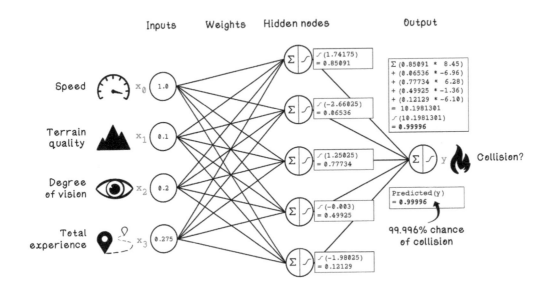

When we run this example through our pretrained ANN, the output is 0.99996, or 99.996 percent, so there is an extremely high chance that a collision will occur. By applying some human intuition to this single example, we can see why a collision is likely. The driver was traveling at the maximum legal speed, on the poorest-quality terrain, with a poor field of vision.

Pseudocode

One of the important functions for activation in our example is the sigmoid function. This method describes the mathematical function that represents the S curve:

```
sigmoid(x):
    return 1 / (1 + exp(-x))
```

← Exp is a mathematical constant called Euler's number, approximately 2.71828.

Notice that the same neural network class defined earlier in the chapter is described in the following code. This time, a `forward_propagation` function is included. This function sums the input and weights between input and hidden nodes, applies the sigmoid function to each result, and stores the output as the result for the nodes in the hidden layer. This is done for the hidden node output and weights to the output node as well:

```
NeuralNetwork(features, labels, hidden_node_count):

    let input equal features

    let weights_input equal a random matrix, size: features * hidden_node_count

    let hidden equal zero array, size: hidden_node_count

    let weights_hidden equal a random matrix, size: hidden_node_count

    let expected_output equal labels

    let output equal zero array, size: length of labels


    forward_propagation():

        let hidden_weighted_sum equal input · weights_input

        let hidden equal sigmoid(hidden_weighted_sum)

        let output_weighted_sum equal hidden · weights_hidden

        let output equal sigmoid(output_weighted_sum)
```

The symbol • implies matrix multiplication.

Backpropagation: Training an ANN

Understanding how forward propagation works is useful for understanding how ANNs are trained, because forward propagation is used in the training process. The machine learning life cycle and principles covered in chapter 8 are important for tackling back-propagation in ANNs. An ANN can be seen as another machine learning model. We still need to have a question to ask. We're still collecting and understanding data in the context of the problem, and we need to prepare the data in a way that is suitable for the model to process.

We need a subset of data for training and a subset of data for testing how well the model performs. Also, we will be iterating and improving through collecting more data, preparing it differently, or changing the architecture and configuration of the ANN.

Training an ANN consists of three main phases. Phase A involves setting up the ANN architecture, including configuring the inputs, outputs, and hidden layers. Phase B is forward propagation. And phase C is backpropagation, which is where the training happens (figure 9.20).

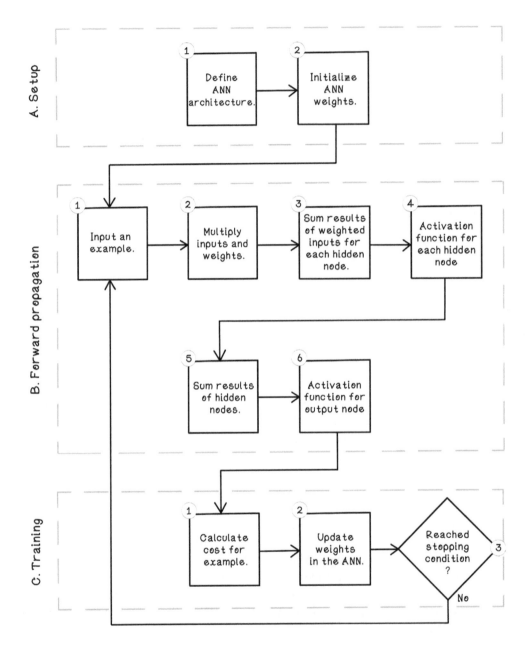

Figure 9.20 Life cycle of training an ANN

Phase A, Phase B, and Phase C describe the phases and operations involved in the back-propagation algorithm.

Phase A: Setup

1. *Define ANN architecture.* This step involves defining the input nodes, the output nodes, the number of hidden layers, the number of neurons in each hidden layer, the activation functions used, and more.

2. *Initialize ANN weights.* The weights in the ANN must be initialized to some value. We can take various approaches. The key principle is that the weights will be adjusted constantly as the ANN learns from training examples.

Phase B: Forward propagation

This process is the same one that we covered in Phase A. The same calculations are carried out. The predicted output, however, will be compared with the actual class for each example in the training set to train the network.

Phase C: Training

1. *Calculate cost.* Following from forward propagation, the cost is the difference between the predicted output and the actual class for the examples in the training set. The cost effectively determines how bad the ANN is at predicting the class of examples.

2. *Update weights in the ANN.* The weights of the ANN are the only things that can be adjusted by the network itself. The architecture and configurations that we defined in phase A don't change during training the network. The weights essentially encode the intelligence of the network. Weights are adjusted to be larger or smaller, affecting the strength of the inputs.

3. *Define a stopping condition.* Training cannot happen indefinitely. As with many of the algorithms explored in this book, a sensible stopping condition needs to be determined. If we have a large dataset, we might decide that we will use 500 examples in our training dataset over 1,000 iterations to train the ANN. In this example, the 500 examples will be passed through the network 1,000 times, and the weights will be adjusted in every iteration.

When we worked through forward propagation, the weights were already defined because the network was pretrained. Before we start training the network, we need to initialize the weights to some value, and the weights need to be adjusted based on training examples. One approach to initializing weights is to choose random weights from a normal distribution.

Figure 9.21 illustrates the randomly generated weights for our ANN. It also shows the calculations for forward propagation for the hidden nodes, given a single training example. The first example input used in the forward propagation section is used here to highlight the differences in output, given different weights in the network.

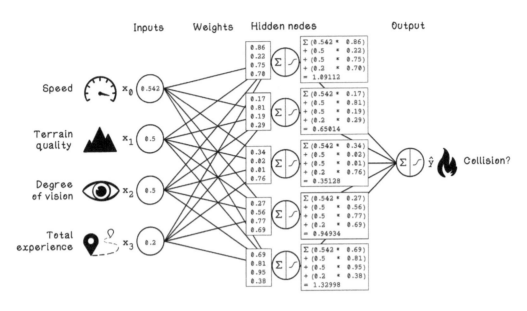

Figure 9.21 Example initial weights for an ANN

The next step is forward propagation (figure 9.22). The key change is checking the difference between the obtained prediction and the actual class.

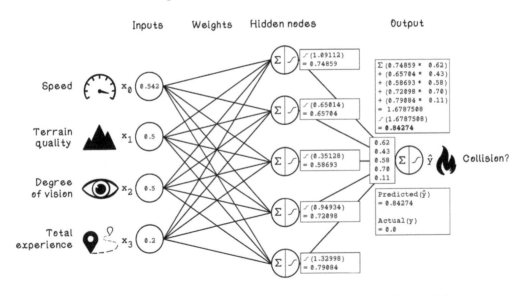

Figure 9.22 Example of forward propagation with randomly initialized weights

By comparing the predicted result with the actual class, we can calculate a cost. The cost function that we will use is simple: subtract the predicted output from the actual output. In this example, 0.84274 is subtracted from 0.0, and the cost is -0.84274. This result indicates how incorrect the prediction was and can be used to adjust the weights in the ANN. Weights in the ANN are adjusted slightly every time a cost is calculated. This happens thousands of times using training data to determine the optimal weights for the ANN to make accurate predictions. Note that training too long on the same set of data can lead to overfitting, described in chapter 8.

Here is where some potentially unfamiliar math comes into play: the Chain Rule. Before we use the Chain Rule, let's gain some intuition about what the weights mean and how adjusting them improves the ANN's performance.

If we plot possible weights against their respective cost on a graph, we find some function that represents the possible weights. Some points on the function yield a lower cost, and other points yield a higher cost. We are seeking points that minimize cost (figure 9.23).

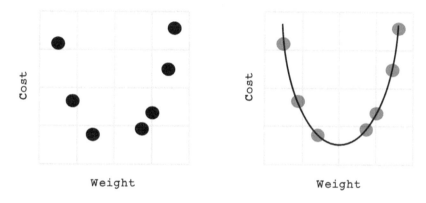

Figure 9.23 Weight versus cost plotted

A useful tool from the field of calculus, called *gradient descent*, can help us move the weight closer to the minimum value by finding the derivative. The *derivative* is important because it measures the sensitivity to change for that function. For example, velocity might be the derivative of an object's position with respect to time; and acceleration is the derivative of the object's velocity with respect to time. Derivatives can find the slope at a specific point in the function. Gradient descent uses the knowledge of the slope to determine which way to move and by how much. Figures 9.24 and 9.25 describe how the derivatives and slope indicate the direction of the minimums.

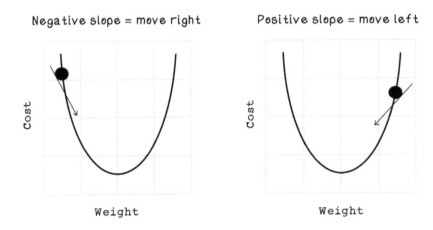

Figure 9.24 Derivatives' slopes and direction of minimums

Figure 9.25 Example of adjusting a weight by using gradient descent

When we look at one weight in isolation, it may seem trivial to find a value that minimizes the cost, but many weights being balanced affect the cost of the overall network. Some weights may be close to their optimal points in reducing cost, and others may not, even though the ANN performs well.

Because many functions comprise the ANN, we can use the Chain Rule. The Chain Rule is a theorem from the field of calculus that calculates the derivative of a composite function. A composite function uses a function g as the parameter for a function f to produce a function h, essentially using a function as a parameter of another function.

Figure 9.26 illustrates the use of the Chain Rule in calculating the update value for weights in the different layers of the ANN.

Calculate update for weights between input nodes and hidden nodes:
input * (2 * cost * sigmoid_derivative(output) * hidden weight) * sigmoid_derivative(hidden)

Calculate update for weights between hidden nodes and output node:
hidden * (2 * cost * sigmoid_derivative(output))

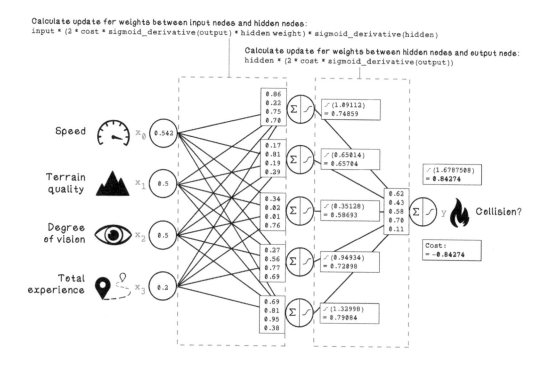

Figure 9.26 Formula for calculating weight updates with the Chain Rule

We can calculate the weight update by plugging the respective values into the formula described. The calculations look scary, but pay attention to the variables being used and their role in the ANN. Although the formula looks complex, it uses the values that we have already calculated (figure 9.27).

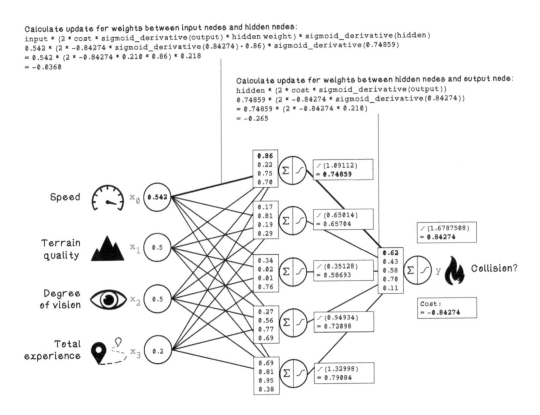

Figure 9.27 Weight-update calculation with the Chain Rule

Here's a closer look at the calculations used in figure 9.27:

```
Calculate update for weights between hidden nodes and output node:
hidden * (2 * cost * sigmoid_derivative(output))

0.74859 * (2 * -0.84274 * sigmoid_derivative(0.84274))
= 0.74859 * (2 * -0.84274 * 0.210)
= -0.265
```

```
Calculate update for weights between input nodes and hidden nodes:
input * (2 * cost * sigmoid_derivative(output) * hidden weight) * sigmoid_derivative(hidden)

0.542 * (2 * -0.84274 * sigmoid_derivative(0.84274) * 0.86) * sigmoid_derivative(0.74859)
= 0.542 * (2 * -0.84274 * 0.210 * 0.86) * 0.218
= -0.0360
```

Now that the update values are calculated, we can apply the results to the weights in the ANN by adding the update value to the respective weights. Figure 9.28 depicts the application of the weight-update results to the weights in the different layers.

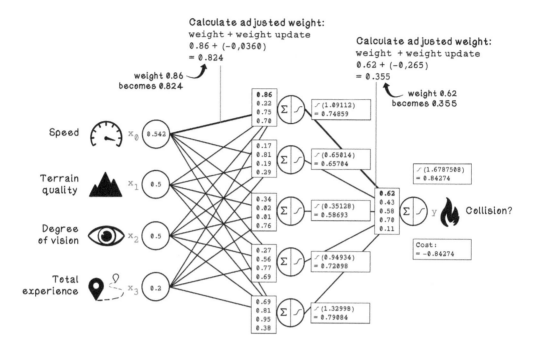

Figure 9.28 Example of the final weight-update for the ANN

EXERCISE: CALCULATE THE NEW WEIGHTS FOR THE HIGHLIGHTED WEIGHTS

Calculate update for weights between input nodes and hidden nodes.

Calculate update for weights between hidden nodes and output node.

SOLUTION: CALCULATE THE NEW WEIGHTS FOR THE HIGHLIGHTED WEIGHTS

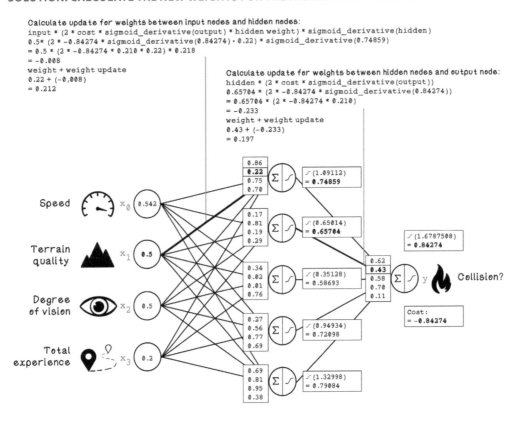

Calculate update for weights between input nodes and hidden nodes:
input * (2 * cost * sigmoid_derivative(output) * hidden weight) * sigmoid_derivative(hidden)
0.5* (2 * -0.84274 * sigmoid_derivative(0.84274) · 0.22) * sigmoid_derivative(0.74859)
= 0.5 * (2 * -0.84274 * 0.210 * 0.22) * 0.218
= -0.008
weight + weight update
0.22 + (-0,008)
= 0.212

Calculate update for weights between hidden nodes and output node:
hidden * (2 * cost * sigmoid_derivative(output))
0.65704 * (2 * -0.84274 * sigmoid_derivative(0.84274))
= 0.65704 * (2 * -0.84274 * 0.210)
= -0.233
weight + weight update
0.43 + (-0.233)
= 0.197

The problem that the Chain Rule is solving may remind you of the drone problem example in chapter 7. Particle-swarm optimization is effective for finding optimal values in high-dimensional spaces such as this one, which has 25 weights to optimize. Finding the weights in an ANN is an optimization problem. Gradient descent is not the only way to optimize weights; we can use many approaches, depending on the context and problem being solved.

Pseudocode

The derivative is important in the backpropagation algorithm. The following piece of pseudocode revisits the sigmoid function and describes the formula for its derivative, which we need to adjust weights:

```
sigmoid(x):
    return 1 / (1 + exp(-x))
```

Exp is a mathematical constant called Euler's number, approximately 2.71828.

```
sigmoid_derivative(x):
    return sigmoid(x) * (1 - sigmoid(x))
```

We revisit the neural network class, this time with a backpropagation function that computes the cost, the amount by which weights should be updated by using the Chain Rule, and adds the weight-update results to the existing weights. This process will compute the change for each weight given the cost. Remember that cost is calculated by using the example features, predicted output, and expected output. The difference between the predicted output and expected output is the cost:

```
NeuralNetwork(features, labels, hidden_node_count):
    let input equal features
    let weights_input equal a random matrix, size: features * hidden_node_count
    let hidden equal zero array, size: hidden_node_count
    let weights_hidden equal a random matrix, size: hidden_node_count
    let expected_output equal labels
    let output equal zero array,size: length of labels


    back_propagation():
        let cost equal expected_output - output
        let weights_hidden_update equal
            hidden · (2 * cost * sigmoid_derivative(output))
        let weights_input_update equal
            input · (2 * cost * sigmoid_derivative(output) * weights_hidden)
            * sigmoid_derivative(hidden)
        let weights_hidden equal weights_hidden + weights_hidden_update
        let weights_input equal weights_input + weights_input_update
```

The symbol • implies matrix multiplication.

Because we have a class that represents a neural network, functions to scale data, and functions for forward propagation and backpropagation, we can piece this code together to train a neural network.

Pseudocode

In this piece of pseudocode, we have a `run_neural_network` function that accepts `epochs` as an input. This function scales the data and creates a new neural network with the scaled data, labels, and number of hidden nodes. Then the function runs `forward_propagation` and `back_propagation` for the specified number of epochs:

```
run_neural_network(epochs):
  let scaled_feature_data equal
    scale_dataset(feature_data, feature_count, features_min, features_max)
  let nn equal NeuralNetwork(scaled_feature_data,
                              scaled_label_data,
                              hidden_node_count)
  for epoch in range(epochs):
    nn.forward_propagation()
    nn.back_propagation()
```

Options for activation functions

This section aims to provide some intuition about activation functions and their properties. In the examples of the Perceptron and ANN, we used a sigmoid function as the activation function, which was satisfactory for the examples that we were working with. Activation functions introduce nonlinear properties to the ANN. If we do not use an activation function, the neural network will behave similarly to linear regression as described in chapter 8. Figure 9.29 describes some commonly used activation functions.

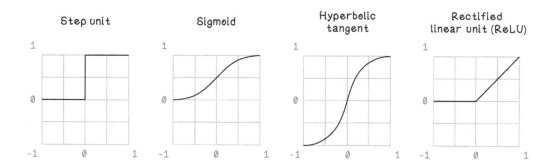

Figure 9.29 Commonly used activation functions

Different activation functions are useful in different scenarios and have different benefits:

- *Step unit*—The step unit function is used as a binary classifier. Given an input between -1 and 1, it outputs a result of exactly 0 or 1. A binary classifier is not useful for learning from data in a hidden layer, but it can be used in the output layer for binary classification. If we want to know whether something is a cat or a dog, for example, 0 could indicate cat, and 1 could indicate dog.

- *Sigmoid*—The sigmoid function results in an S curve between 0 and 1, given an input between -1 and 1. Because the sigmoid function allows changes in x to result in small changes in y, it allows for learning and solving nonlinear problems. The problem sometimes experienced with the sigmoid function is that as values approach the extremes, derivative changes become tiny, resulting in poor learning. This problem is known as the *vanishing gradient problem*.

- *Hyperbolic tangent*—The hyperbolic tangent function is similar to the sigmoid function, but it results in values between -1 and 1. The benefit is that the hyperbolic tangent has steeper derivatives, which allows for faster learning. The vanishing gradient problem is also a problem at the extremes for this function, as with the sigmoid function.

- *Rectified linear unit (ReLU)*—The ReLU function results in 0 for input values between -1 and 0, and results in linearly increasing values between 0 and 1. In a large ANN with many neurons using the sigmoid or hyperbolic tangent function, all neurons activate all the time (except when they result in 0), resulting in lots of computation and many values being adjusted finely to find solutions. The ReLU function allows some neurons to not activate, which reduces computation and may find solutions faster.

The next section touches on some considerations for designing an ANN.

Designing artificial neural networks

Designing ANNs is experimental and dependent on the problem that is being solved. The architecture and configuration of an ANN usually change through trial and error as we attempt to improve the performance of the predictions. This section briefly lists the parameters of the architecture that we can change to improve performance or address different problems. Figure 9.30 illustrates an artificial neural network with a different configuration to the one seen throughout this chapter. The most notable difference is the introduction of a new hidden layer and the network now has two outputs.

> **NOTE** As in most scientific or engineering problems, the answer to "What is the ideal ANN design?" is often "It depends." Configuring ANNs requires a deep understanding of the data and the problem being solved. A clear-cut generalized blueprint for architectures and configurations doesn't exist . . . yet.

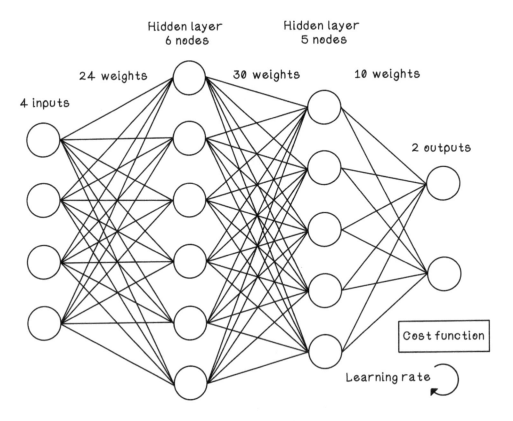

Figure 9.30 An example of a multilayer ANN with more than one output

Inputs and outputs

The inputs and outputs of an ANN are the fundamental parameters for use of the network. After an ANN model has been trained, the trained ANN model will potentially be used in different contexts and systems, and by different people. The inputs and outputs define the interface of the network. Throughout this chapter, we saw an example of an ANN with four inputs describing the features of a driving scenario and one output describing the likelihood of a collision. We may have a problem when the inputs and outputs mean different things, however. If we have a 16- by 16-pixel image that represents a handwritten digit, for example, we could use the pixels as inputs and the digit they represent as the output. The input would consist of 256 nodes representing the pixel values, and the output would consist of 10 nodes representing 0 to 9, with each result indicating the probability that the image is the respective digit.

Hidden layers and nodes

An ANN can consist of multiple hidden layers with varying numbers of nodes in each layer. Adding more hidden layers allows us to solve problems with higher dimensions and more complexity in the classification discrimination line. In the example in figure 9.8, a simple straight line classified data accurately. Sometimes, the line is nonlinear but fairly simple. But what happens when the line is a more-complex function with many curves potentially across many dimensions (which we can't even visualize)? Adding more layers allows these complex classification functions to be found. The selection of the number of layers and nodes in an ANN usually comes down to experimentation and iterative improvement. Over time, we may gain intuition about suitable configurations, based on experiencing similar problems and solving them with similar configurations.

Weights

Weight initialization is important because it establishes a starting point from which the weight will be adjusted slightly over many iterations. Weights that are initialized to be too small lead to the vanishing gradient problem described earlier, and weights that are initialized to be too large lead to another problem, the *exploding gradient problem*—in which weights move erratically around the desired result.

Various weight-initialization schemes exist, each with its own pros and cons. A rule of thumb is to ensure that the mean of the activation results in a layer is 0—the mean of all results of the hidden nodes in a layer. Also, the variance of the activation results should be the same: the variability of the results from each hidden node should be consistent over several iterations.

Bias

We can use bias in an ANN by adding a value to the weighted sum of the input nodes or other layers in the network. A bias can shift the activation value of the activation function. A bias provides flexibility in an ANN and shifts the activation function left or right.

A simple way to understand bias is to imagine a line that always passes through 0,0 on a plane; we can influence this line to pass through a different intercept by adding +1 to a variable. This value will be based on the problem to be solved.

Activation functions

Earlier we covered the common activation functions used in ANNs. A key rule of thumb is to ensure that all nodes on the same layer use the same activation function. In multi-layer ANNs, different layers may use different activation functions based on the problem to be solved. A network that determines whether loans should be granted, for example, might use the sigmoid function in the hidden layers to determine probabilities and a step function in the output to get a clear 0 or 1 decision.

Cost function and learning rate

We used a simple cost function in the example described earlier where the predicted output is subtracted from the actual expected output, but many cost functions exist. Cost functions influence the ANN greatly, and using the correct function for the problem and dataset at hand is important because it describes the goal for the ANN. One of the most common cost functions is *mean square error*, which is similar to the function used in the machine learning chapter (chapter 8). But cost functions must be selected based on understanding of the training data, size of the training data, and desired precision and recall measurements. As we experiment more, we should look into the cost function options.

Finally, the learning rate of the ANN describes how dramatically weights are adjusted during backpropagation. A slow learning rate may result in a long training process because weights are updated by tiny amounts each time, and a high learning rate might result in dramatic changes in the weights, making for a chaotic training process. One solution is to start with a fixed learning rate and to adjust that rate if the training stagnates and doesn't improve the cost. This process, which would be repeated through the training cycle, requires some experimentation. Stochastic gradient descent is a useful tweak to the optimizer that combats these problems. It works similarly to gradient descent but allows weights to jump out of local minimums to explore better solutions.

Standard ANNs such as the one described in this chapter are useful for solving non-linear classification problems. If we are trying to categorize examples based on many features, this ANN style is likely to be a good option.

That said, an ANN is not a silver bullet and shouldn't be the go-to algorithm for anything. Simpler, traditional machine learning algorithms described in chapter 8 often perform better in many common use cases. Remember the machine learning life cycle. You may want to try several machine learning models during your iterations while seeking improvement.

Artificial neural network types and use cases

ANNs are versatile and can be designed to address different problems. Specific architectural styles of ANNs are useful for solving certain problems. Think of an ANN architectural style as being the fundamental configuration of the network. The examples in this section highlight different configurations.

Convolutional neural network

Convolutional neural networks (CNNs) are designed for image recognition. These networks can be used to find the relationships among different objects and unique areas within images. In *image recognition*, convolution operates on a single pixel and its neighbors within a certain radius. This technique is traditionally used for edge detection, image sharpening, and image blurring. CNNs use convolution and pooling to find relationships among pixels in an image. *Convolution* finds features in images, and *pooling* downsamples the "patterns" by summarizing features, allowing unique signatures in images to be encoded concisely through learning from multiple images (figure 9.31).

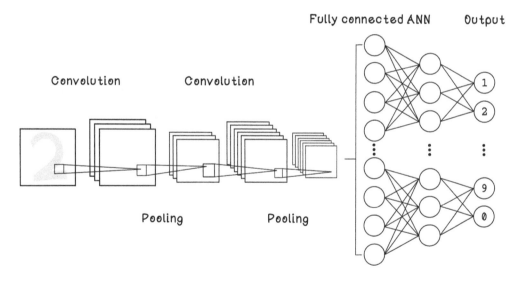

Figure 9.31 Simple example of a CNN

CNNs are used for image classification. If you've ever searched for an image online, you have likely interacted indirectly with a CNN. These networks are also useful for optical character recognition for extracting text data from an image. CNNs have been used in the medical industry for applications that detect anomalies and medical conditions via X-rays and other body scans.

Recurrent neural network

Whereas standard ANNs accept a fixed number of inputs, *recurrent neural networks* (RNNs) accept a sequence of inputs with no predetermined length. These inputs are like spoken sentences. RNNs have a concept of memory consisting of hidden layers that represent time; this concept allows the network to retain information about the relationships among the sequences of inputs. When we are training a RNN, the weights in the hidden layers throughout time are also influenced by backpropagation; multiple weights represent the same weight at different points in time (figure 9.32).

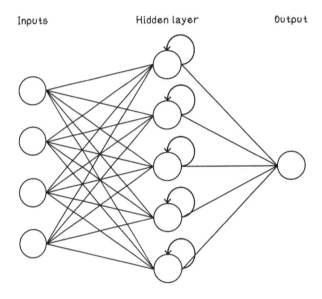

Figure 9.32 Simple example of a RNN

RNNs are useful in applications pertaining to speech and text recognition and prediction. Related use cases include autocompletion of sentences in messaging applications, translation of spoken language to text, and translation between spoken languages.

Generative adversarial network

A *generative adversarial network* (GAN) consists of a generator network and a discriminator network. For example, the *generator* creates a potential solution such as an image or a landscape, and a *discriminator* uses real images of landscapes to determine the realism or correctness of the generated landscape. The error or cost is fed back into the network to further improve its ability to generate convincing landscapes and determine their correctness. The term *adversarial* is key, as we saw with game trees in chapter 3. These two components are competing to be better at what they do and, through that competition, generate incrementally better solutions (figure 9.33).

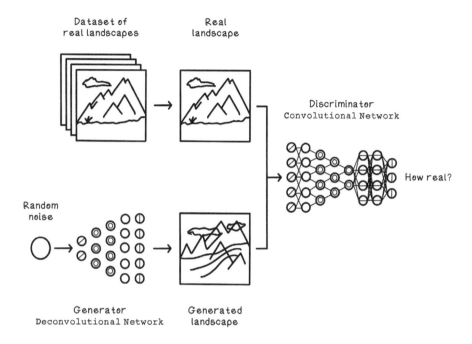

Figure 9.33 Simple example of a GAN

GANs are used to generate convincing fake videos (also known as deepfakes) of famous people, which raises concern about the authenticity of information in the media. GANs also have useful applications such as overlaying hairstyles on people's faces. GANs have been used to generate 3D objects from 2D images, such as generating a 3D chair from a 2D picture. This use case may seem to be unimportant, but the network is accurately estimating and creating information from a source that is incomplete. It is a huge step in the advancement of AI and technology in general.

This chapter aimed to tie together the concepts of machine learning with the somewhat-mysterious world of ANNs. For further learning about ANNs and deep learning, try *Grokking Deep Learning* (Manning Publications); and for a practical guide to a framework for building ANNs, see *Deep Learning with Python* (Manning Publications).

SUMMARY OF ARTIFICIAL NEURAL NETWORKS

Artificial neural networks are inspired by the brain and can be seen as just another ML model.

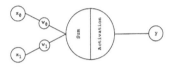

ANNs are based on the idea of the Perceptron.

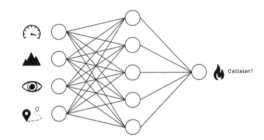

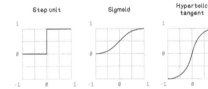

Activation functions help solve nonlinear problems.

Forward propagation is used to use the ANN to make predictions and is also used in training.

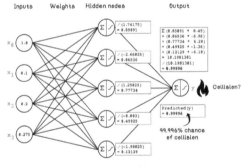

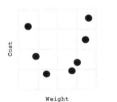

Gradient descent optimization is one of many weight optimization options.

ANNs are flexible and can be adapted to solve many different problems.

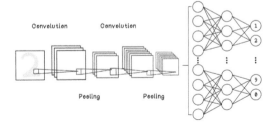

10

This chapter covers

- Understanding the inspiration for reinforcement learning

- Identifying problems to solve with reinforcement learning

- Designing and implementing a reinforcement learning algorithm

- Understanding reinforcement learning approaches

What is reinforcement learning?

Reinforcement learning (RL) is an area of machine learning inspired by behavioral psychology. The concept of reinforcement learning is based on cumulative rewards or penalties for the actions that are taken by an agent in a dynamic environment. Think about a young dog growing up. The dog is the agent in an environment that is our home. When we want the dog to sit, we usually say, "Sit." The dog doesn't understand English, so we might nudge it by lightly pushing down on its hindquarters. After it sits, we usually pet the dog or give it a treat. This process will need to be repeated several times, but after some time, we have positively reinforced the idea of

323

sitting. The trigger in the environment is saying "Sit"; the behavior learned is sitting; and the reward is pets or treats.

Reinforcement learning is another approach to machine learning alongside *supervised learning* and *unsupervised learning*. Whereas supervised learning uses labeled data to make predictions and classifications, and unsupervised learning uses unlabeled data to find clusters and trends, reinforcement learning uses feedback from actions performed to learn what actions or sequence of actions are more beneficial in different scenarios toward an ultimate goal. Reinforcement learning is useful when you know what the goal is but don't know what actions are reasonable to achieve it. Figure 10.1 shows the map of machine learning concepts and how reinforcement learning fits in.

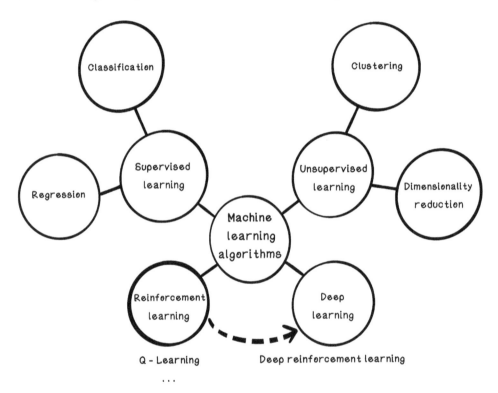

Figure 10.1 How reinforcement learning fits into machine learning

Reinforcement learning can be achieved through classical techniques or deep learning involving artificial neural networks. Depending on the problem being solved, either approach may be better.

Figure 10.2 illustrates when different machine learning approaches may be used. We will be exploring reinforcement learning through classical methods in this chapter.

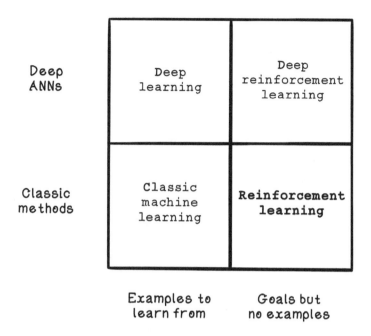

Figure 10.2 Categorization of machine learning, deep learning, and reinforcement learning

The inspiration for reinforcement learning

Reinforcement learning in machines is derived from behavioral psychology, a field that is interested in the behavior of humans and other animals. Behavioral psychology usually explains behavior by a reflex action, or something learned in the individual's history. The latter includes exploring reinforcement through rewards or punishments, motivators for behaviors, and aspects of the individual's environment that contribute to the behavior.

Trial and error is one of the most common ways that most evolved animals learn what is beneficial to them and what is not. Trial and error involves trying something, potentially failing at it, and trying something different until you succeed. This process may happen many times before a desired outcome is obtained, and it's largely driven by some reward.

This behavior can be observed throughout nature. Newborn chicks, for example, try to peck any small piece of material that they come across on the ground. Through trial and error, the chicks learn to peck only food.

Another example is chimpanzees learning through trial and error that using a stick to dig the soil is more favorable than using their hands. Goals, rewards, and penalties are important in reinforcement learning. A goal for a chimpanzee is to find food; a reward or penalty may be the number of times it has dug a hole or the time taken to dig a hole. The faster it can dig a hole, the faster it will find some food.

Figure 10.3 looks at the terminology used in reinforcement learning with reference to the simple dog-training example.

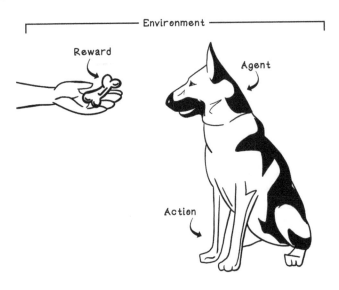

Figure 10.3 Example of reinforcement learning: teaching a dog to sit by using food as a reward

Reinforcement learning has negative and positive reinforcement. *Positive reinforcement* is receiving a reward after performing an action, such as a dog getting a treat after it sits. *Negative reinforcement* is receiving a penalty after performing an action, such as a dog getting scolded after it tears up a carpet. Positive reinforcement is meant to motivate desired behavior, and negative reinforcement is meant to discourage undesired behavior.

Another concept in reinforcement learning is balancing instant gratification with long-term consequences. Eating a chocolate bar is great for getting a boost of sugar and energy; this is *instant gratification*. But eating a chocolate bar every 30 minutes will likely cause health problems later in life; this is a *long-term consequence*. Reinforcement learning aims to maximize the long-term benefit over short-term benefit, although short-term benefit may contribute to long-term benefit.

Reinforcement learning is concerned with the long-term consequence of actions in an environment, so time and the sequence of actions are important. Suppose that we're stranded in the wilderness, and our goal is to survive as long as possible while traveling as far as possible in hopes of finding safety. We're positioned next to a river and have two options: jump into the river to travel downstream faster or walk along the side of the river. Notice the boat on the side of the river in figure 10.4. By swimming, we will travel faster but might miss the boat by being dragged down the wrong fork in the river. By walking, we will be guaranteed to find the boat, which will make the rest of the journey much easier, but we don't know this at the start. This example shows how important the sequence of actions is in reinforcement learning. It also shows how instant gratification may lead to long-term detriment. Furthermore, in a landscape that didn't contain a boat, the consequence of swimming is that we will travel faster but have soaked clothing, which may be problematic when it gets cold. The consequence of walking is that we will travel slower but not wet our clothing, which highlights the fact that a specific action may work in one scenario but not in others. Learning from many simulation attempts is important to finding more-generalist approaches.

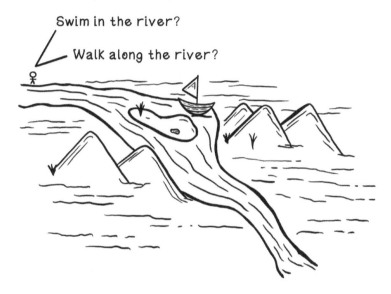

Figure 10.4 An example of possible actions that have long-term consequences

Problems applicable to reinforcement learning

To sum it up, reinforcement learning aims to solve problems in which a goal is known but the actions required to achieve it are not. These problems involve controlling an agent's actions in an environment. Individual actions may be rewarded more than others, but the main concern is the cumulative reward of all actions.

Reinforcement learning is most useful for problems in which individual actions build up toward a greater goal. Areas such as strategic planning, industrial-process automation, and robotics are good cases for the use of reinforcement learning. In these areas, individual actions may be suboptimal to gain a favorable outcome. Imagine a strategic game such as chess. Some moves may be poor choices based on the current state of the board, but they help set the board up for a greater strategic win later in the game.

Reinforcement learning works well in domains in which chains of events are important for a good solution.

To work through the steps in a reinforcement learning algorithm, we will use the example car-collision problem from chapter 9 as inspiration. This time, however, we will be working with visual data about a self-driving car in a parking lot trying to navigate to its owner. Suppose that we have a map of a parking lot, including a self-driving car, other cars, and pedestrians. Our self-driving car can move north, south, east, and west. The other cars and pedestrians remain stationary in this example.

The goal is for our car to navigate the road to its owner while colliding with as few cars and pedestrians as possible—ideally, not colliding with anything. Colliding with a car is not good because it damages the vehicles, but colliding with a pedestrian is more severe. In this problem, we want to minimize collisions, but if we have a choice between colliding with a car and a pedestrian, we should choose the car. Figure 10.5 depicts this scenario.

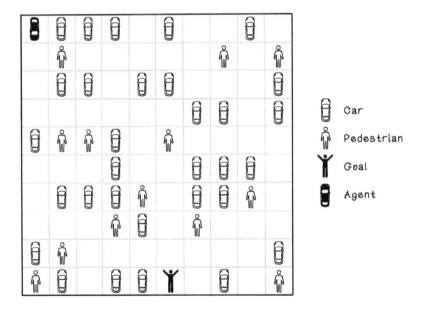

Figure 10.5 The self-driving car in a parking lot problem

We will be using this example problem to explore the use of reinforcement learning for learning good actions to take in dynamic environments.

The life cycle of reinforcement learning

Like other machine learning algorithms, a reinforcement learning model needs to be trained before it can be used. The training phase centers on exploring the environment and receiving feedback, given specific actions performed in specific circumstances or states. The life cycle of training a reinforcement learning model is based on the *Markov Decision Process*, which provides a mathematical framework for modeling decisions (figure 10.6). By quantifying decisions made and their outcomes, we can train a model to learn what actions toward a goal are most favorable.

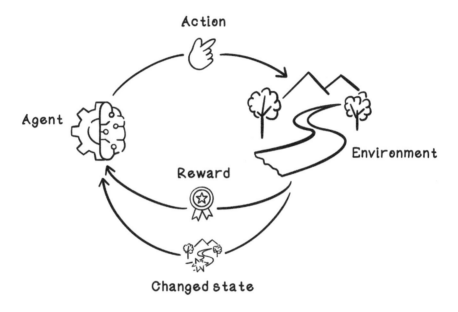

Figure 10.6 The Markov Decision Process for reinforcement learning

Before we can start tackling the challenge of training a model by using reinforcement learning, we need an environment that simulates the problem space we are working in. Our example problem entails a self-driving car trying to navigate a parking lot filled with obstacles to find its owner while avoiding collisions. This problem needs to be modeled as a simulation so that actions in the environment can be measured toward the goal. This simulated environment is different from the model that will learn what actions to take.

Simulation and data: Make the environment come alive

Figure 10.7 depicts a parking-lot scenario containing several other cars and pedestrians. The starting position of the self-driving car and the location of its owner are represented as black figures. In this example, the self-driving car that applies actions to the environment is known as the *agent*.

The self-driving car, or agent, can take several actions in the environment. In this simple example, the actions are moving north, south, east, and west. Choosing an action results in the agent moving one block in that direction. The agent can't move diagonally.

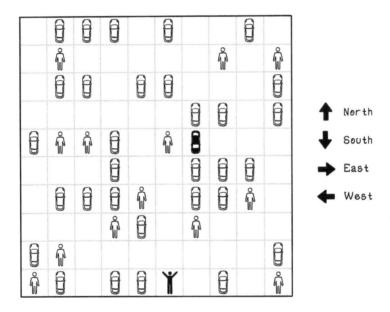

Figure 10.7 Agent actions in the parking-lot environment

When actions are taken in the environment, rewards or penalties occur. Figure 10.8 shows the reward points awarded to the agent based on the outcome in the environment. A collision with another car is bad; a collision with a pedestrian is terrible. A move to an empty space is good; finding the owner of the self-driving car is better. The specified rewards aim to discourage collisions with other cars and pedestrians, and to encourage moving into empty spaces and reaching the owner. Note that there could be a reward for out-of-bounds movements, but we will simply disallow this possibility for the sake of simplicity.

Move into car.   -100

Move into pedestrian.   -1,000

Move into empty space.   +100

Move into goal.   +500

Figure 10.8 Rewards due to specific events in the environment due to actions performed

NOTE An interesting outcome of the rewards and penalties described is that the car may drive forward and backward on empty spaces indefinitely to accumulate rewards. We will dismiss this as a possibility for this example, but it highlights the importance of crafting good rewards.

The simulator needs to model the environment, the actions of the agent, and the rewards received after each action. A reinforcement learning algorithm will use the simulator to learn through practice by taking actions in the simulated environment and measuring the outcome. The simulator should provide the following functionality and information at minimum:

- *Initialize the environment.* This function involves resetting the environment, including the agent, to the starting state.

- *Get the current state of the environment.* This function should provide the current state of the environment, which will change after each action is performed.

- *Apply an action to the environment.* This function involves having the agent apply an action to the environment. The environment is affected by the action, which may result in a reward.

- *Calculate the reward of the action.* This function is related to applying the action to the environment. The reward for the action and effect on the environment need to be calculated.

- *Determine whether the goal is achieved.* This function determines whether the agent has achieved the goal. The goal can also sometimes be represented as is complete. In an environment in which the goal cannot be achieved, the simulator needs to signal completion when it deems necessary.

Figures 10.9 and 10.10 depict possible paths in the self-driving-car example. In figure 10.9, the agent travels south until it reaches the boundary; then it travels east until it reaches the goal. Although the goal is achieved, the scenario resulted in five collisions with other cars and one collision with a pedestrian—not an ideal result. Figure 10.10 depicts the agent traveling along a more specific path toward the goal, resulting in no collisions, which is great. It's important to note that given the rewards that we have specified, the agent is not guaranteed to achieve the shortest path; because we heavily encourage avoiding obstacles, the agent may find any path that is obstacle-free.

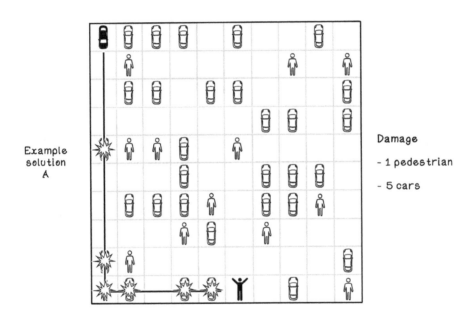

Figure 10.9 A bad solution to the parking-lot problem

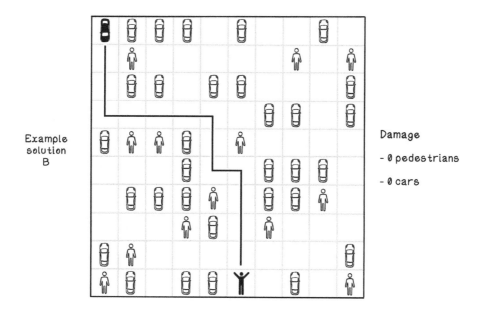

Figure 10.10 A good solution to the parking-lot problem

At this moment, there is no automation in sending actions to the simulator. It's like a game in which we provide input as a person instead of an AI providing the input. The next section explores how to train an autonomous agent.

Pseudocode

The pseudocode for the simulator encompasses the functions discussed in this section. The simulator class would be initialized with the information relevant to the starting state of the environment.

The `move_agent` function is responsible for moving the agent north, south, east, or west, based on the action. It determines whether the movement is within bounds, adjusts the agent's coordinates, determines whether a collision occurred, and returns a reward score based on the outcome:

```
Simulator(road, road_size_x, road_size_y,
          agent_start_x, agent_start_y, goal_x, goal_y):

  move_agent(action):
    if action equals COMMAND_NORTH:
      let next_x equal agent_x - 1
      let next_y equal agent_y
    else if action equals COMMAND_SOUTH:
      let next_x equal agent_x + 1
      let next_y equal agent_y
    else if action equals COMMAND_EAST:
      let next_x equal agent_x
      let next_y equal agent_y + 1
    else if action equals COMMAND_WEST:
      let next_x equal agent_x
      let next_y equal agent_y - 1
    if is_within_bounds(next_x, next_y) equals True:
      let reward_update equal cost_movement(next_x, next_y)
      let agent_x equal next_x
      let agent_y equal next_y
    else:
      let reward_update equal ROAD_OUT_OF_BOUNDS_REWARD
    return reward_update
```

Here are descriptions of the next functions in the pseudocode:

- The `cost_movement` function determines the object in the target coordinate that the agent will move to and returns the relevant reward score.

- The `is_within_bounds` function is a utility function that makes sure the target coordinate is within the boundary of the road.

- The `is_goal_achieved` function determines whether the goal has been found, in which case the simulation can end.

- The `get_state` function uses the agent's position to determine a number that enumerates the current state. Each state must be unique. In other problem spaces, the state may be represented by the actual native state itself.

```
cost_movement(next_x, next_y):
  if road[next_x][next_y] equals ROAD_OBSTACLE_PERSON:
    return ROAD_OBSTACLE_PERSON_REWARD
  else if road[next_x][next_y] equals ROAD_OBSTACLE_CAR:
    return ROAD_OBSTACLE_CAR_REWARD
  else if road[next_x][next_y] equals ROAD_GOAL:
    return ROAD_GOAL_REWARD
  else:
    return ROAD_EMPTY_REWARD


is_within_bounds(next_x, next_y):
  if road_size_x > next_x >= 0 and road_size_y > next_y >= 0:
    return True
  return False


is_goal_achieved():
  if agent_x equals goal_x and agent_y equals goal_y:
    return True
  return False


get_state():
  return (road_size_x * agent_x) + agent_y
```

Training with the simulation using Q-learning

Q-learning is an approach in reinforcement learning that uses the states and actions in an environment to model a table that contains information describing favorable actions based on specific states. Think of Q-learning as a dictionary in which the key is the state of the environment and the value is the best action to take for that state.

Reinforcement learning with Q-learning employs a reward table called a *Q-table*. A Q-table consists of columns that represent the possible actions and rows that represent the possible states in the environment. The point of a Q-table is to describe which actions are most favorable for the agent as it seeks a goal. The values that represent favorable actions are learned through simulating the possible actions in the environment and learning from the outcome and change in state. It's worth noting that the agent has a chance of choosing a random action or an action from the Q-table, as shown later in figure 10.13. The Q represents the function that provides the reward, or quality, of an action in an environment.

Figure 10.11 depicts a trained Q-table and two possible states that may be represented by the action values for each state. These states are relevant to the problem we're solving; another problem might allow the agent to move diagonally as well. Note that the number of states differs based on the environment and that new states can be added as they are discovered. In state 1, the agent is in the top-left corner, and in state 2, the agent is in the position below its previous state. The Q-table encodes the best actions to take, given each respective state. The action with the largest number is the most beneficial action. In this figure, the values in the Q-table have already been found through training. Soon, we will see how they're calculated.

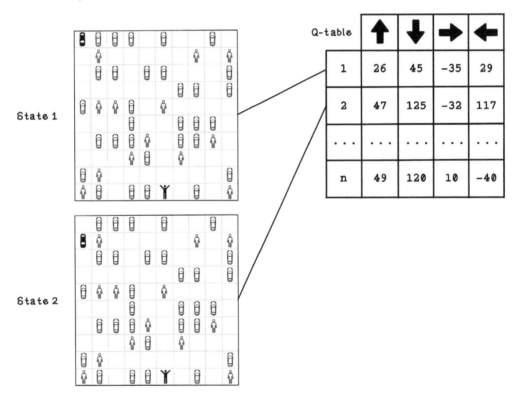

Figure 10.11 An example Q-table and states that it represents

The big problem with representing the state using the entire map is that the configuration of other cars and people is specific to this problem. The Q-table learns the best choices only for this map.

A better way to represent state in this example problem is to look at the objects adjacent to the agent. This approach allows the Q-table to adapt to other parking-lot configurations, because the state is less specific to the example parking lot from which it is learning. This approach may seem to be trivial, but a block could contain another car or a pedestrian, or it could be an empty block or an out-of-bounds block, which works out to four possibilities per block, resulting in 65,536 possible states. With this much variety, we would need to train the agent in many parking-lot configurations many times for it to learn good short-term action choices (figure 10.12).

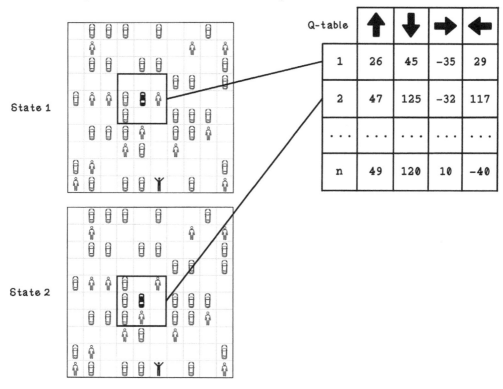

Figure 10.12 A better example of a Q-table and states that it represents

Keep the idea of a reward table in mind as we explore the life cycle of training a model using reinforcement learning with Q-learning. It will represent the model for actions that the agent will take in the environment.

Let's take a look at the life cycle of a Q-learning algorithm, including the steps involved in training. We will look at two phases: initialization, and what happens over several iterations as the algorithm learns (figure 10.13):

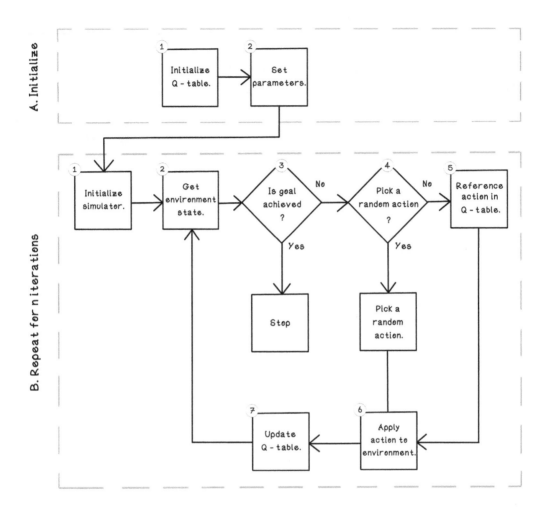

Figure 10.13 Life cycle of a Q-learning reinforcement learning algorithm

- *Initialize.* The initialize step involves setting up the relevant parameters and initial values for the Q-table:

  1. *Initialize Q-table.* Initialize a Q-table in which each column is an action and each row represents a possible state. Note that states can be added to the table as they are encountered, because it can be difficult to know the number of states in the environment at the beginning. The initial action values for each state are initialized with 0s.

  2. *Set parameters.* This step involves setting the parameters for different hyperparameters of the Q-learning algorithm, including:

- *Chance of choosing a random action*—This is the value threshold for choosing a random action over choosing an action from the Q-table.

- *Learning rate*—The learning rate is similar to the learning rate in supervised learning. It describes how quickly the algorithm learns from rewards in different states. With a high learning rate, values in the Q-table change erratically, and with a low learning rate, the values change gradually but it will potentially take more iterations to find good values.

- *Discount factor*—The discount factor describes how much potential future rewards are valued, which translates to favoring immediate gratification or long-term reward. A small value favors immediate rewards; a large value favors long-term rewards.

- *Repeat for n iterations.* The following steps are repeated to find the best actions in the same states by evaluating these states multiple times. The same Q-table will be updated over all iterations. The key concept is that because the sequence of actions for an agent is important, the reward for an action in any state may change based on previous actions. For this reason, multiple iterations are important. See an iteration as a single attempt to achieving a goal:

    1. *Initialize simulator.* This step involves resetting the environment to the starting state, with the agent in a neutral state.

    2. *Get environment state.* This function should provide the current state of the environment. The state of the environment will change after each action is performed.

    3. *Is goal achieved?* Determine whether the goal is achieved (or the simulator deems the exploration to be complete). In our example, this goal is picking up the owner of the self-driving car. If the goal is achieved, the algorithm ends.

    4. *Pick a random action.* Determine whether a random action should be selected. If so, a random action will be selected (north, south, east, or west). Random actions are useful for exploring the possibilities in the environment instead of learning a narrow subset.

    5. *Reference action in Q-table.* If the decision to select a random action is not selected, the current environment state is transposed to the Q-table, and the respective action is selected based on the values in the table. More about the Q-table is coming up.

    6. *Apply action to environment .*This step involves applying the selected action to the environment, whether that action is random or one selected from the Q-table. An action will have a consequence in the environment and yield a reward.

7.   *Update Q-table.* The following material describes the concepts involved in updating the Q-table and the steps that are carried out.

The key aspect of Q-learning is the equation used to update the values of the Q-table. This equation is based on the *Bellman equation*, which determines the value of a decision made at a certain point in time, given the reward or penalty for making that decision. The Q-learning equation is an adaptation of the Bellman equation. In the Q-learning equation, the most important properties for updating Q-table values are the current state, the action, the next state given the action, and the reward outcome. The learning rate is similar to the learning rate in supervised learning, which determines the extent to which a Q-table value is updated. The discount is used to indicate the importance of possible future rewards, which is used to balance favoring immediate rewards versus long-term rewards:

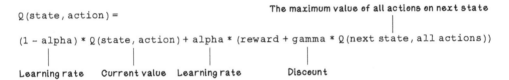

Because the Q-table is initialized with 0s, it looks similar to figure 10.14 in the initial state of the environment.

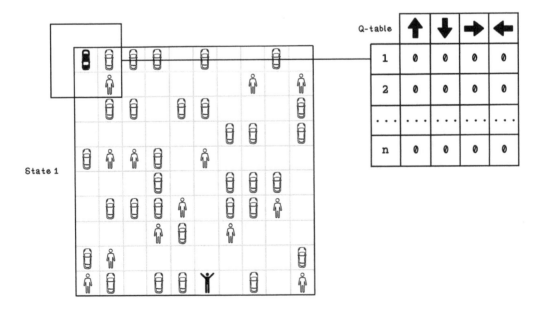

Figure 10.14 An example initialized Q-table

Next, we explore how to update the Q-table by using the Q-learning equation based on different actions with different reward values. These values will be used for the learning rate (alpha) and discount (gamma):

- Learning rate (alpha): 0.1

- Discount (gamma): 0.6

Figure 10.15 illustrates how the Q-learning equation is used to update the Q-table, if the agent selects the East action from the initial state in the first iteration. Remember that the initial Q-table consists of 0s. The learning rate (alpha), discount (gamma), current action value, reward, and next best state are plugged into the equation to determine the new value for the action that was taken. The action is East, which results in a collision with another car, which yields -100 as a reward. After the new value is calculated, the value of East on state 1 is -10.

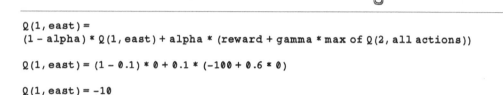

```
Q(1, east) =
(1 - alpha) * Q(1, east) + alpha * (reward + gamma * max of Q(2, all actions))

Q(1, east) = (1 - 0.1) * 0 + 0.1 * (-100 + 0.6 * 0)

Q(1, east) = -10
```

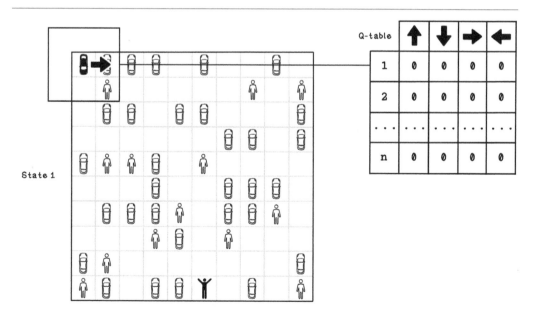

Figure 10.15 Example Q-table update calculation for state 1

The next calculation is for the next state in the environment following the action that was taken. The action is South and results in a collision with a pedestrian, which yields -1,000 as the reward. After the new value is calculated, the value for the South action on state 2 is -100 (figure 10.16).

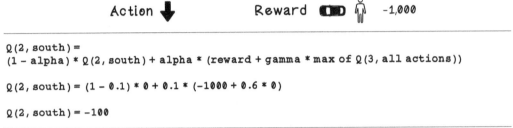

```
Q(2, south) =
(1 - alpha) * Q(2, south) + alpha * (reward + gamma * max of Q(3, all actions))

Q(2, south) = (1 - 0.1) * 0 + 0.1 * (-1000 + 0.6 * 0)

Q(2, south) = -100
```

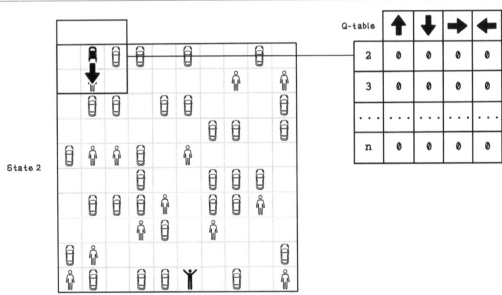

Figure 10.16 Example Q-table update calculation for state 2

Figure 10.17 illustrates how the calculated values differ in a Q-table with populated values because we worked on a Q-table initialized with 0s. The figure is an example of the Q-learning equation updated from the initial state after several iterations. The simulation can be run multiple times to learn from multiple attempts. So, this iteration is succeeding many before it, where the values of the table have been updated. The action for East results in a collision with another car and yields -100 as a reward. After the new value is calculated, the value for East on state 1 changes to -34.

Action ➡   Reward 🔋🗑 -100

Q(1, east) =
(1 - alpha) * Q(1, east) + alpha * (reward + gamma * max of Q(2, all actions))

Q(1, east) = (1 - 0.1) * -35 + 0.1 * (-100 + 0.6 * 125)

Q(1, east) = -34

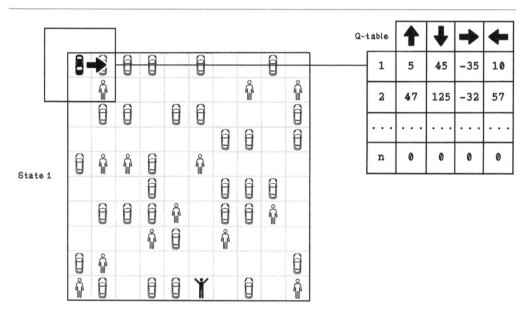

Figure 10.17 Example Q-table update calculation for state 1 after several iterations

EXERCISE: CALCULATE THE CHANGE IN VALUES FOR THE Q-TABLE

Using the Q-learning update equation and the following scenario, calculate
the new value for the action performed. Assume that the last move was East
with a value of -67:

Q(state, action) =

(1 - alpha) * Q(state, action) + alpha * (reward + gamma * Q(next state, all actions))

Learning rate   Current value   Learning rate   Discount

The maximum value of all actions on next state

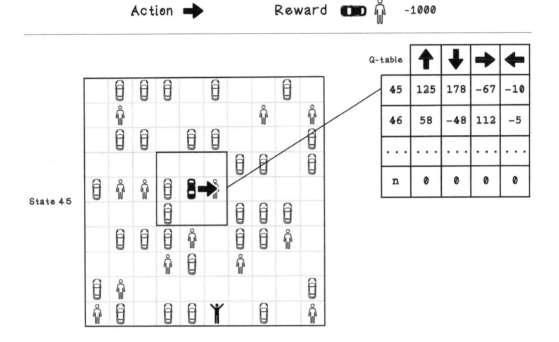

SOLUTION: CALCULATE THE CHANGE IN VALUES FOR THE Q-TABLE

The hyperparameter and state values are plugged into the Q-learning equation, resulting in the new value for Q(1, east):

- Learning rate (alpha): 0.1

- Discount (gamma): 0.6

- Q(1, east): -67

- Max of Q(2, all actions): 112

```
Q(1, east) =
(1 - alpha) * Q(1, east) + alpha * (reward + gamma * max of Q(2, all actions))

Q(1, east) = (1 - 0.1) * -67 + 0.1 * (-100 + 0.6 * 112)

Q(1, east) = -64
```

Pseudocode

This pseudocode describes a function that trains a Q-table by using Q-learning. It could be broken into simpler functions but is represented this way for readability. The function follows the steps described in this chapter.

The Q-table is initialized with 0s; then the learning logic is run for several iterations. Remember that an iteration is an attempt to achieve the goal.

The next piece of logic runs while the goal has not been achieved:

1. Decide whether a random action should be taken to explore possibilities in the environment. If not, the highest value action for the current state is selected from the Q-table.

2. Proceed with the selected action, and apply it to the simulator.

3. Gather information from the simulator, including the reward, the next state given the action, and whether the goal is reached.

4. Update the Q-table based on the information gathered and hyperparameters. Note that in this code, the hyperparameters are passed through as arguments of this function.

5. Set the current state to the state outcome of the action just performed.

These steps will continue until a goal is found. After the goal is found and the desired number of iterations is reached, the result is a trained Q-table that can be used to test in other environments. We look at testing the Q-table in the next section:

```
train_with_q_learning(observation_space, action_space,
                      number_of_iterations, learning_rate,
                      discount, chance_of_random_move):
  let q_table equal a matrix of zeros [observation_space, action_space]
  for i in range(number_of_iterations):
    let simulator equal Simulator(DEFAULT_ROAD, DEFAULT_ROAD_SIZE_X,
                                  DEFAULT_ROAD_SIZE_Y, DEFAULT_START_X,
                                  DEFAULT_START_Y, DEFAULT_GOAL_X,
                                  DEFAULT_GOAL_Y)
    let state equal simulator.get_state()
    let done equal False
    while not done:
      if random.uniform(0, 1) > chance_of_random_move:
        let action equal get_random_move()
      else:
        let action max(q_table[state])

      let reward equal simulator.move_agent(action)
      let next_state equal simulator.get_state()
      let done equal simulator.is_goal_achieved()

      let current_value equal q_table[state, action]
      let next_state_max_value equal max(q_table[next_state])

      let new_value equal (1 - learning_rate) * current_value + learning_rate *
                      (reward + discount * next_state_max_value)

      let q_table[state, action] equal new_value
      let state equal next_state

  return q_table
```

Testing with the simulation and Q-table

We know that in the case of using Q-learning, the Q-table is the model that encompasses the learnings. When presented with a new environment with different states, the algorithm references the respective state in the Q-table and chooses the highest-valued action. Because the Q-table has already been trained, this process consists of getting the current state of the environment and referencing the respective state in the Q-table to find an action until a goal is achieved (figure 10.18).

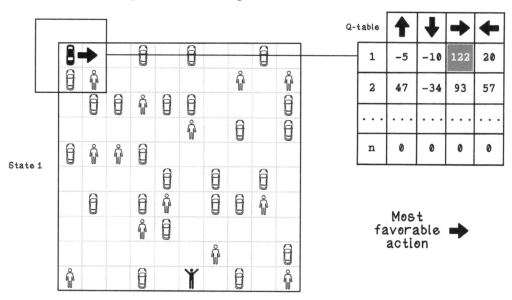

Figure 10.18 Referencing a Q-table to determine what action to take

Because the state learned in the Q-table considers the objects directly next to the agent's current position, the Q-table has learned good and bad moves for short-term rewards, so the Q-table could be used in a different parking-lot configuration, such as the one shown in figure 10.18. The disadvantage is that the agent favors short-term rewards over long-term rewards because it doesn't have the context of the rest of the map when taking each action.

One term that will likely come up in the process of learning more about reinforcement learning is *episodes*. An *episode* includes all the states between the initial state and the state when the goal is achieved. If it takes 14 actions to achieve a goal, we have 14 episodes. If the goal is never achieved, the episode is called *infinite*.

Measuring the performance of training

Reinforcement learning algorithms can be difficult to measure generically. Given a specific environment and goal, we may have different penalties and rewards, some of which have a greater effect on the problem context than others. In the parking-lot example, we heavily penalize collisions with pedestrians. In another example, we may have an agent that resembles a human and tries to learn what muscles to use to walk naturally as far as possible. In this scenario, penalties may be falling or something more specific, such as too-large stride lengths. To measure performance accurately, we need the context of the problem.

One generic way to measure performance is to count the number of penalties in a given number of attempts. Penalties could be events that we want to avoid that happen in the environment due to an action.

Another measurement of reinforcement learning performance is *average reward per action*. By maximizing the reward per action, we aim to avoid poor actions, whether the goal was reached or not. This measurement can be calculated by dividing the cumulative reward by the total number of actions.

Model-free and model-based learning

To support your future learning in reinforcement learning, be aware of two approaches for reinforcement learning: *model-based* and *model-free*, which are different from the machine learning models discussed in this book. Think of a model as being an agent's abstract representation of the environment in which it is operating.

We may have a model in our heads about locations of landmarks, intuition of direction, and the general layout of the roads within a neighborhood. This model has been formed from exploring some roads, but we're able to simulate scenarios in our heads to make decisions without trying every option. To decide how we will get to work, for example, we can use this model to make a decision; this approach is model-based. Model-free learning is similar to the Q-learning approach described in this chapter; trial and error is used to explore many interactions with the environment to determine favorable actions in different scenarios.

Figure 10.19 depicts the two approaches in road navigation. Different algorithms can be employed to build model-based reinforcement learning implementations.

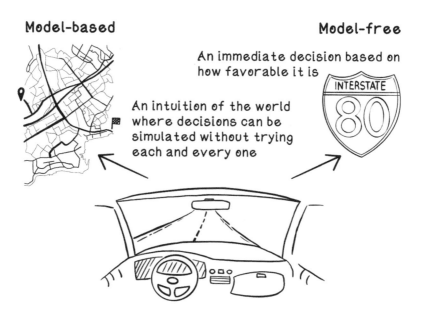

Figure 10.19 Examples of model-based and model-free reinforcement learning

Deep learning approaches to reinforcement learning

Q-learning is one approach to reinforcement learning. Having a good understanding of how it functions allows you to apply the same reasoning and general approach to other reinforcement learning algorithms. Several alternative approaches depend on the problem being solved. One popular alternative is *deep reinforcement learning*, which is useful for applications in robotics, video-game play, and problems that involve images and video.

Deep reinforcement learning can use artificial neural networks (ANNs) to process the states of an environment and produce an action. The actions are learned by adjusting weights in the ANN, using the reward feedback and changes in the environment. Reinforcement learning can also use the capabilities of convolutional neural networks (CNNs) and other purpose-built ANN architectures to solve specific problems in different domains and use cases.

Figure 10.20 depicts, at a high level, how an ANN can be used to solve the parking-lot problem in this chapter. The inputs to the neural network are the states; the outputs are probabilities for best action selection for the agent; and the reward and effect on the environment can be fed back using backpropagation to adjust the weights in the network.

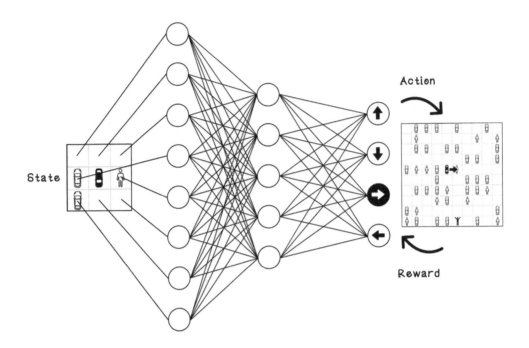

Figure 10.20 Example of using an ANN for the parking-lot problem

The next section looks at some popular use cases for reinforcement learning in the real world.

Use cases for reinforcement learning

Reinforcement learning has many applications where there is no or little historic data to learn from. Learning happens through interacting with an environment that has heuristics for good performance. Use cases for this approach are potentially endless. This section describes some popular use cases for reinforcement learning.

Robotics

Robotics involves creating machines that interact with real-world environments to accomplish goals. Some robots are used to navigate difficult terrain with a variety of surfaces, obstacles, and inclines. Other robots are used as assistants in a laboratory, taking instructions from a scientist, passing the right tools, or operating equipment. When it isn't possible to model every outcome of every action in a large, dynamic environment, reinforcement learning can be useful. By defining a greater goal in an environment and introducing rewards and penalties as heuristics, we can use reinforcement learning to train robots in dynamic environments. A terrain-navigating robot, for example, may learn which wheels to drive power to and how to adjust its suspension to traverse difficult terrain successfully. This goal is achieved after many attempts.

These scenarios can be simulated virtually if the key aspects of the environment can be modeled in a computer program. Computer games have been used in some projects as a baseline for training self-driving cars before they're trained on the road in the real world. The aim in training robots with reinforcement learning is to create more-general models that can adapt to new and different environments while learning more-general interactions, much the way that humans do.

Recommendation engines

Recommendation engines are used in many of the digital products we use. Video streaming platforms use recommendation engines to learn an individual's likes and dislikes in video content and try to recommend something most suitable for the viewer. This approach has also been employed in music streaming platforms and e-commerce stores. Reinforcement learning models are trained by using the behavior of the viewer when faced with decisions to watch recommended videos. The premise is that if a recommended video was selected and watched in its entirety, there's a strong reward for the reinforcement learning model, because it has assumed that the video was a good recommendation. Conversely, if a video never gets selected or little of the content is watched, it's reasonable to assume that the video did not appeal to the viewer. This result would result in a weak reward or a penalty.

Financial trading

Financial instruments for trading include stock in companies, cryptocurrency, and other packaged investment products. Trading is a difficult problem. Analysts monitor patterns in price changes and news about the world, and use their judgment to make a decision to hold their investment, sell part of it, or buy more. Reinforcement learning can train models that make these decisions through rewards and penalties based on income made or loss incurred. Developing a reinforcement learning model to trade well takes a lot of trial and error, which means that large sums of money could be lost in training the agent. Luckily, most historic public financial data is freely available, and some investment platforms provide sandboxes to experiment with.

Although a reinforcement learning model could help generate a good return on investment, here's an interesting question: if all investors were automated and completely rational, and the human element was removed from trading, what would the market look like?

Game playing

Popular strategy computer games have been pushing players' intellectual capabilities for years. These games typically involve managing many types of resources while planning short-term and long-term tactics to overcome an opponent. These games have filled arenas, and the smallest mistakes have cost top-notch players in many matches. Reinforcement learning has been used to play these games at the professional level and beyond. These reinforcement learning implementations usually involve an agent watching the screen the way a human player would, learning patterns, and taking actions. The rewards and penalties are directly associated with the game. After many iterations of playing the game in different scenarios with different opponents, a reinforcement learning agent learns what tactics work best toward the long-term goal of winning the game. The goal of research in this space is related to the search for more-general models that can gain context from abstract states and environments and understand things that cannot be mapped out logically. As children, for example, we never got burned by multiple objects before learning that hot objects are potentially dangerous. We developed an intuition and tested it as we grew older. These tests reinforced our understanding of hot objects and their potential harm or benefit.

In the end, AI research and development strives to make computers learn to solve problems in ways that humans are already good at: in a general way, stringing abstract ideas and concepts together with a goal in mind and finding good solutions to problems.

SUMMARY OF REINFORCEMENT LEARNING

Reinforcement learning is applicable when a goal is known but examples to learn from are not.

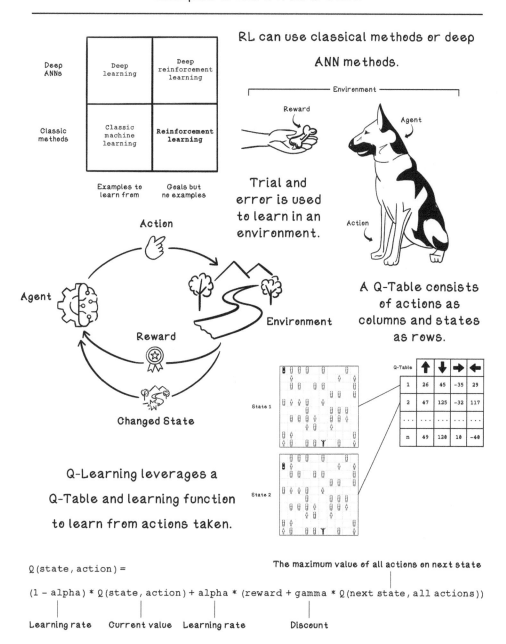

RL can use classical methods or deep ANN methods.

Trial and error is used to learn in an environment.

A Q-Table consists of actions as columns and states as rows.

Q-Learning leverages a Q-Table and learning function to learn from actions taken.

$Q(state, action) =$

$(1 - alpha) * Q(state, action) + alpha * (reward + gamma * Q(next state, all actions))$

Learning rate   Current value   Learning rate   Discount

The maximum value of all actions on next state

index

RELATED MANNING TITLES

Grokking Algorithms
by Aditya Y. Bhargava

ISBN 9781617292231
256 pages
eBook: $35.99/Print book + eBook: $44.99
May 2016

Grokking Deep Learning
by Andrew W. Trask

ISBN 9781617293702
336 pages
eBook: $39.99/Print book + eBook: $49.99
January 2019

Grokking Bitcoin
by Kalle Rosenbaum
Foreword by David A. Harding

ISBN 9781617294648
480 pages
eBook: $31.99/Print book + eBook: $39.99
April 2019

For ordering information go to www.manning.com

RELATED MANNING TITLES

Deep Learning with Python, Second Edition
by François Chollet

ISBN 9781617296864
400 pages *(estimated)*
eBook: $19.99/Print book + eBook: $24.99
Fall 2020 *(estimated)*

Deep Learning with Pytorch
by Eli Stevens, Luca Antiga, and Thomas Viehmann
Foreword by Soumith Chintala

ISBN 9781617295263
520 pages
eBook: $39.99/Print book + eBook: $49.99
July 2020

Machine Learning with Tensorflow
by Nishant Shukla
with Kenneth Fricklas

ISBN 9781617293870
272 pages
eBook: $35.99/Print book + eBook: $44.99
January 2018

For ordering information go to www.manning.com

Machine Learning with R,
the tidyverse, and mlr
by Hefin I. Rhys

ISBN 9781617296574
536 pages
eBook: $39.99/Print book + eBook: $49.99
March 2020

Deep Learning with JavaScript
Shanqing Cai, Stanley Bileschi, Eric D. Nielsen, and
Francois Chollet
Foreword by Nikhil Thorat and Daniel Smilkov

ISBN 9781617296178
560 pages
eBook: $39.99/Print book + eBook: $49.99
January 2020

GANs in Action
by Jakub Langr and Vladimir Bok

ISBN 9781617295560
240 pages
eBook: $39.99/Print book + eBook: $49.99
September 2019

For ordering information go to www.manning.com

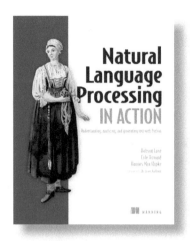

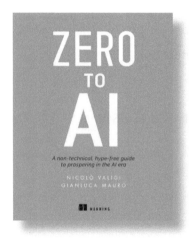